TO THE RIGHT

TO THE RIGHT

*The Transformation of
American Conservatism*

JEROME L. HIMMELSTEIN

UNIVERSITY OF CALIFORNIA PRESS
BERKELEY   LOS ANGELES   OXFORD

University of California Press
Berkeley and Los Angeles, California

University of California Press, Ltd.
Oxford, England

© 1990 by
The Regents of the University of California

First Paperback Printing 1992

Library of Congress Cataloging-in-Publication Data

Himmelstein, Jerome L.
 To the Right : The transformation of American conserv-
atism / Jerome L. Himmelstein.
  p. cm.
 Bibliography: p.
 Includes index.
 ISBN 0-520-08042-4
 1. Conservatism—United States—History—20th cen-
tury. 2. United States—Politics and government—1945– I.
Title.
JA84.U5H55 1990
320.5'2'0973—dc20   89-31599
                                                              CIP

Printed in the United States of America
2 3 4 5 6 7 8 9

*To Evy,
and to our little guys,
Daniel and Joel*

Contents

Acknowledgments

My first contacts with conservative political thought came as an undergraduate in the late 1960s, first in Sam Coleman's wide-ranging, wonderful courses in social philosophy at Columbia University and later at Michael Oakeshott's lectures at the London School of Economics. I became interested in American conservatism in particular as a sociological topic, however, only sometime in the 1970s while I was a graduate student at the University of California, Berkeley. The broader intellectual concern that motivated my interest initially was with ideology, with how our assumptions about the world are socially structured and how these assumptions in turn shape our perceptions and actions. That concern arose from, and was nurtured by, my participation in Leo Lowenthal's culture seminar, an intellectual enterprise that defied the normal limits of semesters and quarters and continued throughout my years at Berkeley. The topics of the seminar ranged widely, but to me the central theme always was that of ideology and its impact on politics. My first round of thanks goes, therefore, to Leo and the ever-changing membership of the seminar, but especially to Jeff Weintraub, Jim Stockinger, and Bob Bell.

An interest in conservatism did not, however, translate into immediate work on the topic. My concern with politics and ideology pushed me in a different direction, to the study of marijuana laws and the public discussion of the drug in America, a matter that occupied most of my last years at Berkeley and led to my writing *The Strange Career of Marihuana*. My study of the Right began in earnest only after I took a postdoctoral fellowship in 1980 at the University of Michigan in a program called "Sociology, Social Policy, and the Professions," funded by the National Institute of Mental Health. There I had the good fortune of working for two years at the Center for Research on Social Organization, an excellent setting for developing an analysis of conservatism as a social movement. I also drew on the many resources of the Institute for Social Research to add analysis of public opinion data to my work. Bill Gamson and Mayer Zald, who first brought me to Michigan, provided the right combination of freedom and intellectual encouragement to get my work under way. They have continued to be important sources of advice and support since then. Thanks also go to the countless others who together made CRSO such a stimulating place, but especially Jim McRae, Ron Kessler, and Bert Useem.

The research I began at CRSO turned into a series of articles and review essays on conservative ideology, conservatism in public opinion, and conservative movements, on which I continued to work after I started teaching at Amherst College in 1982. That fall I joined a faculty seminar on the New Right sponsored by the Center for the Advanced Study of the Humanities at the University of Massachusetts. I am grateful to the seminar for keeping the momentum of my work going and for helping me focus more clearly on specific elements of American conservatism in the 1970s and 1980s, especially the New Religious Right and corporate conservatism. I extend thanks to all the seminar members, including Allen Hunter, who organized it, Dan Clawson, Jim Ault, and Steve Arons.

The following summer I participated in a seminar on feminist and antifeminist movements in America, sponsored by the National Endowment for the Humanities, at Duke University. There I gained an understanding of how issues like abortion and the Equal Rights Amendment polarized women and what role they played in the rise of the Right. I also became fascinated with the world of North Carolina politics. Above all, I found another rich, supportive intellectual environment. I am indebted to all the seminar members, but especially to the seminar organizers, Bill Chafe, Jane deHart Mathews, and Don Mathews.

In the ensuing years I worked out many of my ideas in collaboration with others. Jim McRae and I coauthored two articles on American public opinion, and I developed my analysis of big business and the state through much discussion with Dan Clawson. Again, my thanks to both of them. Thanks also to Brian Elliott, James L. Guth,

Paul Luebke, and Corwin Smidt, with whom I have discussed one part or another of this work.

In 1985 I began to pull together the various elements of my research on conservatism into what would become this book. I am grateful to Amherst College for a Trustee Faculty Fellowship, which gave me the time away from teaching to get the project started.

As I did the final revisions on the book in 1988, I had the pleasure of participating in both a Sloan Workshop on Political Technology at the Rose Institute of State and Local Government in Claremont, California, and in a conference on Gender, Politics, and Religion at Smith College. My thanks to Alan Heslop, director of the Rose Institute, and to Arthur Parsons, Susan S. Bourque, and the Project on Women and Social Change at Smith.

Finally, I want to thank Susan Urquhart, who by now has typed and word processed so many pages of my work that I have long since lost count, and my editors at the University of California Press, Naomi Schneider, Amy Klatzkin, and Richard Miller.

Introduction

Sociology, Social Commentary,
and the Rise of the Right

"So inevitable, yet so completely unforeseen," said Tocqueville by way of explaining the puzzle that the French Revolution posed for the historical observer. Nothing quite so sweeping can be said about the rise of the Right in America in the late 1970s and early 1980s, but it was certainly not something for which American sociologists were prepared. Liberal sociologists in the early 1960s spent considerable time on what they called the "radical Right," but largely to stress how peripheral it was to the dominant directions of social and political change. Radical sociologists in the late 1960s and into the 1970s simply took the predominance of liberalism in capitalist America for granted and aimed their criticism accordingly. Both these perspectives may provide some tools for understanding the rise of the Right in the late 1970s and early 1980s, but only if this phenomenon is viewed with fresh eyes.

"The ideological age has ended," wrote Daniel Bell with finality and hope in the early 1960s. The old ideologies of left and right no longer held sway, at least among intellectuals: the old images of laissez-faire in which every government intervention put society on a slippery slope to totalitarianism were as dead as those of socialist utopias achieved through revolution and planning. In their place a rough consensus had emerged on the desirability of the Welfare State, a mixed economy, decentralized power, and political pluralism.

This image of the "end of ideology" of course was not idiosyncratically Bell's; it reflected the pervasive intellectual mood of the time.[1]

To be sure, Bell and his like-minded colleagues recognized the persistence of a right wing in American politics that angrily dissented from the consensus, and they wrote extensively about it. The classic 1955 volume *The New American Right,* which dissected McCarthyism, was updated in 1962 as *The Radical Right* to cover as well the efflorescence of the John Birch society, the Christian Crusade, and the like. The contributors to these volumes were men who made their imprint on a generation of sociologists and other social observers: Bell, Seymour Martin Lipset, Talcott Parsons, David Riesman, Nathan Glazer, and Richard Hofstadter, among others.[2]

The image of the Right that emerged from their essays was largely consistent with the broader theme of the "end of ideology." The radical Right appeared as an episodic disruption of American political life, a futile cry of protest against inexorable social change, a transient emotional response to social dislocation. This assessment was not always made explicitly, but it was always implicit in the way the contributors to *The Radical Right* discussed their subject. Their understanding of why people supported McCarthy or joined the John Birch Society or the Christian Crusade was embodied in their shared notion of status politics. The American emphasis on success and the considerable social fluidity of American society, Hofstadter argued, made Americans especially preoccupied with their status, that is, their relative economic and social standing. Social groups undergoing rapid downward or upward mobility tended to deal with their status anxieties by projecting them onto the political realm in the form of a concern with moral decay or political subversion. Status politics, understood as politics concerned with broad values (as opposed to interest or class politics concerned with material goals) tended to be especially prevalent during times of prosperity. With this argument, the contributors to *The Radical Right* explained, or claimed to explain, why diverse groups—new wealth in the Southwest, upwardly mobile Catholic ethnics, and Protestant fundamentalists in cultural eclipse—flocked at one point or another in the 1950s and early 1960s to the support of the Right.[3]

Whatever the validity of this argument (to which I return in Chapter 3), it tended to treat the right-wing resurgence as a transitory phenomenon, an episodic eruption rather than a sustained movement.

Status politics appeared as the product of a group's transition from one socioeconomic or cultural rank to another, which by implication could be expected to subside once adjustments to a new status were made. It appeared as a simple cry of pain, without any clear program, and lacked sustained form and direction.

The contributors to *The Radical Right*, moreover, consistently pictured the radical Right as running counter to fundamental, inexorable currents of social change in America. Hofstadter put it simply: "The extreme right suffers from what America has become in the twentieth century." Parsons saw in the Right an individualism of "pristine simplicity" quite out of place in an industrial society with its inherent complex division of labor and large-scale organization. Bell at one point pictured the Right as rebelling against "deep changes taking place in the social structure": the replacement of wealth and property by political position and technical skill as bases of power; the primacy of education over inheritance or entrepreneurship as a route to privilege; the linking of individual achievement, status, and prestige to collectivities; and the emergence of a new elite of professional and technical intellectuals. At another point he simply noted that "what the right wing is fighting, in the shadow of Communism, is essentially 'modernity.' "[4]

This last word, *modernity*, sums up the attitude of a generation of sociologists and social observers to the Right as a political force. Modernity implies something monolithic and inexorable, the inescapable result of overwhelming forces of change. To revolt against modernity is a futile gesture. To regard the Right, therefore, as a "revolt against modernity"—a phrase that recurs often in sociological writing—is to dismiss it as a political force of long-term significance.

The late 1960s witnessed the collapse of the intellectual consensus of which Bell et al. spoke and the resurgence of radical ideas in the social sciences. Sociologists came to disagree among themselves about many things, but not about the marginality of the Right to American politics. The premise of most radical sociology in the ensuing years was that American capitalism flourished within a liberal political shell. Revising the history of liberal reform in the twentieth century, some argued that these reforms, far from signaling the political defeat of the capitalist class, had been decisively shaped by its more enlightened members, representing the larger corporations and banks, especially those that were internationally oriented and technology-intensive. Faced with economic crisis or social unrest, these leaders headed off more radical social change by instituting reforms that would stabilize the capitalist system—government regulation of the economy, social-welfare legislation, even collective bargaining. From this viewpoint, summarized so ably by G. William Domhoff in *The Higher Circles*, the men who dominated the capitalist class were internationalists abroad and moderate liberals at home; above all, within the constraints of their class interests, they were "rational, reasonable, and forward-looking."[5]

If capitalists embraced a moderate liberalism, others argued, it was because liberalism and a growing state, far from transforming or threatening capitalism, helped it to function. Especially as corporate monopoly capitalism superseded competitive capitalism, the simple scale of investment and time frame required the state to guarantee long-term markets, underwrite costs of production, and maintain social order and legitimacy. The corporate and state sectors of the economy came to live in something approaching symbiosis. From this vantage point virtually any kind of government spending could be seen as contributing to the essential health of the system. By building highways, ports, and airports, providing gas, electricity, and water, or funding education and research and development, government enhanced productivity, argued James O'Connor in his classic, *The Fiscal Crisis of the State*.[6] Moreover, by providing social insurance of various kinds, sponsoring suburban development and urban renewal, and underwriting child care and hospital facilities, government reduced the costs of reproducing labor. According to O'Connor, welfare spending helped cool out the surplus labor population that capitalism produced, and military spending helped keep the world safe for the economic expansion propelled by surplus capital. To be sure, O'Connor did not see this fit between a growing state (in both liberal and illiberal forms) and capitalism as perfect. Capitalism, he thought, certainly placed limits on liberal reform, and high levels of government spending could certainly precipitate a fiscal crisis of the state as expenditures easily outran revenues. Nonetheless, a hard-line conservative resistance to the growth of the state seemed more and more atavistic in a corporate capitalist world and scarcely drew the attention of a generation of radical sociologists. Terms like *monopoly capitalism* and *advanced capitalism* played the same role in the discourse of radicals as *modernity* played in that of liberals: they made the Right seem irrelevant.

From the vantage point of the end of 1980s, the Right hardly seems atavistic or peripheral. The elements of the radical Right studied by Bell and his colleagues were not episodic eruptions of mindless anger and pain. They were part of the sustained growth of a continuous social movement with a clear, systematic ideology that led ultimately to the New Right and the New Religious Right. Nor was big business so wedded to a corporate liberalism, or American capitalism so tied to a growing state, that conservative leaders and ideas hostile to much of big government could not come to power. More broadly, an advanced industrial society might inevitably encourage both rationalization (the growth of large-scale organization and planning) and secularization (the decline of religious beliefs), but these trends did not prevent the rise to power of an ideology and movement that celebrated a simple individualism and a fervent religiosity.[7]

Its unexpectedness from a sociological perspective makes the rise of the Right in America a compelling issue. It justifies not only an effort to understand why it occurred but also a broader reassessment of the whole phenomenon of conservatism in America. That is what this book is all about.

Of course, my analysis does not emerge from a vacuum. Sociology did not remain frozen in the molds of the 1960s and early 1970s. On the one hand, the sociology of social movements came to view collective action not simply as a reflexlike reaction to social dislocation and discontent but also as a systematic, rational effort to mobilize people and resources toward a political goal. On the other, political sociology quickly recognized that the growth of the domestic state was neither the simple product of a capitalist ruling class nor the simple concomitant of monopoly capitalism. In other words, it gave a greater role to conflict and contradiction. My analysis draws on both these developments and others as well. At the same time, there has hardly been a dearth of commentary, both sociological and otherwise, on the rise of the Right. The present study is both a reflection on much of this work and an effort to carve out a distinct position.

The question of why the Right rose to power is really at least two distinct questions. First, what social conditions created the political opportunities for the Right? Second, how did the Right build and sustain itself as a plausible political alternative capable of seizing those opportunities? This book is concerned with the intersection of these two questions, or more precisely, with using answers to the first to help construct answers to the second.

The story has been told often enough of the multiple crises that beset American society in the late 1960s and the 1970s and rendered the existing political direction—whether called liberalism, political capitalism, or the growth coalition—increasingly troubled. A sputtering economy; a world order less and less amenable to American influence and interests; growing domestic conflict over family, gender roles, and basic values; radical social movements that questioned basic features of American society; and a state the demands on which outran its resources—all these factors contributed to a general crisis of confidence in American institutions and created a political opening for possible alternatives. Given the historical limits of the Left in America, this alternative naturally came from the Right, which presented itself in the late 1970s as a "revitalization movement" (to use Walter Dean Burnham's term).[8]

Of interest here is how conservatism managed to be in a position to take up the reins for a time. While the sorry state of the economy made it likely that a Republican would win the presidency in 1980, it did not dictate that the victor would be a committed conservative with the organized backing to propose and enact a conservative agenda. How did conservatism come to be a viable alternative in American politics by the late 1970s, and how did it make use of the multiple crises of the time to get into power?

My answer begins from the premise that the rise of the Right should be understood in two analytic and historical parts—how the Right became an effective political contender between the mid-1950s and the mid-1970s, and how it came to dominate American politics in the late 1970s and the 1980s. The mid-1970s are a likely dividing line because only after that point did the general direction of American politics shift decisively to the right on a wide range of issues and did many of the most important elements of the Right as a coherent political tendency take shape, including the New Right, the New Religious Right, and corporate conservatism.

The Right, or conservatism, began as the hard-line opposition to the New Deal. As a provisional definition (to be fleshed out later), we can say that its central political assumption has been that the main problem facing America, and indeed all of humanity, is collectivism, the tendency for the state to organize and control all social life. As Chapter 1 argues, the 1950s were a pivotal time for this conservatism: New Deal liberalism had receded but had left an indelible mark on

American politics. Tide after tide of political reaction had crested and fallen back without washing out this mark, and conservatives, it became clear, could no longer rely on the natural rhythms of American politics to put them back into serious political contention. The dominant political consensus, sometimes called cold-war liberalism, assumed that America should play a leadership role in the international effort to contain communism and that government at home should play a positive role in promoting economic growth and maintaining the health of capitalism. Conservatives, of course, were also anticommunist and procapitalist, but in quite different ways from liberals, and that is where their problem lay. Their anticommunism was isolationist, not internationalist, and the capitalism they sought to defend was of the laissez-faire, pristine variety.

To become a political contender again, conservatives had to reconstruct their ideology and build a sustained, independent movement. Chapter 2 examines how conservatives transformed their case against collectivism, foreign and domestic, by on the one side jettisoning their isolationism and crafting a different kind of internationalism and on the other side developing a defense of laissez-faire capitalism that did not rely on the themes of growth and prosperity that cold-war liberalism had so convincingly appropriated. These ideological projects formed the basis for the often far-ranging intellectual self-scrutiny among conservatives in the 1950s and early 1960s and led to the creation of what we recognize today as conservatism. I approach this reconstruction process with an eye not only to how the finished product emerged—a matter covered in considerable detail by George Nash in *The Conservative Intellectual Movement in America*—but also to what got left out and why conservatives went to so much trouble to begin with.[9]

Chapter 3 traces the growth of the network of conservative organizations and activists from the late 1950s through the late 1970s, ending with an examination of the continuities between the Old Right and the New Right. I take issue both with those, like the contributors to *The Radical Right*, who saw in the development of the movement only irrational eruptions of status anxiety and with those official movement historians, like William Rusher in *The Rise of the Right*, who view it as pure insurgency or rebellion, albeit of a more rational kind. Instead, I argue that the secret to the growth of the conservative movement lay in a paradoxical combination of respectability and rebelliousness. The conservative movement combined solid socioeconomic and political roots and the access to resources these provided with a broadly antiestablishment ideology that allowed it to appeal to the growing range of discontents bequeathed by the 1960s. The cadre of political activists known as the New Right was simply the culmination of this movement, not a right-wing populist break with conservatism as some (Alan Crawford in *Thunder on the Right*, Kevin Phillips in *Post-Conservative America*) have argued.[10]

If conservatism had become a serious political contender by the early 1970s, however, it failed to have a decisive impact until the end of the decade. The march of the Right to power in the late 1970s and early 1980s fed upon three developments, the rise of the New Religious Right, the mobilization of corporate conservatism, and the revitalization of the Republican party. Each of these involved not so much the emergence of something new as the strengthening of a relationship that had already been central to the life of conservatism— to religious traditionalism, to big business, and to the GOP. In addition, each of these developments captures one important way that social commentators have characterized the rise of the Right—as a successful social movement, as a realignment of elites, and as a transformation of the electorate. Finally, each provides a lens through which to view some of the broader changes in American society that shaped the fortunes of the Right.

The religiously based conservative political organizations and activists known as the New Religious Right, Chapter 4 argues, emerged from the interaction of the so-called social issues and the growth of the evangelical-fundamentalist religious world. For a considerable time, beginning in the late 1960s, it was common to argue that a range of issues having to do with morality, social order, family and gender roles, and the like would be the new cutting edge of American politics, creating new political cleavages and alignments. (Kevin Phillips made the argument in various forms in a series of books starting with *The Emerging Republican Majority*; Everett Carll Ladd, Jr., and Charles D. Hadley did so in *Transformations of the American Party System*; and Ronald Inglehart generalized the argument to Western societies in *The Silent Revolution*.)[11] It is clear from the vantage point of the late 1980s that they have had no such revolutionary effect. Issues like abortion and the Equal Rights Amendment have played the more modest role, however, of mobilizing new cohorts of conservative activists, often from traditional religious backgrounds. This has been especially so among evangelical Christians, where discontent about a permissive secular culture and a growing network of religious and cultural organizations together provided fertile conditions for political mobilization, conditions carefully cultivated by the leaders of the conservative movement. The rise of the New Religious Right, in short, fed on several of the conditions that theories of social movements generally emphasize—heightened discontent, a growing capacity for collective action, and the intensified efforts of social-movement professionals.

The mobilization of big business around a conservative agenda lay at the heart of a developing set of linkages between conservative and neoconservative intellectuals, corporate money, and political power—what Sidney Blumenthal has termed the "rise of the Counter-Establishment" or a "realignment of elites." These linkages made it easier for conservative ideas and policymakers to have political impact. Although much has been said about corporate conservatism (in Thomas Ferguson and Joel Rogers's *Right Turn* and Thomas Edsall's *The New Politics of Inequality,* for example), much about it remains puzzling.[12] Chapter 5 examines the impact of corporate conservatism on business lobbying, election funding, and support for policy-planning organizations and shows not only that big business did indeed mobilize but also that corporate conservatism was *hegemonic* in character; that is, it drew broad-based corporate support and involved an effort to influence politics in the interest not of specific firms or industries but of capitalists generally. I examine the problems this corporate conservatism poses for most theories about the political role of big business. If capitalists are a ruling class, as many have argued, why did they have to mobilize and why did they rebel against their state? If they are not a ruling class and indeed lack the ability to pursue their class interests, how did they suddenly gain the capacity to act in such a coherent, broad-based fashion? Chapter 5 confronts various theories of the state with the phenomenon of corporate conservatism and concludes in effect that the nature of capitalist power, whether ruling-class or not, varies with historical circumstances.

The partial revitalization of the Republican party after several decades of distinctly minority status and the debacle of Watergate has invariably been viewed through the prism of realignment: was there a fundamental shift in the political allegiances of the American electorate akin to what occurred in the 1930s or at previous nodal points in American history? Although Chapter 6 examines the likely answers to this question, its central thesis is that the question itself is misleading. A general realignment, however defined, probably did not occur, but the Republican party nonetheless gained, and the electorate changed in significant ways that the preoccupation with realignment obscures. Among some groups, notably white southerners and evangelicals, something akin to realignment did occur. Among other voters, a growing tendency to make race-by-race decisions about specific candidates rather than rely on deeper party loyalties probably helped Republicans, whose superior centralized control of money allowed them to target undecided voters in close races and make effective use of new political technologies. Finally, the general tendency of the electorate to cast their votes on the basis of general economic conditions also aided the Republicans as more and more voters came to see the GOP, rather than the Democrats, as the "party of prosperity." In short, selective realignment, dealignment, and economic voting each gave small advantages to the Republican party in the late 1970s and early 1980s.

The rise of the New Religious Right, the mobilization of corporate conservatism, and the reinvigoration of the Republican party together embody or reflect many of the important social and political changes that turned conservatism from political contender to political victor. But they do not constitute one grand, integrated explanation for the rise of the Right, for that rise did not result from one massive wave of social change but from a number of smaller ones.

The six chapters that follow provide a composite portrait of American conservatism as a social phenomenon, pulling together studies of public opinion and ideological texts, theories of the state in advanced capitalism and theories of postindustrial society, images of the Right as insurgent political outsider and as well-connected insider. The result is an assessment of the emergence of the New Right and its sources of strength.

Part One

Becoming a Contender

One

Historical Prologue

Revolution and Delayed Reaction

"Last November's victory was singularly your victory," President Ronald Reagan told the Conservative Political Action Conference in March 1981. "Fellow citizens, fellow conservatives—our time is now, our moment has arrived."[1] The political movement that Reagan addressed was hardly three decades old when it savored its greatest triumph. American conservatism had certainly existed before the 1950s, but during that decade conservatives substantially transformed themselves. They reconstructed their ideology, discarding some themes, adding others, modifying still others. They began to build a long-term movement to gain broad political power. They even for the first time agreed on *conservative* as the name for their new ideology and their fledgling movement—a symbolic expression of a new political beginning. Understanding American conservatism in the age of Reagan requires starting with the historical context in which it emerged in the 1950s.

First of all, however, let us be clear about what this conservatism is. The constellation of economic, social, and national-security themes that define recent American conservatism as a worldview is no doubt clear enough. In economics, conservatives have stressed freeing the market from the constraints of government. They have consistently equated less government with more freedom and greater prosperity: cutting taxes, domestic spending, and regulation would lead to greater freedom for Americans to produce, create, and

13

achieve and hence to increased national wealth. On social issues, conservatives have condemned the secular, humanistic bent of American culture and its corrosive effects on the traditional family, gender roles, religion, and morality. In regard to national security, conservatives have urged greater spending on the American military to counter the growth of the Soviet military and restrict Soviet power. In their view, the conflict between the United States and the Soviet Union is a struggle not simply between superpowers but between good and evil, civilization and barbarism; it suffuses not just the immediate relationship between the two countries but also most conflicts around the world where U.S. interests are threatened.

We can call these three elements of conservatism respectively *economic libertarianism*, *social traditionalism*, and *militant anticommunism*. To be sure, not all political issues fit neatly within rubrics. Nor is being a conservative an all-or-nothing proposition: one may be an economic conservative without being a social one, or vice versa. One may be more or less conservative within each category; one may advocate conservatism in principle in any of these areas while compromising it in practice—for example, by conceding a minimal "safety net" of welfare programs, downplaying the importance of social issues like abortion, or even negotiating arms agreements with the Soviet Union. What matters is that what has come to be called conservatism and the way that conservatives have defined themselves involve the conjunction of these three elements.

The core assumption that binds these three elements is the belief that American society on all levels has an organic order—harmonious, beneficent, and self-regulating—disturbed only by misguided ideas and policies, especially those propagated by a liberal elite in the government, the media, and the universities. From a fully developed conservative perspective, America's problems result not from the inherent contradictions or conflicts of a capitalist economy, a patriarchal family, or an unequal international world order but from liberal tampering with otherwise harmonious, self-sustaining systems. The free-market capitalist economy would function well except for government grown too big and too powerful because of liberal social-welfare and regulatory programs. Family, morality, religion, and gender roles would be smoothly intact if liberal elites had not encouraged permissiveness, secularism, alternative life-styles, and feminism. The Soviet Union would not pose so great a threat to American security and international affairs would prove amenable to American interests and actions if liberals had not hobbled defense spending for so long and been soft on communism. Perhaps many conservatives would not put things so baldly, but implicit in their ideology is, first, the identification of liberal elites and ideas as a central cause of America's problems and, second, a belief in the possibility of a natural, pristine harmony within existing institutions.

Conservatives themselves have been quick to identify the 1950s as the seminal decade in their collective political and ideological life. Writing in the early 1960s, Frank Meyer, an editor of the *National Review* and one of the central architects of a reconstructed conservative ideology, remarked: "The crystallization in the past dozen years or so of an American conservative movement is a *delayed* reaction to the *revolutionary* transformation of America that began with the election of Franklin Roosevelt in 1932." Most internal histories of the conservative movement since then have identified a similar starting point.[2]

Meyer's words may sound strange to nonconservative ears. To many historians and social scientists, the New Deal, far from being a "revolutionary transformation," was a set of moderate reforms that undercut any possibility of such a transformation. The reaction to the New Deal, the hard-line effort to undo it, did not wait for the mid-1950s to coalesce: witness the activities of Herbert Hoover, Robert Taft, the American Liberty League, and the *American Mercury* in the 1930s and 1940s. Understanding the roots of contemporary American conservatism nonetheless requires seeing how the New Deal, whether a revolution or not, transformed the American political landscape and how the reaction to the New Deal, if not beginning in the 1950s, transformed itself at that time.

The New Deal "Revolution"

Despite the assertion of conservatives like Meyer, in many ways the New Deal was clearly not revolutionary.[3] It was a practical, fairly moderate collection of programs aimed at dealing with the almost total economic collapse of the Great Depression. It brought together a variegated set of reformers, who enacted an eclectic set of programs between 1933 and 1938—immediate relief for the unemployed, home owners, farmers, and bank depositors; tentative efforts at economic planning and government-owned enterprise; the beginnings of a welfare state; progressive tax reform; antitrust legislation aimed at utility holding companies and a general inquiry into the concentration of property ownership; and legislation promoting collective bargaining and unions. Certainly, FDR never succeeded in transforming American politics to pave the way for economic planning or social democracy. His plans for reorganizing the executive branch of government got nowhere; his efforts to purge the Democratic party of conservatives were late and half-hearted; and, above all, he failed to articulate a reform ideology, an alternative to the fundamentally individualist, antistatist American political tradition. As a result, the New Deal never created the comprehensive welfare state or the forms of economic planning characteristic of many European capitalist countries.[4]

Despite occasionally radical rhetoric, New Dealers typically saw themselves as saviors of capitalism at a time when economic hardship was breeding leaders and movements of much greater radical potential. Senator Huey Long of Louisiana, until his assassination in 1935 probably the most popular politician in America after FDR, toured the country advocating a major redistribution of income and starting Share Our Wealth societies. Father Charles Coughlin, a parish priest from Royal Oak, Michigan, enthralled a huge radio audience with a proposal to nationalize the banks. (His anti-Semitism, for which he is better known to posterity, came later, after his political clout and popularity had begun to wane.) Francis Townsend, a California physician, received considerable support for his $200-a-month pension for all persons over sixty, and Townsend clubs sprang up across the country. Also in California, author Upton Sinclair, the best-known socialist in America, started the popular End Poverty in California movement and won the Democratic nomination for governor in 1934, getting 40 percent of the vote in the general election. Progressive and Farmer-Labor movements held political power in Wisconsin and Minnesota, and a new wave of militant union organizing spread throughout the industrial heartland. Compared to all these proposals and movements, the New Deal was hardly radical.

The New Deal nonetheless significantly transformed American politics in at least two ways. First, whatever its limits, it did insert the federal government more deeply into American life than ever before. The federal government became committed to providing at least some social-insurance programs and to exerting at least some control over economic life. Although New Deal ideas and programs often seemed to echo those of the Progressive Era, the overall ethos and effect were different: operating during general prosperity, most progressives were content to involve government in limited ways to correct the abuses and inequalities of an otherwise sound society. Attempting to cope with almost total economic collapse, the New Deal, without acknowledging it, gave government a more permanent and pervasive role, pushing it further along the continuum from judge or policeman to manager or protector and placing it at the heart of national life.[5]

Second, the New Deal entailed the biggest political realignment in American political life since the Civil War. From the 1860s to the early 1930s, and especially after the elections of 1896, the Republican party had all but dominated American politics. From 1896 to 1932 Democrats controlled the House and the Senate each in only three of eighteen Congresses. They won the White House only twice—once in 1912, when the Republicans split between William Howard Taft and Theodore Roosevelt, and again in 1916, with Democratic incumbent Woodrow Wilson in the White House. Neither time did Wilson get a majority of the popular vote. Republicans won consecutive presidential elections in 1920, 1924, and 1928 by landslides, the Democratic candidate never getting more than 41 percent of the vote.

In this context the early 1930s did indeed represent a political earthquake. Democrat Franklin D. Roosevelt won the White House in 1932 with 57 percent of the popular vote—the first time since James Buchanan in 1856 that a Democrat had captured the presidency with a popular majority. Democrats made gains in both houses of Congress in an unprecedented four consecutive elections from 1930 to 1936, gaining 170 seats in the House and 36 in the Senate. The Seventy-fifth Congress convened in 1937 with lopsided Democratic majorities of 333–89 in the House and 75–17 in the Senate.

The Democrats rode to power on a major political realignment that, beginning in the mid-1920s and accelerating in the 1930s, brought a large constituency of urban ethnic and working-class voters outside the South into the Democratic fold. Voter turnout in the North and the West increased from an all-time low of 54 percent in the 1920 presidential election to 74 percent in 1940. Northern and western cities, longtime Republican strongholds, slid back into the Democratic camp. The electorate changed in a fundamental way: the

[handwritten margin note: but different parties then ?.]

once respected *Literary Digest* straw poll, which had accurately predicted the results of the 1928 and 1932 elections, failed miserably in
1936, giving Republican candidate Alf Landon about twenty percentage points more than he actually got. Survey samples drawn from
telephone directories and presumably biased to the higher socioeconomic strata no longer accurately reflected the electorate as a whole.

The realignment also changed the balance of power and the political divisions within each party. The Democratic party ceased to be a
largely southern party with a few northern appendages. As a new
urban ethnic and working-class constituency came to the fore, the
northern segment of the party came to predominate in the mid-1930s,
and the social basis of support for liberal or progressive economic
programs changed at least partly from rural to urban. New Deal programs after 1936 shifted accordingly, and resistance to the New Deal
among southern and western Democrats—and with it a "conservative" coalition with Republicans—emerged. At the same time, the
geographical cleavages within the Republican party reversed themselves. In the East, a bastion of the old guard, or conservative wing,
of the party, Republicans found they had to accommodate to New
Deal issues to compete for the votes of the new constituencies. In the
Midwest and West, formerly the home of the progressive wing of the
party, Democrats attracted many of the GOP's progressive elements,
while Republicans picked up isolationist defectors from the Democratic ranks. As a result, where eastern old-guard Republicans had
once faced progressive midwestern and western Republicans, now
more and more the Eastern moderates faced midwestern and western
conservatives.[6] It was, in short, a changed political world in more
ways than one, and these changes revolved around the New Deal.

The "Delayed" Reaction

The activist phase of the New Deal came to an end in 1938, the year
that saw the last of FDR's major legislation, including the Fair Labor
Standards Act and a new Agricultural Adjustment Act; yet its opponents were too weak to organize a full-scale reaction. In the ensuing
years—1938, 1946, and the early 1950s—wave after wave of reaction
fell short of putting into power a leadership able and willing to undo
New Deal gains. The result was a political stalemate that persisted
into the 1950s and beyond.

The New Deal in fact lost its momentum very soon after its landslide victory in the 1936 elections. After five years of economic recovery, the gross national product and industrial production fell sharply in 1937 in what opponents dubbed the "Roosevelt recession." Sitdown strikes and labor militancy among industrial workers increasingly alarmed middle-class voters, and FDR's efforts to gain a liberal majority on the U.S. Supreme Court by expanding its membership to fourteen provoked widespread opposition and damaged his prestige. Southern and western Democrats came to oppose New Deal initiatives. In late 1937, on one important vote on the fair labor standards bill, which proposed to set a minimum wage and maximum working hours, one-third of House Democrats joined most Republicans in voting successfully to recommit the bill to committee. While 101 of 152 southern and western Democrats defected, only 31 of 177 other Democrats did.[7] Seventy-four percent of the defectors were from rural districts. Finally, in the 1938 midterm elections Republicans posted their first gains since 1928, picking up eighty House and six Senate seats, while FDR's belated effort to defeat conservative Democrats fell flat.

The opposition to the New Deal, however, remained weak and disorganized. The Republican party was a small minority in both chambers of Congress and lacked clear leadership. The nascent conservative coalition in Congress never fully solidified; its support shifted from issue to issue and fell apart totally in such areas as farm legislation. Furthermore, it never got beyond rearguard actions, often supporting and winning only small changes in New Deal legislation. Finally, the major independent anti–New Deal organization, the American Liberty League, effectively fell apart after the 1936 elections (though it continued in existence until 1940) despite substantial support from big business.

World War II put domestic political conflict on ice in the early 1940s. Whether the New Deal would have regained momentum in the absence of war, or conservative reaction would have pushed FDR out of office in 1940, is a tantalizing question that we need not address here. As it happened, America emerged from the war still in political stalemate. New Deal activists sought unsuccessfully to press forward with social change.[8] In 1944 FDR had pledged to enact an economic "bill of rights," guaranteeing decent housing, education, and health care for all Americans. After the war New Dealers argued that the wartime experience, during which the gross national product doubled in an economy under considerable government control, showed that government investment could keep the economy booming. They proposed an increased role for the government in planning and investment, which would include, among other things, responsibility for full employment and national health insurance. In foreign affairs they emphasized the importance of world peace as central to America's national interest, a peace to be insured through cooperation between the victors in World War II, world government, and a more equitable world order. Little of this came to be; postwar liberal legislation was either never enacted (national health insurance) or was enacted in eviscerated form (full-employment legislation). The new Democratic president, Harry Truman, shied away from the more ambitious ideas and stocked his administration with Democratic moderates. The party itself lost control of Congress in the 1946 elections as Republicans gained fifty-six new House seats and thirteen new seats in the Senate.

The extension of the New Deal failed for many reasons, but two seem especially important. First, continuing economic prosperity dulled the appetite of many Americans for additional social reform. That this prosperity itself benefited from government spending on highways, mortgage subsidies, and GI benefits was simply an irony of history. Second, the growing fear of communism abroad and at home ultimately shifted the emphasis to opposing the Soviet Union and rooting out subversion at home.

A full-scale conservative reaction, however, did not replace New Deal activism. If Americans had little taste for extending the New Deal, they adamantly rejected any hint of undoing it. The 1948 elections drove that point home. Republicans expected to finish the job begun in 1946 by taking back the White House for the first time in sixteen years. The political mood seemed conservative. Truman was hardly the charismatic leader that FDR had been, and the Democratic Party was badly split: its more liberal elements gravitated to former vice president Henry Wallace and his Progressive party, while Southern segregationists, angry at the Democrats' nascent concern with civil rights, defected to Governor Strom Thurmond of South Carolina, running on a states' rights platform. Voter turnout also favored the Republicans as it fell to 53 percent, the lowest since the 1920s. Yet Truman rode to a most improbable victory over Republican Thomas E. Dewey, and Democrats retook the Congress, picking up seventy-five House and nine Senate seats. Truman's campaign made appeals to many constituencies, but the overarching theme was an attack on the Republicans as "gluttons of privilege" eager "to do a hatchet job on the New Deal" and make "America an economic colony of Wall Street." Class polarization of the presidential vote was the highest ever recorded, with middle-class voters going heavily Republican and working-class voters heavily Democratic.[9]

The 1948 elections, however, represented a mere interruption in the rumblings of conservative reaction. Unable to make headway by attacking Democrats on domestic New Deal legislation, Republicans and conservatives more and more emphasized Democratic and liberal softness on communism, both the Soviet threat abroad and subversion at home. They in effect chose to run against the spirit and leadership of liberalism, not its economic substance, by accusing liberals of softness, even treason, on the issue of communism. Americans since the beginning of the New Deal seemed to have embraced New Deal programs without wholly forsaking the philosophy of free enterprise. FDR had even encouraged this attitude by ultimately justifying his programs as restoring individual opportunity. Conservatives could most easily advance their fortunes, therefore, by attacking liberals themselves and their allegedly collectivist ideology in a way that did not immediately implicate specific programs. Allegations that Democrats and liberals were sympathetic to, soft on, or even in cahoots with communism were an effective tactic. Conservatives could even use such charges to reverse the rhetoric of class conflict. If Truman had appealed to workers and farmers against Wall Street and its Republican representatives, Senator Joseph McCarthy could appeal to the plain people of America against a treasonous political elite, "the bright young men who are born with silver spoons in their mouths"; and Whittaker Chambers, the accuser of Alger Hiss, could claim to speak for "the plain men and women of America" against "the enlightened and the powerful." The meaning of McCarthyism, Frank Meyer argued later in the 1950s, was that liberals were unfit to lead a free society because their worldview and sympathies were unsuitable.[10]

Of course, communism did not suddenly emerge as an issue in 1948. Republicans had long linked the New Deal to communism, and they used their control of Congress after the 1946 elections to press investigations by the House Un-American Activities Committee into alleged cases of subversion. Nor was communism the preserve of Republicans alone. For their part, Democrats and many liberals had moved after World War II against both domestic communism and the Soviet Union. Federal loyalty and security programs scrutinized the political credentials of government appointees; the Democratic party purged itself of leftists; the Congress of Industrial Organizations expelled communist-led unions; the top membership of the Communist party was convicted under the Smith Act; and liberal anticommunist organizations like Americans for Democratic Action policed the left flank of liberalism. In addition, the Truman administration embarked on an anticommunist foreign policy with the Marshall Plan for rebuilding Western Europe, the creation of the North Atlantic Treaty Organization, and the promulgation of the Truman Doctrine, a commitment "to support free peoples who are resisting attempted subjugation by armed minorities or by outside pressures"—in effect, to resist communist aggression or subversion around the world.[11] Meant partly as a defense against conservative charges, this liberal anticommunism may well have helped make communism more of an issue.

What certainly increased the importance of the communism issue and placed it firmly in the Republicans' lap were several events in 1949 and 1950—the announcement of the explosion of the first Soviet atomic bomb coupled with evidence that American atomic secrets had been passed to the Soviet Union; the victory of the Chinese revolution; and the conviction of Alger Hiss, a major New Deal figure, for perjury in denying charges that he had spied for the Soviet Union. It was in this atmosphere that a minor speech by an obscure Republican senator, Joseph R. McCarthy of Wisconsin, on February 9, 1950, in Wheeling, West Virginia, launched a renewed conservative assault on the New Deal around the issue of domestic communist subversion—an assault that became known as McCarthyism. The outbreak of the Korean War later in the year encouraged its growth.

This wave of reaction too, however, fell short. The issues of "corruption, Korea, and Communism" may have helped the Republicans win the presidency and both houses of Congress in 1952, and Republican control of government gave McCarthy control of a Senate subcommittee from which to pursue his investigations.[12] In the long run, whatever its impact on individual lives, McCarthyism did not lead to a major change in policies. Eisenhower was not a liberal activist, but neither was he a conservative. His administration was a period of some retrenchment and much consolidation but not of wholesale revocation of New Deal legislation. An expanded domestic role for government was here to stay. After flirting with the idea of liberating Eastern Europe and other communist-controlled areas, Eisenhower settled down to a policy of containment mixed with occasional negotiations. McCarthy himself lost much of his official support in 1954 when he started investigating subversion in the U.S. Army. The 1954 midterm elections returned the Democrats to power in Congress, and a year later the Senate censured McCarthy.

The broader political trend of the late 1940s and the 1950s, moreover, was away from the Republican party. In a sense the New Deal realignment was still unfolding. In states from New England to the West Coast a new generation of elected Democratic leaders emerged: Senator Hubert Humphrey in Minnesota, Governor G. Mennen Williams in Michigan, Governor Edmund Muskie in Maine, Senator William Proxmire in Wisconsin (replacing the deceased McCarthy in 1957), and Governor Pat Brown in California. With them, Democratic party organizations established themselves in states where a sustained Democratic presence had been lacking for generations. The 1958 midterm elections gave Democrats forty-nine new House and fifteen new Senate seats, their biggest majorities since the height of the New Deal and, above all, a majority in the House of Representatives even without counting the southern seats. Eisenhower left office in 1960 with the Republicans in their weakest position of the postwar years; once neck-and-neck in party affiliation among voters in the late 1940s, Republicans now trailed Democrats by a wide margin. The solidly Democratic South, to be sure, was beginning to crack, but this split would not have its full impact until well into the 1960s.[13]

Finally, a generally healthy economy, though dampening the desire for further liberal reform, also minimized public openness to the major redirection of American politics conservatives proposed. The gross national product and productivity generally rose, as did real income.

What came to dominate American politics in the 1950s was neither an extension of the New Deal liberalism nor conservative reaction. Many have called it cold-war liberalism, stressing its combination of anticommunist foreign policy and the slow growth of the domestic state. Others have called it interest-group liberalism, emphasizing the extent to which debate over clear political options gave way to jockeying among interest groups for governmental favors. Alan Wolfe has named it the Growth Coalition to underline the importance given to economic growth as a solution to all political conflicts, while Godfrey Hodgson has called it simply, and misleadingly, the liberal consensus.[14] Whatever its name, the basic elements of this consensus were the following:

1. An affirmation of American capitalism, as reformed or amended since the New Deal, as an unparalleled source of both material abundance and social justice.

2. A belief that enough economic growth would mute social conflict over scarce resources and obviate hard political choices concerning how society ought to be organized.

3. An affirmation of a positive role for government in economic life, not primarily to redistribute wealth or plan production, but rather to promote economic growth by pumping money into the economy and to solve what were regarded as the vestigial injustices of a basically sound society.

4. An acceptance of a permanent American role in international affairs, understood as necessary to protect American interests around the globe and to contain communism.

Within this consensus there remained much room for debate and disagreement. Of more relevance for this discussion, however, is what got left out. On the one side was a tiny, defeated left that doubted the viability or fairness of even a reformed capitalism, questioned the centrality of economic growth, rejected the subordinate role given government in economic life, and criticized American foreign policy as an effort to maintain an American empire rather than as an attempt at true internationalism. On the other side was a sizable conservative force, critical of the new consensus even while sharing common ground with it. From the conservative perspective the new consensus was simply a continuation of New Deal liberalism. Conservatives regarded reform and the growing role of government as detracting from, rather than enhancing, American capitalism. Economic growth would be achieved, wrote Barry Goldwater in 1960, "not by government harnessing the nation's economic forces, but by emancipating them." Conservatives viewed American foreign policy as a crazy mixture of half-hearted tries at containing communism and doomed attempts to negotiate with it rather than as a forthright effort to roll back communist advance. Goldwater scolded both Republican and Democratic leaders for not making "victory the goal of American policy." [15]

In general, conservatives in the 1950s were in a contradictory political position. They had shown themselves a force to be reckoned with although unable to get into power—not even in the Republican party, let alone in the country. A national mood of self-satisfaction and quiescence had smothered liberal activism but had not sufficiently promoted conservative reaction. More important, conservatives found themselves rejecting vehemently what they regarded as the liberalism dominant in American politics even while making the same procapitalist, anticommunist appeals. Because they shared two such potent symbols with the dominant consensus, they had sure access to the political arena. At the same time, the liberal consensus gave both those symbols contents different from what conservatives wanted them to have. Procapitalism had come to imply not laissez-faire but an active, if modest, role for the state as macroeconomic manager and guarantor of social welfare; and anticommunism meant not the isolationist ideal of avoiding political involvement in European affairs but a complicated internationalist effort at containment, mixed with negotiation.

In short, political common sense—the content of the dominant political symbols—had changed. Consequently, conservatives could no longer rely on easy appeals to that common sense to put them back into power. They needed to remake in new terms the case for a *pristine* capitalism—a capitalism devoid of a major role for the state. They needed to stake out a kind of anticommunism at once different from that of the liberal consensus yet shorn of the vestiges of isolationism with which conservatives entered the 1950s. To become an effective political contender, conservatives had to reconstruct their ideology.

At the same time, if the policies of the Eisenhower administration represented the extent to which the political pendulum would swing back after the New Deal swing forward, then conservatives had to concede that the natural rhythms of American politics would not return them to power. The New Deal realignment had by the 1950s created a greatly strengthened Democratic party, well entrenched throughout the north and west, and new constituencies for that party's liberal wing. To become an effective political contender, conservatives had to build their own movement, look for support in new places, and dig in for the long haul. They had to mobilize.

As if in recognition of the political changes they were undergoing, conservatives finally decided what to call themselves. By the late 1950s they generally agreed that *conservative* was their proper name, not *individualist, true liberal,* or *libertarian.* Up to that point, the label *conservative* had led a rather homeless existence in American political discourse.[16] Throughout most of the nineteenth century it was conspicuous by its absence (as was its companion term, *liberal*). In the European politics of that day, conservative referred generally to the resistance to the major features of modern Western society—industrial capitalism, political democracy, and an individualist culture—in the name of an agrarian, aristocratic, communal social order. Liberal referred generally to support for those same changes. Because those changes came relatively easily in the United States and conflict over them was relatively muted, there was little use for the terms that described the opposing sides in those conflicts.

In the early twentieth century, conservative and liberal, their meanings substantially altered, did become common labels for describing opposing positions in American politics. Conservatism came to mean the defense of laissez-faire capitalism against government-sponsored reforms as well as opposition to internationalism and world government and to women's rights, and support for traditional religion and morality. Liberalism came to mean the opposite in each case. In the 1930s FDR chose to call his New Deal programs liberal and tarred his opponents as conservatives; general usage followed suit.

Nonetheless *conservative* remained a partisan political label. FDR might have called his opponents conservatives, but former president Herbert Hoover insisted that he was the "true liberal," while writer Albert Jay Nock called himself a "radical," an "individualist," or an "anarchist," anything but a "conservative."[17] Entering the 1950s, hard-line opponents of the New Deal legacy still went by a variety of names, or by none at all. *The Freeman,* the early-1950s mouthpiece of that opposition, described itself in its first issue as a "traditional liberal" journal. William F. Buckley's first book, *God and Man at Yale,* defended "individualism" and "Christianity" against "collectivism" and "Agnosticism" without calling its position conservative. Frank

Chodorov, for a time editor of both *The Freeman* and *Human Events,* another important hard-line journal, usually called himself an "individualist" and named the primary organization he founded the Intercollegiate Society of Individualists.[18]

As the movement and its reworked ideology coalesced, however, *conservative* became the label of choice. *National Review,* which was founded in 1955 and rapidly became the movement's premier journal, called itself a "conservative journal of opinion." Buckley's 1959 volume, *Up from Liberalism,* made it clear that the destination of its ascent was "conservatism." Works with *conservative* in their titles proliferated—Goldwater's *The Conscience of a Conservative,* Willmoore Kendall's *The Conservative Affirmation,* Frank Meyer's *What Is Conservatism?* In the fall of 1960 the founders of Young Americans for Freedom referred to themselves as "young conservatives." Indeed, conservatives quickly became protective of their new name, fiercely defending their right to use it against external critics; by 1964 Buckley could comfortably proclaim that any usage that did not center on his *National Review* and the movement it represented had simply become eccentric.[19]

The story of American conservatism in the 1950s and 1960s and into the 1970s is about how conservatives both reconstructed an ideology and built a movement. The important point here is that the 1950s represented for conservatives a new beginning, or, in Meyer's word, a "crystallization." Reaction, though not delayed, was transformed.

Two

Reconstructing an Ideology

Continuities and Changes

American conservative ideology in the 1980s, as exemplified in Ronald Reagan's speeches and in the writings of his followers, developed in the 1950s and early 1960s. Its distinctive themes were articulated in a number of places, the most influential and symptomatic of which was the *National Review,* founded in 1955 by William F. Buckley, Jr. One ought not to be misled by the fashionable tendency since the mid-1970s to see new beginnings on the right: however much American conservatism has changed since the 1950s in its strategy, its sources of support, and its propensity to compromise on one issue or hew strictly to principle on another, its ideology has remained fundamentally the same. One also ought not to be seduced by the kind of intellectual history that sees an unchanging conservatism extending back over the generations—perhaps to Edmund Burke and nineteenth-century celebrants of tradition and organic order or alternatively to the nineteenth-century purveyors of laissez-faire, social Darwinism, and atomized individualism. American conservatism as we know it is neither brand-new nor timeless; it has a history of some three decades.

The 1950s, as I showed in Chapter 1, were contradictory times for conservatives. Economic prosperity and political reaction stifled any revival of New Deal activism but did not lead to a wholesale undoing of existing New Deal reforms. What emerged instead was the compromise sometimes called the liberal consensus, which emphasized the active use of government to consolidate American power and contain communism abroad and to promote economic growth through private enterprise at home. Conservatives shared the pro-capitalism and anticommunism of this consensus but gave both terms quite different meaning. To the extent that they simply acquiesced in the dominant political ethos, they risked political homogenization; to the extent that they departed from it, they risked political oblivion.

Caught in political stalemate and faced with a difficult ideological dilemma, conservatives fell to ideological self-scrutiny, the result of which was the growth of what historian George Nash calls the "conservative intellectual movement." This movement found its voice in a growing number of journals, first *Human Events* and *The Freeman*, later the *National Review, Modern Age,* and many others.[1]

The fruit of this self-scrutiny was the active reconstruction of conservative beliefs. The conservative ideology that developed in the 1950s and early 1960s preserved the core concern of anti–New Deal conservatism with the problem of collectivism but greatly changed the ways in which that problem was understood. To understand American conservative ideology in the age of Reagan, we need to understand which of its features came through the reconstruction process intact, which features changed, and why they changed. We need to look behind conservative ideology as a finished historical product to see how it was constructed and how its constituent elements fit together.

What has stayed the same in American conservative ideology since the 1930s has been its core opposition not simply to the New Deal but, more importantly and more accurately, to the broader trends that the New Deal was said to represent. This continuity is what makes the conservative intellectuals of the 1950s and 1960s sound a lot like Herbert Hoover or the American Liberty League and what makes Ronald Reagan sound a lot like all of them. To get at this core stance let us return to the writings of Frank Meyer, longtime *National Review* editor and one of the most important formulators of a reconstructed conservative ideology in the 1950s and 1960s. Immediately after characterizing the American conservative movement as the "delayed reaction" to the "revolutionary transformation" of America begun by the New Deal, Meyer went on to say:

> That revolution itself has been a gentler, more humane, bloodless expression in the United States of the revolutionary wave that has swept the globe in the twentieth century. Its grimmest, most total manifestations have been the phenomena of Communism and Nazism. In rather peculiar forms in late years it

has expressed itself in the so-called nationalism typified by Nasser, Nkrumah, and Sukarno; in Western Europe it has taken the forms of the socialism of England or that of Scandinavia. Everywhere, however open or masked, it represents the aggrandizement of the power of the state over the lives of individual persons. Always that aggrandizement is cloaked in a rhetoric and a program putatively directed to and putatively concerned for "the masses."[2]

This passage nicely captures the assessment of the modern world that lies at the heart of American conservative ideology. Note the assumptions made explicit here or lurking just beneath the surface:

1. The central peril facing humankind in the twentieth century is the "aggrandizement of the power of the state," the growing tendency of the state to organize or plan social life (a trend that conservatives call statism, collectivism, rationalism, or, at an extreme, totalitarianism).

2. The growth of the state results primarily from—or is at least justified as—an effort "putatively directed to and putatively concerned for 'the masses.'" That is, it has occurred in the name of equality, social welfare, or building an earthly utopia.

3. A variety of apparently different political phenomena, including communism, fascism, Third World nationalism, European social democracy, and American New Deal liberalism, are all in essence similar because they all tend toward statism or collectivism.

4. By implication, only two kinds of society are possible—collectivism and what most conservatives would call free society, which is in effect capitalism understood in a particular way. In principle, at least, to depart from the latter substantially is to put oneself on a slippery slope to totalitarianism; the middle ground is precarious.

Although their core concern remained the same, conservatives transformed their case against collectivism both abroad and at home in the 1950s and early 1960s. First, conservatism moved dramatically from an isolationist to an interventionist anticommunism. Coming out of World War II, conservatism, while certainly anticommunist, maintained the classic objections of prewar isolationism to an active international role in the United States. Isolationism, however, was increasingly out of step with political reality, or at least with the dominant interpretation of that reality. In the early 1950s conservatism shifted to an interventionist anticommunism, which managed to distinguish itself from liberal anticommunism by stressing liberation rather than containment. In this way conservatism accommodated to the dominant political consensus while remaining critical of it.

Second, conservatives attempted to revise their argument against the growing domestic state and their defense of laissez-faire (or what I shall soon call "pristine") capitalism. As the 1950s approached, the conservative position tended to have a utilitarian bent, criticizing big government for hampering economic prosperity, and celebrating unfettered capitalism for promoting it. Although this argument obviously has never disappeared, it lost credibility for a time in the 1950s and 1960s as increased government spending seemed to coincide with economic health and as the liberal consensus successfully appropriated the language of economic growth and prosperity to justify a growing, if circumscribed, role for government. Conservatives, as a result, sought to make their case in an alternative way as well, arguing that whatever their short-term consequences, unfettered capitalism and the kind of economic freedom that goes with it were inherently good. That is, they attempted to make a moral case for capitalism to go along with the utilitarian one. The conservative concern with how best to promote unfettered capitalism provided the rationale for a philosophical discussion about how to bring together two very different kinds of conservative language—a libertarianism that emphasized individualism and freedom, and a traditionalism that stressed moral order and community.

The Transformation of Anticommunism

As it emerged from World War II, conservative thought was largely isolationist or noninterventionist. It was wary of the broad new role the United States was taking in the world in the name of anticommunism and critical of high levels of defense spending and the growing power of the president in military and foreign affairs. It feared that an anticommunist crusade would simply be an excuse for supporting old corrupt empires and governments or for establishing a new American imperialism; it worried that global overcommitment would wreck the American economy or lead to a third world war with more dire consequences than the first two; it believed that mobilizing to oppose the Soviet Union might be a greater threat to American liberty than the Soviet Union itself. This is not to say that conservatives yielded anything to liberals and Democrats in regard to anticommunism but merely that their anticommunism was initially of a different kind, one that would prove unviable in the postwar world.

Beginning roughly in 1947, the year James Burnham published his influential *The Struggle for the World,* a second kind of conservative anticommunism, interventionist in nature, began to appear; by 1955, the year the *National Review* began publishing, it had all but pushed aside noninterventionist anticommunism among conservatives. Rather than being skeptical of America's new global role as leader of an anticommunist crusade, it pressed this crusade with a vengeance. It was critical of the foreign policy of the Truman administration for doing too little and being too disorganized, not for doing too much.

The shift from noninterventionism to interventionism was the occasion for a split on the Right between self-labeled conservatives and self-labeled libertarians. The latter, who did not make the transition and thus found themselves outside the new conservative camp, often pictured the transition as an abrupt break or a brazen intellectual theft. Libertarian Murray Rothbard contrasts the Right of the 1930s and 1940s, which worried about the growth of the "leviathan state" abroad as well as at home and which provided "the main political opposition to the Cold War," to the newer Right of the 1950s and 1960s, whose only goal, he argued, was the annihilation of the Soviet Union. Conservative historian George Nash, however, emphasizes the ease with which the transition took place. Nash is more nearly correct: noninterventionist anticommunism gave way relatively smoothly to interventionist anticommunism, partly because historical circumstances had rendered the former obsolete and partly because despite their obvious differences, the two had some less obvious similarities. Noninterventionist anticommunism could become interventionist after selective, if dramatic, ideological pruning.[3]

Prewar Noninterventionism.   To understand postwar noninterventionist anticommunism, one needs first to understand the so-called isolationism of prewar years; and the first step in doing that is to recognize that the label is misleading in at least two ways.[4] First, isolationism did not mean total noninvolvement of the United States with the rest of the world. What isolationists typically rejected were long-term or entangling *political* commitments, especially involving *European* affairs. In this sense, the term *noninterventionism* is probably more accurate, especially in the context of the 1930s and early 1940s, when the central issue was nonintervention or neutrality toward the growing conflicts in Europe, which in effect meant not going to war with Germany.

Second, there were many isolationisms, not just one. Rather than being one consistent ideology or movement, isolationism or noninterventionism was a feature of a variety of political positions and drew on a range of arguments. Some students of the movement err by focusing wholly on its conservative, anticommunist tendencies; others by highlighting its radical, anti-imperialist variants. Thus, some noninterventionists were pacifists; others, like the America First Committee, advocated strong air and naval forces to defend the Western Hemisphere. Some were noninterventionist out of ethnic sensibilities—the anti-English bias of Irish Americans or the pro-German bias of German Americans; others were noninterventionist out of a broader anti-imperialism. Some were anti-Semitic, blaming war on Jews, though most were not. Some were conservative advocates of a laissez-faire capitalism; others were liberals, progressives, and socialists. The Midwest may have been especially fertile ground for isolationism, but regional sensibilities were not essential to it. Certainly through the mid-1930s noninterventionism had broad and diverse support, and it would be wrong to see it simply as a product of the Midwest, specific ethnic minorities, fascist sympathies, or xenophobia.[5]

In the late 1930s, to be sure, public support for noninterventionism declined markedly as the practical difficulties of neutrality became manifest, as evidence of German aggression increased, and as public sympathy shifted to Britain and France. Noninterventionism, moreover, became more closely allied to anti–New Deal conservatism. While noninterventionist organizations still spanned the political spectrum, the major liberal journals were strongly in favor of going to war against fascism; the leading noninterventionist organization, the America First Committee, tilted distinctly to the right; and noninterventionist liberals often found themselves pushed in that direction for want of an audience on their customary political terrain.

Despite the drift to the right, however, noninterventionists on the eve of American entry into World War II still drew on a diverse repertoire of arguments. Among the most prominent arguments against going to war, especially with Germany, were the following:

1. America should avoid entangling alliances and expensive long-term commitments that undermine its independence, threaten to bankrupt its economy, and limit its ability to retain control over its own foreign policy. The crucial feature of a viable foreign policy, in short, should be *unilateralism.*

2. Europe is so corrupt and problem-ridden that America can do nothing to help it. Getting involved will simply drag America down.

3. War or a war-oriented economy necessarily aggrandizes the state, concentrates power in the presidency, and otherwise threatens democracy and freedom at home. War has never done anything to spread democracy and freedom abroad.

4. There is no compelling moral reason for America to go to war against Nazi Germany, a country that is no worse than Britain or France. Going to war against Germany inevitably would mean American support for British and French imperialism and perhaps ultimately the growth of an American empire. European conflicts, and perhaps wars in general, are not ideological or moral battles in which one side is markedly better than the other; they are economic and territorial contests between self-interested states.

5. Going to war with Nazi Germany would mean an alliance with the Soviet Union, which would ultimately promote communism.

6. The Nazi regime in Germany may be horrible, but it is practically no direct threat to the United States. We can hardly expect a German invasion across the Atlantic Ocean, especially if we maintain strong air and naval defenses. Moreover, Germany's natural aspirations lie to the east, where we can hope Nazi Germany and Soviet Russia will bleed themselves to death in a prolonged war.

7. Wars are always the result of conspiracy and manipulation; they are fought not because of external threats but to deal with domestic problems. Bankers, munitions makers, and other war profiteers manipulated the United States into World War I. Faced with the domestic failures of the New Deal, FDR is maneuvering us into war with Germany and Japan.

In short, prewar noninterventionism appealed to a range of themes: unilateralism, dislike of Europe, antistatism, anticommunism, anti-imperialism, realpolitik, and a distrust of elites.

Noninterventionist Anticommunism. At the close of World War II the conservative noninterventionist could advance many of the same arguments to oppose the foreign policy of the Truman administration. Everything from the United Nations to the Atlantic Pact to the Truman Doctrine smacked of entangling alliances and overreaching commitments. The high levels of defense spending and the secrecy with which a number of postwar agreements and policies was made threatened to increase state power and undermine democracy. If conservatives agreed on the evil of the Soviet Union, they hardly looked favorably on our allies, especially Britain, which was doubly damned for its empire and its Labour government. The Soviet Union, many conservatives argued, was not a direct threat to the United States; we would overburden ourselves if we tried to protect every nation potentially threatened by it. A third world war against Russia, moreover, might paradoxically lead to the strengthening of world communism just as the first two wars had. The real communist threat was domestic and took two forms: first, policies of appeasement, and perhaps outright treason, that since the wartime and postwar conferences had ceded big pieces of the world to the communists; and second, the economic crisis and totalitarianism that militarization and global overinvolvement might bring.

A prime example of noninterventionist anticommunism was the speech delivered to the Senate by Senator Robert Taft, the acknowledged leader of the Republican party in Congress and a longtime noninterventionist, on January 5, 1951, part of the "great debate" on American foreign policy. Taft was unequivocal that the Soviet Union was an aggressive totalitarian power bent on world domination and that America "must be the leader in the battle to prevent the spread of communism and defend liberty." Yet he had little good to say about the anticommunist foreign policy of the Truman administration.[6]

Taft strongly criticized the secret, centralized, undebated way that policy was being made—the very way, he added, that Democratic administrations in the 1930s and 1940s had made the policies that had appeased the Soviet Union, helped make it a world power, and led to the problem that current policies were trying to solve. "It is part of our American system that the basic elements of foreign policy shall be openly debated," Taft argued, but the Roosevelt and Truman administrations had concentrated foreign policy–making power in the executive and "assumed complete authority to make in secret the most vital decisions and commit this country to the most important and dangerous obligations." A "dangerous" new theory of bipartisanship had even arisen that "there shall be no criticism of the foreign policy of the administration" because such criticism undermined national unity and aided the enemy. President Truman had committed American troops to Korea without consulting Congress; now, Taft warned, the president even claimed the right to use atomic weapons without consultation, and a secret agreement seemed to be in the offing to send American troops to Europe.

Taft also attacked what he regarded as three false premises underlying Truman administration policies: that the United States had broad moral responsibilities around the globe; that the Soviet Union sought direct military conquest of the world and hence that war with it was inevitable; and that a high level of defense spending was necessary and acceptable. The goals of American foreign policy ought to be limited and realistic, he argued, not "to reform the entire world or spread sweetness and light and economic prosperity" but simply to maintain American liberty. Although the Soviet Union certainly planned to spread communism throughout the world, Taft continued, it hardly envisioned military conquest or a war with the United States. Stationing American troops in Europe, however, might provoke war with the Soviet Union because "however defensive and pacific our intentions, the building up of this force must look like aggression when it is completed." Finally, Taft argued that the high level of military spending required by the foreign policy of the Truman administration would lead to high taxes and inflation, domestic economic disaster, and, ultimately, loss of liberty.

In short, Taft combined classic noninterventionist positions—a limited international role for the United States, the downplaying of the immediate enemy threat, a fear of military spending, and even the thinly veiled accusation that the administration was warmongering—with a compelling sense that America nonetheless had to act forthrightly against the Soviet Union. The specific proposals in Taft's speech reflected this mix of views. He rejected stationing American troops in Europe, criticized the Korean War as unwise, and counseled against any obligations that required extensive use of land-based forces. Instead he advocated reliance on sea and air power to defend the Western Hemisphere, "island nations" like Japan and Great Britain, and potentially Western Europe as well; a counteroffensive by Chiang Kai-shek against the Communist Chinese, at least until peace was made in Korea; "aggressive methods of propaganda" for promoting the "philosophy of liberty"; and efforts to organize insurgencies in Soviet satellite countries. Taft also urged his fellow senators to recognize that in reality the United States was at war with China in Korea and to "untie the hands of our military commanders."

Other conservatives made a noninterventionist case similar to Taft's. Former president Herbert Hoover, a senior statesman of conservative Republicanism, ringingly condemned the evils of communism and chastised the Democrats for years of "acquiescences and appeasements" but nonetheless opposed the Truman administration's military buildup to fight communism as disastrous for the American economy. Rather than shouldering the entire burden of defending the world against communism, Hoover counseled, America should either convince its allies to join the mobilization or, failing that, retreat to a defensive posture, developing its air and sea power to defend the "Western Hemisphere Gibraltar of western civilization," and perhaps Great Britain and Japan, but no more.[7]

Felix Morley, founder and onetime editor of *Human Events* before it forsook noninterventionism, argued that the militarism and military establishment that inevitably went with an interventionist anticommunist foreign policy would lead to imperialism abroad and concentration of power at home—both policies incompatible with "republican institutions." Frank Chodorov, who edited both *Human Events* and *The Freeman*, ratified this argument and added that if communism came to America, it would not be by conquest—the Soviet Union was not strong enough for that—but because Americans wanted an expanded state: "Communism will not be imported from Moscow; it will come out of Wall Street and Main Street." Murray Rothbard, already distancing himself in the early 1950s from the main conservative camp in favor of a purer libertarianism, argued that the real enemy was not the Soviet Union or even communism but the state itself. Because all states were inherently coercive, repressive at home and imperialist abroad, the proper goal was limiting state power in general.[8]

Interventionist Anticommunism.   By way of contrast with noninterventionism, consider the writings of the most able and influential interventionist conservative, James Burnham, later an editor at the *National Review,* who presented his position in a series of books in the first decade after the war: *The Struggle for the World* (1947), *The Coming Defeat of Communism* (1950), and *Containment or Liberation?* (1953). Although the emphasis and argument of each of these books differ somewhat, reflecting in part the last stages of Burnham's odyssey from left to right, together they present a fairly consistent stance.[9]

Even before World War II had ended, Burnham argued, World War III had begun between the United States and the Soviet Union, a struggle that would decide who would control the world. The Soviet Union brought to this conflict immense population and resources; the United States, a more economically, politically, and culturally advanced society. What had been telling thus far, however, was that the Soviet Union recognized that it was at war and pursued its goal of world dominance single-mindedly and wholeheartedly. The United States, because of its immaturity on the world stage, had failed to grasp geopolitical realities, take on its new international responsibilities, and mobilize accordingly. The crucial factor, therefore, Burnham argued, would be "politics and political will."

Burnham had nothing but scorn either for advocates of appeasement, who counseled getting along with the Soviet Union, or for the isolationists, who resisted America's new global role and seemed willing to surrender the European continent. He aimed his main criticism, however, at the emerging doctrine of containment, as codified in George Kennan's writings and put into practice in the Truman Doctrine, the Marshall Plan, the North Atlantic Treaty Organization, aid to Greece and Turkey, and American rearmament. As its name indicates, this policy sought to contain Soviet expansionism wherever it might strike in the hope that such determination would eventually pressure Soviet leaders into giving up their expansionary goals and moderating their policies. To be sure, Burnham saw containment as a step in the right direction, and he believed the coherence of U.S. foreign policy to be greatly enhanced by the centralization of policymaking in the executive branch that accompanied it—the creation of the National Security Council, the Department of Defense, the Joint Chiefs of Staff, and the Policy Planning Staff of the State Department.

Nonetheless, Burnham regarded containment as fatally flawed on a number of grounds. Containment seemed to imply that the United States could ultimately coexist peacefully with the Soviet Union once its leaders had modified their geopolitical goals. As a purely defensive strategy, it in effect let the Soviet Union choose the time and place of confrontation to its own advantage; it also did nothing to weaken Soviet power in its European base or its subversive, aggressive power abroad. Above all, containment was not a sufficiently lofty or inspiring goal to sustain the "moral and spiritual demands" required by the "heavy expenditures of resources, talents, and courage" that fighting communism required. "Who," Burnham asked, "will willingly suffer, sacrifice, and die for containment?"[10]

Underlying all these flaws, Burnham argued, lay a failure to recognize three realities of the postwar world. First, the United States and the Soviet Union were already at war; the apparent peace was illusory. Second, in the modern world the lines between war and peace, military and civilian, had broken down. War was now fought by a host of nonmilitary—political and ideological—means. Third, the Soviet Union was not a conventional state but the "main base of a world communist movement, an unprecedented enterprise" that was at once a secular religion, a world conspiracy, and new kind of army, irrevocably pledged to world domination.[11]

What, then, was to be done? According to Burnham, the United States had to make the "destruction of the power of Soviet-based communism" the central objective of foreign policy and focus its energy accordingly. To accomplish this objective would require, first of all, stopping communist expansion not only through direct containment but also by breaking the power of communist movements within noncommunist countries. More important, it demanded an *offensive* strategy, what Burnham variously called a "policy of liberation" or an "Eastern European strategy," which would openly seek to overthrow communist regimes in the Soviet Union and Eastern Europe through "political-subversive" warfare—a massive propaganda campaign and the support of refugee liberation movements.[12]

Burnham, in short, summoned the United States to take an active leadership role in the world and to mobilize for the war for world power already under way with the Soviet Union. He believed the stakes were high, the moment late, the enemy dangerous and powerful, and victory attainable only with immense sacrifice and expense. Yet if the United States did mobilize, he thought, the Soviet

Union would be overwhelmed. The Soviets' great advantage lay in the capacity of their leadership to define and pursue wholeheartedly the goal of world domination. If American leaders showed a similar determination, that advantage would evaporate and the inherent weaknesses of the Soviet Union would come to the fore. But for all his talk about war, Burnham did not expect his policy of liberation to lead to direct armed conflict between the United States and the Soviet Union.

The Transition.   Despite their shared anticommunism, the noninterventionist and interventionist positions were clearly as different as day and night. The noninterventionists in effect called for retrenchment, a foreign policy of limited goals and limited means. They pictured a United States with clearly circumscribed world responsibilities. They were wary of political power and its unintended consequences and hidden motives. The interventionists called for total mobilization, for throwing all resources into the struggle to defeat communism utterly. They envisioned a United States as leader of nothing less than a world empire. They were virtually intoxicated with power, with the capacity to define, pursue, and attain goals. They worried little about abuses of American power or its unintended consequences.

Yet after all was said and done, the shift from noninterventionism to interventionism occurred rather smoothly. To be sure, conservatives sometimes debated the alternatives angrily, and a few agonized in print over the choices. There was, however, surprisingly little wrangling, and once the transition had taken place, largely with the founding of the *National Review* in 1955, conservatives hardly gave it a second thought.

One reason for the smoothness of the transition undoubtedly was the emergence of a new generation of conservative leaders in politics and political journalism who no longer viewed the 1950s through the lens of the 1930s and 1940s. The Goldwaters replaced the Tafts, and the Buckleys replaced the Chodorovs. They were heavily influenced as well by writers whose background lay not in conservative Republicanism but in various kinds of radicalism from which they were in flight—James Burnham, Whittaker Chambers, and William Schlamm, to name three.[13]

More fundamentally, the transition went off smoothly because in the political context of the 1950s noninterventionist anticommunism had become an ideological liability. Its problems are manifest in Taft's speech. It was anticommunism with a troubled conscience: Taft urged America to take the lead against the Soviet menace, but he raised all sorts of scruples about the international use of American power. It was anticommunism fraught with contradiction: Taft condemned the Truman administration for at once being too aggressive and not aggressive enough; he simultaneously rejected troops in Europe as unnecessarily provocative and supported other measures that were at least as provocative; he condemned the decision to send troops to Korea but urged taking the war to China. Finally, noninterventionist anticommunism was vulnerable to liberal counterattacks precisely because of its scruples and contradictions: in the debate following his speech, Taft found himself under attack from Senators J. William Fulbright and Wayne Morse (who in later years would take the lead in opposing the Vietnam War) for being, in effect, soft on communism or at least unwilling to do what was necessary to confront the Soviet Union.

The liabilities became increasingly clear to conservatives themselves. In a famous exchange in *The Freeman* in 1954, interventionist William Schlamm drove the point home in an exchange with noninterventionist Frank Chodorov. Surely, Chodorov argued, the lesson of the 1940s was clear enough: mobilizing against the external enemies of freedom inevitably diminishes freedom at home by enlarging the state, raising taxes, and generally militarizing society. Schlamm replied that it was no longer 1940, when conservatives could hope that if the United States stayed out of the European war, Nazi Germany and the Soviet Union would destroy each other. In the world of the 1950s there was no effective counter to Soviet power but that of the United States, hence it was simply contradictory to inveigh against the ultimate evil of the Soviet Union and world communism while voicing grave doubts about the rectitude of an all-out anticommunist crusade.[14]

One need not share Schlamm's politics to recognize that given the dominant political assumptions of America in the 1950s, the noninterventionist anticommunist had a choice to make. He could be an anticommunist or a noninterventionist but he could not be both—at least not convincingly. In a political context in which it was assumed that the Soviet Union was not only evil but also intent on world conquest and capable of carrying out that intent, noninterventionist anticommunism had become anticommunism hobbled by its moral scruples. Interventionist anticommunism so readily won conservatives over precisely because it had none of the liabilities of noninterventionism. In adopting it, conservatives simply gave up a collective bad conscience about the use of state power in one sphere.

Interventionism also triumphed so easily because although it required conservatives to give up a host of moral and political concerns about the military power of the state, it still incorporated two important noninterventionist themes intact, unilateralism and a preoccupation with liberal perfidy. First, interventionists as well as noninterventionists sought a foreign policy that would preserve the independence of the United States by avoiding entangling alliances and open-ended commitments. They criticized the Truman Doctrine from different perspectives but agreed that its essentially defensive strategy threatened to bog America down in an unending struggle. Noninterventionists could agree with the interventionist enthusiasm for an offensive policy of liberation, which seemed to offer a less costly, less entangling alternative. Both groups shared a frustration at apparent American impotence and a preference for quick solutions. Noninterventionists might assert that the Korean war—a land war against numerically superior forces undertaken by a president without consultation with Congress—was dreadfully wrong, but they often believed that once involved, the United States ought to take the war to China by bombing supply lines and staging areas. From this perspective the danger lay not in the anticommunist crusade itself but in one that was half-hearted and led to stalemate. Interventionists might castigate noninterventionists for their immaturity in foreign-policy matters and call for America to assume the role of world leadership. They might picture the struggle against communism as long-term and costly. Still, they also argued that given determined leadership, political will, and correct strategies, the United States would overwhelm the Soviet Union.

Second, interventionists could agree with noninterventionists that decades of appeasement by Democratic and liberal leadership had created the communist menace and that the Soviet threat was largely a function of liberal lack of determination and flawed policies. They thus shared a gut distrust of any policy, whatever its content, that developed under the auspices of liberals and Democrats. Both of them favored the rooting out of the sympathizers, fellow travelers, and subversives from American government.

Emblematic of their large areas of agreement, noninterventionists and interventionists alike could rally behind Senator Joseph McCarthy on the issue of domestic communism and General Douglas MacArthur on issues of military strategy. Senator Taft, who never fully made the transition, remained a hero for all conservatives long after the triumph of interventionism.

In a broad sense the shared emphases on unilateralism and liberal perfidy reinforced each other. The former demanded a world in which problems were subject to straightforward solutions; the latter proclaimed that only wrongheaded leadership prevented finding such a solution for the problem of communism. The penchant for what Eric Goldman called the "quick, total solution of any world problem" informed conservative interventionism as much as noninterventionism, especially in contrast to the anticommunism of the liberal consensus, with its commitment to an open-ended process of containment.[15]

The greater political suitability of interventionism and its incorporation of some noninterventionist themes made the transition so smooth that those who lived through it seemed quickly to lose all memory that conservatives had ever believed otherwise. The intellectual journey of William F. Buckley, Jr., in this regard is instructive. As an adolescent in 1940, Buckley had supported the America First Committee. As late as 1954 Buckley's writings still reflected noninterventionist themes; one article of his in *The Freeman* criticized military training for encouraging unquestioning deference to authority, the suppression of individuality, and regimentation. Such traits, he argued, were undoubtedly good for "effective war-making" but hardly constituted the "trademarks of the free man." What the demobilized military personnel needed, Buckley suggested half-seriously, was a libertarian deorientation.[16]

In August 1954 Buckley noted with concern that conservative anticommunists were implicitly dividing themselves into noninterventionist and interventionist camps, disagreeing over the immediacy of the Soviet threat and the dangers posed by militarizing American society. He offered no immediate resolution of these differences.[17] In early 1955, after these two camps explicitly clashed in the Chodorov-Schlamm debate, Buckley wrote to *The Freeman* that he had "dejectedly" made his choice. Yes, going to war against the Soviet Union would aggrandize the American state, and undoing that aggrandizement afterward would be difficult. Still, he decided, there would be a better chance against an aggrandized American state than against passively accepted Soviet tyranny. For that reason, Buckley concluded, "I number myself, dejectedly, among those who favor a carefully planned showdown, and who are prepared to go to war to frustrate communist designs."[18]

In this carefully measured decision the ultimate choice has openly acknowledged costs and stands only as the lesser of two evils. What is striking about the newly founded *National Review* a few months later is that although Buckley's decision stood, the agony, dejection, and weighing of costs that went into its making ceased to be discussed. Once made, the choice appeared self-evident, and its costs were conveniently forgotten, buried in silence. A whole set of noninterventionist arguments, which had been common in the pages of *The Freeman*, were abandoned by its effective successor, the *National Review*, even as topics for debate. The magazine's writers spent little time worrying about imperialism or militarism, the domestic consequences of anticommunist mobilization, or defense spending and the military establishment. By the early 1960s Frank Meyer could dismiss criticism of anticommunist militarism from a fundamentally noninterventionist position as something alien to the conservative political universe.[19]

Banished from conservative discourse, the debate over interventionism persisted instead on the fringes of conservatism as a battle between conservatives and those who called themselves libertarians. Libertarians took the conservative abandonment of noninterventionism as the prime example of a broader retreat from a principled antistatism on the right. Conservatives, libertarians charged, not only promoted a belligerent foreign policy and sanctioned imperialism abroad but also sought to suppress civil liberties and extend the power of the state in other ways at home. The conservatives responded that libertarians indulged in a dogmatic or fundamentalist antistatism whereas they themselves held a more flexible presumption against state power that they were willing to modify as circumstances warrant, the better to fight communism, preserve domestic order, combat drug abuse, and the like.[20]

From Barry Goldwater's *Conscience of a Conservative* (1960) to Richard Viguerie's *The New Right: We're Ready to Lead* (1980), the basic tenets of interventionist conservatism remained the same: an emphasis on American weakness and vulnerability due to a failure of liberal political leadership and will; a call for recognizing the de facto state of war with the Soviet Union and making victory in that war the central goal of foreign policy; and a summons to total mobilization against the enemy. Similar themes, in less extreme form, appeared in Ronald Reagan's rhetoric throughout much of his presidency and expressed themselves as well in his administration's liberation strategy of supporting insurgencies in Nicaragua, Angola, and Afghanistan.[21]

The Synthesis of Libertarianism and Traditionalism

The reconstruction of the conservative case against domestic collectivism took the form of a debate over whether that case could best be made in a libertarian language that stressed the decline of individualism and freedom, a traditionalist language that emphasized the loss of moral order and community, or some combination of the two. Conservatives never fully resolved the issue; indeed, given the different, even contradictory, natures of the two languages, they could not. The center of ideological attention became an attempted synthesis most commonly called *fusionism*, and the two languages came to coexist more or less harmoniously in a revised conservative ideology.

Why conservatives tried so hard to combine such disparate ideas and how they did so are questions that cannot be answered by viewing the effort as a philosophical matter of deciding on first principles, as most observers have done. At stake as well was precisely the concrete social and political problem of how best to make a case for laissez-faire capitalism. Conservatives turned to traditionalist themes to help construct a moral defense of capitalism to supplement the utilitarian one that usually emerged from libertarianism. To be sure, traditionalism at first seems an odd place to look since most of its variants were heavily critical of both capitalism and individualist philosophies. Still, conservatives attempted to isolate from traditionalism an emphasis on transcendent moral truths and integrate it into a basically libertarian outlook.

Libertarianism.   The libertarianism discussed in this section is different from the particular antistatist, noninterventionist movement that has called itself *libertarian* and that I have just discussed in the previous section. It refers to a broad philosophical perspective characteristic of a wide range of politicians and intellectuals on the right—leaders of the Old Republican Right like Herbert Hoover and Robert Taft; neoclassical economists like Friedrich Hayek, Ludwig von Mises, and Milton Friedman; and a variety of iconoclastic individualists and objectivists like Albert Jay Nock and Ayn Rand, as well as self-labeled libertarians. Despite their obvious differences, all share a basic worldview that its proponents have variously called individualism, true liberalism, philosophy of liberty, or libertarianism.

The central features of the generic libertarian position are the following:

1. The root problem of the modern world is the loss of individual freedom. For libertarianism, freedom is primarily understood in the negative: Its major precondition is an absence of coercion, by force or fraud, of life, limb, or property. The most dangerous source of this coercion is the state since it monopolizes the legitimate use of force; hence a limited state (or even no state at all) is the precondition for freedom. The primary freedom, moreover, is economic, both as precondition and paradigm: the unrestricted right to use one's property, spend one's money, and sell one's skills and labor. To be sure, libertarianism recognizes other valuable freedoms, but it regards economic freedom as necessary for other freedoms and as a model for understanding them.

2. Freedom so understood presupposes an individualist image of society. In the libertarian view, society is nothing more than an association of self-directed (but not necessarily selfish) individuals. It is not itself an entity; it has no goals, interests, or rights other than those of all the individuals who make it up. Any effort to hypostatize society, to impute to it an existence of its own or to define a distinct common good, necessarily undermines individual freedom by providing the potential basis for collectivism. The libertarian view of society assumes that individuals have the capacity for self-control and self-direction, but it rarely examines how that capacity develops. It also assumes that these self-directed individuals intent on purely personal goals can live together harmoniously in society. Finally, since it treats values as the province of the individual, it rarely asks how individuals come to have certain values or which ones they ought to have.

3. The main supports of individual freedom in the modern world are the major elements of capitalism—private property, the market, and the organization of economic life around private profit. The major threat to individual freedom is the growing state direction of economic life. In the libertarian view, freedom and capitalism are two sides of the same coin. The defense of one implies the defense of the other.

It is important to note for understanding both libertarianism and the conservative synthesis of which it is a part that the libertarian defense of capitalism is a defense of not just any capitalism, nor is it just any defense of capitalism. Libertarianism is above all a defense of what is best called *pristine* capitalism, the more common term *laissez-faire* being too narrow. Pristine capitalism is capitalism in which the original, most distinctive features of the system do not give way to their opposites in the normal course of development. In pristine capitalism the market and commodity relations do not give way to a growing state role in structuring economic relations and distributing income; individual entrepreneurship does not give way to the bureaucratic corporation; competition, to monopoly; concrete, owner-controlled property, to abstract stock ownership; individualism and contractual relations, to growing rationalization. The existence of the latter elements is not denied; they are simply regarded as extrinsic and inessential to the system. This image of pristine capitalism is implicit in both libertarianism and the conservatism that incorporates it.

The libertarian defense of this pristine capitalism has often tended to be materialist and secular in nature. Capitalism is justified by its superior efficiency, its promotion of technological innovation and material progress, and its ability to deliver goods. The appeal is to individual self-interest: capitalism maximizes individual prosperity, happiness, and the capacity to pursue personal goals.

Libertarian arguments were the mainstay of the anti–New Deal politics of the 1930s and 1940s. They dominated the arguments of right-wing Republicans like Hoover and Taft and the pamphlets of the American Liberty League.[22] In the postwar years perhaps the most powerful libertarian influence on conservatism was Friedrich Hayek's *The Road to Serfdom*. Hayek situated himself squarely in the individualist tradition, the development of which he traced from the

Renaissance to the nineteenth century. This tradition stressed "respect for the individual man qua man," which meant treating each person's own views and tastes as supreme in his or her own life and believing that "men should develop their own individual gifts and bents." It dictated as well that in constructing society, "we should make as much use as possible of the spontaneous forces of society, and resort as little as possible to coercion." It encouraged a belief in the "unbounded possibilities" of improving the human condition and a "new sense of power" over human fate.[23]

Since the late 1800s, however, this tradition had been in eclipse, Hayek argued, as Western societies had sought to replace "the impersonal and anonymous mechanism of the market by collective and 'conscious' direction of all social forces to deliberately chosen goals." This is what Hayek called "collectivism," and he argued that all collectivisms, whatever their goals, tended alike toward totalitarianism. What mattered were the means, not the ends:

> The various kinds of collectivism, communism, fascism, etc., differ among themselves in the nature of the goal toward which they want to direct the efforts of society. But they all differ from liberalism and individualism in wanting to organize the whole of society and all its resources for this unitary end and in refusing to recognize autonomous spheres in which the ends of individuals are supreme. In short, they are totalitarian in the true sense of this new word.[24]

Any attempt to direct society toward a collective goal, Hayek maintained, necessarily encroached on democracy because it required central planning and a degree of consensus that democratic decision making could not yield. It undermined the rule of law because governmental planning required a degree of discretion that was incompatible with the predictability and regularity of laws. Finally, it diminished individual freedom because central planning necessarily led to state control over consumption (hence what goods people could buy) and production (hence who got what jobs).

Nor could one confine planning to limited economic goals, such as an equal distribution of income, and leave society otherwise untouched, Hayek continued. Economic control meant power over the resources needed for pursuing all noneconomic ends and thus conferred the power to define which ends were desirable. Once the market was impeded, moreover, the need for planning multiplied; once people decided that government was responsible for their fate, their demands on it rose. In short, no middle ground was possible.

Above all, Hayek stressed that at the heart of collectivism lay a false view of morality and the role of the state. "It [collectivism] presupposes . . . the existence of a complete ethical code in which all the different human values are allotted their due place." That is, it assumed some transcendent or absolute scheme of values on which collective goals could be based. "We do not possess moral standards which would enable us to settle those questions," Hayek argued. "The growth of civilization," in fact, coincided with "a steady diminution of the sphere in which individual actions are bound by fixed rules. The rules of which our common moral code consists have progressively become fewer and more general in character." Given this, values must be the province of the individual. "It is this recognition of the individual as the ultimate judge of his ends," Hayek maintained, "that forms the essence of the individualistic position" (rather than the belief that "man is egoistic or selfish"). Such a view does not rule out common action for social ends, but it regards such ends as "merely identical ends of many individuals" and thus limits common action "to the fields where people agree on common ends." Usually common ends will not be ultimate goals "but means which different persons can use for different purposes" because consensus is more likely on such things. The state, then, has a role to play, but it is largely limited to setting the terms for individual pursuit of individual goals, not to defining the goals themselves. In Hayek's terms, its role is utilitarian rather than moral.[25]

Traditionalism. The traditionalism that conservatives sought to add to libertarianism, like its counterpart, embraced a range of positions and a diversity of thinkers. It included arguments rooted in natural law, Christian theology, and nineteenth-century European conservatism and its notions of tradition. Among its proponents in the late 1940s and 1950s who influenced the developing conservative synthesis were Leo Strauss, Eric Voegelin, Robert Nisbet, Russell Kirk, and Richard Weaver, to name but a few.[26] Despite the diversity, a distinct set of arguments emerged from most traditionalist writing:

1. The major problems of the modern world, according to traditionalists, are the decay of belief in a divinely rooted, objective moral

order and the decline of community, processes that have unfolded over several centuries. The loss of transcendent, spiritual values—a belief in an absolute good independent of human preferences and desires—has left human beings without an overarching purpose and justification for life other than the worldly, materialist goals of pleasure, success, and worldly perfection. The decline of shared beliefs and of institutions like family, church, community, and guild that bind individuals to each other have left human beings atomized and rootless. The ultimate effect of these twin processes is totalitarian, because they leave human beings craving for both the promise of an earthly utopia and a substitute sense of belonging.

2. Underlying this analysis is an image of society as more than an association of individuals who pursue purely personal goals and are tied to others purely by bonds of self-interest. It requires moral or emotional bonds, a set of compelling shared beliefs, and it easily falls apart in the absence of a shared sense of moral order or public virtue. The task of maintaining these shared beliefs may fall to the state or "intermediate" institutions like families, neighborhoods, or churches. The individual capacity for self-control, and hence freedom, requires such a society—as a moral order and a network of binding institutions.

3. A decay in the belief in absolutes and the decline of community are tied closely to the general development of modern Western society over several centuries, including the growth of capitalism. For most traditionalists, collectivism and totalitarianism are not twentieth-century departures from the general direction of Western societies but their logical culmination. Furthermore, in the traditionalist view, capitalism often appears not at all in its pristine image: a growing state, the large corporation, abstract property, monopoly, and rationalization appear to be part of the logic of the system, rather than as alien, extrinsic growths.

Of all the important traditionalist texts, Richard Weaver's *Ideas Have Consequences* (1948) was probably the most revered and influential among conservatives. The central philosophical question for Weaver was "whether there is a source of truth higher than, and independent of, man," and he regarded the answer to that question as "decisive for one's view of the nature and destiny of humankind."

The root problem of modern human beings, he argued, is that they have become "moral idiots": they have lost the capacity to believe in any transcendent or absolute moral standards, a loss that Weaver located as far back as the fourteenth-century doctrine of nominalism, which denies that universal concepts have any real existence.[27]

The denial of a higher truth, Weaver continued, undermines both social stability and individual self-control. A common "metaphysical dream," a shared image of how the world ought to be, is the necessary basis for coherent individual action and for cohesive community. Without it, societies fall apart: hierarchical relations and social norms lose all justification; no one has a fixed place in society; persons of different social ranks no longer feel they participate in a common enterprise. Consequently, suspicion, hostility, and rootlessness abound. In the absence of any compelling goals or values outside themselves, individuals lose all capacity for self-control, becoming enslaved to their own passions and preoccupied with material comfort.

Weaver saw capitalism ("the bourgeois ascendancy") as the very embodiment of the "materialistic civilization" that emerged from the loss of transcendent truths. He rejected socialism as merely the "materialistic offspring of bourgeois capitalism," in which the state simply takes over the responsibility of ensuring the comfort and security demanded by the people.[28] Central to the obsession with material progress in modern society, Weaver added, is the use of science and technology to subdue nature. The decline of belief in a transcendent order undermines the idea that nature is fundamentally good or sacred. The result is a "metaphysic of progress through aggression," which Weaver deemed central to the "modern western mentality": "For centuries now we have been told that our happiness requires an unrelenting assault upon [the order of nature]. . . . Somehow the notion has been loosed that nature is hostile to man or that her ways are offensive or slovenly, so that every step of progress is measured by how far we have altered these."[29]

In addition, Weaver argued, the denial of absolute truths leads to the degradation of work by undermining the notion that work can be an effort to embody an ideal in material form. Capitalism reinforces this destructive process by reducing both labor and its products to commodities and by driving "a wedge between the worker and his product." Craftsmanship cannot survive commercialism.[30]

A this-worldly, materialist society, Weaver concluded, is bound to lead to totalitarianism. The denial of transcendental goals and hence all compelling forms and duties undermines any basis for self-control, leaving human beings open to external direction. The "failure to maintain internal discipline," Weaver argued, "is followed by some rationalized organization in the service of a single powerful will. In this particular, at least, history, with all her volumes vast, has but one page." The emphasis on material comfort and happiness leads to the same end. People who expect that "redemption lies through the conquest of nature," "progress is automatic," and happiness in this world is a veritable right are headed toward that "disillusionment and resentment which lay behind the mass psychosis of fascism."[31]

What, then, is to be done? Not surprisingly, Weaver contended that "the first positive step must be a driving afresh of the wedge between the material and the transcendental," a denial that "whatever is, is right." He added that this begins with "the right of private property, which is, in fact, the last metaphysical right remaining to us." Modern society has swept away all other absolute rights, but "the relationship of a man to his own has until the present largely escaped attack." Because "the middle class rose to power on property," it consecrated "property rights at the same time that it was liquidating others." However, Weaver hastened to note, this defense of property did not extend to prevalent forms of capitalist property, which violate "the very notion of *proprietas*":

> The abstract property of stocks and bonds . . . actually destroy[s] the connection between man and his substance [and] makes impossible the sanctification of work. . . .
> Big business and the rationalization of industry thus abet the evils we seek to overcome. . . . Respecters of private property are really obligated to oppose much that is done today in the name of private enterprise, for corporate organization and monopoly are the very means whereby property is casting aside its privacy.[32]

What Weaver had in mind instead was "the distributive ownership of small properties"—independent farms, small businesses, owner-occupied homes, and the like—"where individual responsibility gives significance to prerogative over property." For the eradication of such property, "monopoly capitalism must be condemned along with communism."[33]

Contrasts and Similarities. Libertarianism and traditionalism certainly shared some common ground. Both were preoccupied with the growth of the state as organizer and planner of all social life. Both sought a more "organic" social order, one that functions and changes like a living organism, without explicit, conscious direction. The libertarian Hayek, while stressing the differences between the two camps, noted that both shared a fondness for "spontaneously grown institutions." The traditionalist Weaver, who more eagerly sought a synthesis, argued that both believed "that there is an order of things which will largely take care of itself if you leave it alone."[34] Both libertarians and traditionalists, moreover, defended private property and were skeptical of any egalitarian impulse.

The differences between the two, however, were greater than their similarities. To begin, they understood the central problem of the modern world very differently. Libertarianism argued that the central problem is the tendency to restrict individual freedom especially in the name of a spurious common good or higher set of values, a tendency that at an extreme leads to totalitarianism. Traditionalism argued, in contrast, that totalitarianism arises in effect from too much individualism, not too little: the real danger is that the breakdown of social bonds and transcendent values will yield a mass of rootless, atomized individuals preoccupied with material goals, who will ultimately yearn for the ersatz community and utopian lure of totalitarianism. Freedom and individualism, in the libertarian view, presuppose a certain dilution of a "common moral code" and the prying loose of individuals from social institutions; for the traditionalist, in contrast, moral order implies constraints on both freedom and individualism.

The two positions also had very different notions of society. Libertarianism pictured society as an association, a set of practical, contractual relations between self-contained, self-directed individuals; it looked askance at any effort to treat society as a reality *sui generis* or to define an overarching common good. Traditionalism viewed society as a community, a web of values and institutions that bind individuals together; it was wary of any effort to treat society simply as a collection of individuals.

These differences between libertarianism and traditionalism were tied as well to different views of self-control and freedom, the nature of morality, and the role of the state. Libertarianism took for granted that the individual has the capacity for self-direction and self-control, for defining and ordering goals, and for pursuing those goals in a disciplined way. It did not spend much time examining how such a capacity develops and the conditions necessary for it. By default, if for no other reason, libertarianism took an optimistic view of the ability of individuals to direct their own lives in the absence of strong shared beliefs and social bonds. Its view of the conditions necessary for individual freedom, therefore, was primarily negative—an absence of constraint. Traditionalism, in contrast, regarded self-control and self-direction as problematic. It spent considerable time examining how these develop. Central to its argument was the insight that self-direction requires compelling shared beliefs and strong social bonds. In their absence individuals lack a clear orientation to the world or orderly way of acting in it. Traditionalism necessarily took a less sanguine view of the ability of individuals standing alone to direct their lives. Its notion of freedom had a positive component: certain social conditions are necessary to enable individuals to be free.

Libertarianism simply assumed that individuals have goals they wish to pursue, and it was scarcely concerned with what those goals ought to be or how one ought to live one's life. It avoided these questions because it was wary of the collectivist implications of any definition of a higher or common good, because it regarded values as largely the province of individuals, and because consequently it believed the central concern of social and political thought should be to establish the conditions under which individuals can pursue their own goals, not to define goals for them. Libertarianism thus tended toward a certain moral agnosticism; it did not so much deny the existence of an absolute good as sidestep the issue.[35] Traditionalism, in contrast, was preoccupied with examining how individuals ought to live because it was wary of the collectivist implications of a moral vacuum, because it regarded values as the province of society as well as the individual, and because consequently it regarded defining the good as central to social and political thought.

Everything about libertarianism reinforced an antistatist stance— its diagnosis of the problems of the modern world, its image of society, its view of self-control and freedom, and its approach to morality.

None of these justified more than the minimal state action required to assure a negative freedom. With traditionalism, the situation was more complicated. Although it was certainly wary of the state, it also defined a sphere of positive state action. Its notion of society as more than a collection of individuals, its unqualified belief in a higher good, and its assumption that certain positive conditions must be maintained for individual self-control and freedom all could justify an active role for the state. From the traditionalist perspective, the goal of politics was more than simply ensuring negative freedom.

Finally, libertarians and traditionalists differed on their stance toward capitalism. The libertarian position saw a pristine capitalism as the solution to the problem of collectivism. The traditionalist position, again, was more complicated. Although not thoroughly anticapitalist, many traditionalists viewed existing capitalism as part of the problem. Capitalism, in their view, opens the way to collectivism by undermining community, centralizing property and transforming its nature, reducing the majority of people to dependent wage and salary earners, alienating the worker from his work, and propagating materialist values. Traditionalists opted for no clear, comprehensive alternative, but the distributist vision of a society of decentralized industry and small property gripped many of them.

The Rationale for a Synthesis.   The contradictions between libertarianism and traditionalism were not lost on conservatives themselves. Attempts at synthesis inevitably met with uneasiness, disagreement, and even rancor from one side or the other. Conservatives never ceased to reexamine the fundamental principles of their thought because they never felt they had fully eliminated the inconsistencies. Even into the 1980s conservative journals continued to bristle with articles expressing the unfinished, uneasy quality of conservative thought: "Conservatives and Libertarians: Uneasy Cousins"; "The American Conservative Movement of the 1980s: Are Traditionalist and Libertarian Elements Compatible?"; "Conservatives and Libertarians View Fusionism: Its Origins, Possibilities, and Problems"; "Traditionalism and Libertarianism: Two Views."[36] The apprehension that conservatives might have no common principles after all voiced itself clearly within conservative ranks over the years. "Self-avowed conservatives are having difficulty agreeing among themselves as to what it is precisely they stand for," wrote one conservative in 1964.

"American conservatism has yet to decide exactly what it is," wrote another in 1970. "On a purely philosophical level, American conservatism did not speak with a single voice," wrote an intellectual historian of the movement in the mid-1970s; "It had never done so and probably never would." The same feeling remained strong as the age of Reagan dawned, with one prominent conservative wondering what, "besides a common dislike of liberals," held conservatives together, and an important conservative newsletter remarking that although conservatives "have always prided themselves on being the party of first principles, . . . the nature of these principles has yet to be agreed on."[37]

In the light of the obvious difficulty of combining libertarianism and traditionalism, why conservatives so persistently sought to do so and how they went about it become all the more intriguing questions. We can answer them by examining the writings of three of the principle architects of fusionism, Frank Meyer, M. Stanton Evans, and William F. Buckley, Jr.

Meyer argued that libertarianism and traditionalism, despite a "fundamental clash of emphasis," were simply different elements of "the consciousness of Western civilization," which had separated from each other as nineteenth-century European conservatism and liberalism. Nineteenth-century conservatism had stressed objective moral order, tradition, and the pursuit of virtue to such an extent that it had tended to support "authoritarian political and social structures" and to de-emphasize individual freedom. Nineteenth-century liberalism had firmly supported individual freedom, a limited state, and a free economy but played down moral order and tradition.

But these fundamental differences, Meyer continued, were of little importance in the context of American political culture. The "American constitutional settlement," he argued, "brought into common synthesis . . . the acceptance of the authority of an organic moral order together with a fierce concern for the freedom of the individual person." Contemporary libertarians and traditionalists, he added, had a good deal in common, not only a reverence for "the Constitution as originally conceived" with its mandate for a "federal system of strictly divided powers" but also an antipathy to utopianism and collectivism, an opposition to state control of the economy, and a recognition that communism is an "armed and messianic threat to the very existence of Western civilization."[38]

Neither shared enemies nor a common reverence for the Constitution, however, got to the heart of what Meyer and other fusionists saw as uniting libertarianism and traditionalism in a common conservative position. The central point for them was that the libertarian concern with individual freedom and the traditionalist concern with objective moral order and virtue, far from being antithetical, actually coincided. To be sure, a doctrinaire libertarianism might reject as coercive any effort to define the good and hence specify the proper goals of human action. Similarly, a doctrinaire traditionalism might support authoritarian political and social structures aimed at encouraging or enforcing a notion of virtue. Historically, though, the fusionists argued, freedom and belief in an objective moral order had been entwined as had collectivism and secularization.

On the one hand, Meyer maintained that the pursuit of virtue is impossible without freedom because an act cannot be virtuous unless freely chosen and because coercion at best yields a merely negative virtue, not "active, positive, creative virtue." On the other hand, freedom would be aimless and empty without a transcendental goal. In this sense, freedom is an end in itself only in the political realm; in the moral realm, it is a means for the human pursuit of the good and the true.[39]

Most important for the fusionists, however, was the argument that unless freedom and the capitalism they deemed integral to freedom are seen as inherently good—in effect divinely ordained—they are easily undermined. Purely secular or materialist justifications simply did not work. In the relatively prosperous days of the 1950s and 1960s, it seemed foolish for conservatives to argue that the welfare state and government regulation of the economy spelled economic disaster. As long as the previously accumulated wealth of capitalism lasts, Meyer argued in 1958, a welfare state or democratic socialism might indeed work. The real objections instead should be moral or spiritual; even if it leads to a better material life, the welfare state inherently undermines human dignity and autonomy.[40]

Buckley made a similar case the following year in *Up from Liberalism*. "The conservative demonstration" failed, he lamented, partly because it presented itself as a "crassly materialist position." Conservatives erred, for example, in opposing Social Security on the grounds that it would bankrupt the nation. Buckley conceded that this claim was probably false: America could afford such a program.

The better argument would be principled, not practical: compulsory programs like Social Security are inherently bad, independent of their material effects, because they violate economic freedom, "the most precious temporal freedom." Evans, writing in 1964, added that appeals to material self-interest are not adequate for defending freedom and capitalism because people are all too eager to give up their freedom for the short-term benefits of the welfare state.[41]

The argument for a distinctly moral defense of individual freedom and capitalism came across, too, in conservative criticism of those who tended toward the libertarian end of the right-wing spectrum. In the case of Hayek, whom conservatives generally revered, Meyer made the point rather gently: despite his stirring critique of the welfare state, Hayek regrettably justified freedom on utilitarian grounds as the condition under which individuals can best achieve their private goals, material progress advances most quickly, and would-be social engineers are most easily held in check. The trouble with such arguments, Meyer noted, is that they assume specific preferences, without which they fall apart. What if people decide that individual goals are unimportant, material progress unnecessary, or social engineering desirable? A firmer case for freedom can be built only by arguing that freedom is "the true condition of man's created being," "the truth of the order of things."[42]

In the case of Ayn Rand, whose militant atheism repelled most conservatives, Whittaker Chambers and Evans made the point with full force. Acknowledging that "a great many of us dislike much that Miss Rand dislikes," Chambers nonetheless condemned her "forthright philosophical materialism," her denial of God, and her enthronement of the pursuit of happiness as the moral purpose of human life. The single-minded pursuit of happiness, Chambers warned, degenerates quickly into the pursuit of mere pleasure (and hence a softening of the human spirit) and from there into a desire for the state to solve all problems. Without some higher purpose or justification, freedom and individualism yield easily to passivity and an openness to manipulation. If human happiness is the justification for freedom, Chambers concluded, then freedom will be jettisoned as soon as it seems not to lead to that end. Evans argued simply that attempting to be at once profreedom (and procapitalist) and anti-Christian flouts the lessons of history because Christianity originated the notion of the sacredness of the individual personality, whereas all collectivist systems espoused "atheist humanism."[43]

In a 1966 article Evans made the general point most sharply and broadly by taking aim at the whole libertarian tradition—the classical liberal tradition, as he called it—from David Hume to Ayn Rand. He agreed with what the exponents of this tradition defend but not with how they defend it: the "economic views of the classical liberals" are fine, and Herbert Spencer's account of the "secular modulations of freedom" is "hard to surpass." Evans, however, parted company with "classical liberalism's most famous spokesmen . . . in their mechanical, materialist, and relativist view of human nature and ethical principles." Their fundamentally secular worldview paved the way for the transformation of classical liberalism, the defender of freedom, into modern liberalism, the purveyor of the welfare state. Classical liberals "helped lay the ethical foundation for the rise of the total state they wanted to avoid." "The maintenance of freedom," Evans concluded, "is not, and cannot be, purely secular." It requires an "underpinning of religion and moral sentiment derived from Judeo-Christian revelation."[44]

Here indeed lay the central rationale of the fusionist synthesis. By trying to join traditionalism to libertarianism, conservative fusionists were above all saying that the decline of freedom and pristine capitalism went hand in hand with the decay of belief in God and absolute truths. Freedom and capitalism required a religious, moral, or spiritual justification. The secular, materialist bent of the mainstream defense of pristine capitalism had paradoxically helped to undermine the system being defended.

What the fusionists sought to articulate, in short, was a religious defense of pristine capitalism. Given this goal, their synthesis of libertarianism and traditionalism leaned heavily to the former. What the fusionists required of libertarianism as they brought it into harness with traditionalism was not that it give up its largely negative, economic concept of freedom, its individualist concept of society, or its preference for pristine capitalism but merely that it base all its arguments on an objective moral order preferably rooted in the Judeo-Christian tradition.

In contrast, the fusionists demanded of traditionalism that it give up virtually everything except its emphasis on objective moral order.

They had little use for the traditionalist notion of society as an organic whole and still less use for its critical insights into capitalism. Meyer argued vehemently that society is "but a set of relations between persons, not . . . an organism morally superior to persons." Any idea that society has an existence and a moral claim of its own, not reducible to individual rights, could justify limitations on individual freedom. The anticapitalist dimension of traditionalism slipped out of sight. Traditionalists like Weaver, preoccupied more with the common collectivist enemy, de-emphasized anticapitalist elements in their later work and, at any rate, wrote mostly about issues in which those elements did not directly figure. Conservative discussion of traditionalist work ignored these elements. In a 1970 appreciation of Richard Weaver, for example, Meyer argued that Weaver's *Ideas Have Consequences* prefigured the union of traditionalism and libertarianism with its traditionalist emphasis on objective moral order and its libertarian stress on private property. In quoting Weaver on private property as the "last metaphysical right," however, Meyer ignored his subsequent condemnation of modern capitalist forms of property as the very negation of what private property ought to be and mean. He also ignored the anticapitalist themes throughout Weaver's book.[45]

For some conservatives, the synthesis of libertarianism and traditionalism seemed commonsensical; for others it was deeply problematic. Either way, however, most conservatives accepted somehow bringing the two languages together to criticize domestic collectivism. For those sympathetic to synthesis, these languages conjoined to provide a unified utilitarian and moral case for pristine capitalism and for freedom understood in capitalist terms. For those who remained skeptical, libertarianism and traditionalism were two distinct languages applicable to distinct issues. If their former use was immediately apparent, their latter use would become evident with the emergence of the distinction between economic and social issues in the 1970s.

From Ideological Liabilities
to Ideological Assets

Reconstructing conservative ideology was the first act in the drama of the rise of the Right in America. From the 1950s into the 1960s, conservatives reworked the terms in which they understood and justified their case against collectivism, both foreign and domestic, to fit new political realities at least as these appeared within the dominant political assumptions that I have called the liberal consensus.

Conservatives entered the 1950s burdened with a doubly problematic ideology. First, they had maintained many noninterventionist scruples about the use of American power abroad, which were ill-suited to a political world in which nearly everyone—conservatives included—took for granted the need for the United States to lead in actively opposing the Soviet Union and world communism. Second, they had continued to make a primarily utilitarian case for pristine capitalism and against government intervention in the economy at a time when the dominant political assumption was that economic growth and prosperity required government action and when in fact the two developed in tandem.

To become effective political contenders, conservatives had to deal with both these ideological problems. They moved fairly easily in the early 1950s from a noninterventionist anticommunism to a distinct kind of interventionist anticommunism. The new position jettisoned the moral objections to the use of American power in the world while preserving the noninterventionist desire for a unilateralist approach to world affairs. Thus was born what Theodore Draper in the mid-1980s called "global unilateralism"—though he erroneously ascribed to it a much more recent vintage—which continued to characterize conservative thought into the age of Reagan.[46]

With more difficulty, conservatives recast their defense of pristine capitalism by making a more explicitly moral, rather than a merely economic, case for it. The result was a complicated combination of libertarian and traditionalist themes that remained a hallmark of conservatism into the 1980s. Together these changes created the distinctive characteristics that constitute conservative ideology as we have known it—militant anticommunism, a libertarian defense of freedom and individualism, and a traditionalist concern with moral order and community.

In each case conservatives reconstructed their ideology in the light of dominant political assumptions even while maintaining its distinctive thrust. Conservative interventionism incorporated the less problematic strategic and practical noninterventionist themes even as it left behind the more troublesome moral ones. The reworked defense of pristine capitalism did not forsake the basic libertarian argument but merely buttressed it with traditionalist themes.

In each case, too, conservatives exchanged ideological liabilities for assets. If noninterventionism had been an obvious contradiction, conservative interventionism was an effective weapon. It pictured a straightforward world situation amenable to American control if only the political will could be mustered and the resources mobilized. If matters appeared otherwise, that was the result of the inadequate political will of liberals and the hesitation and unevenness of their policies. Similarly, if a purely libertarian defense of pristine capitalism often seemed implausible, the addition of traditionalist themes gave conservatives alternative arguments. Just as important, from a combined libertarian-traditionalist position pristine capitalism appeared immune to the twin deformations of collectivism and secularization. Conservatives imagined a capitalism in which the pursuit of profit and worldly success led neither to the decline of individual entrepreneurship and the market nor to the decay of belief in transcendent moral values. Again, if the ideal did not match the reality, the blame fell on liberal policies that unnecessarily encouraged the growth of the state and liberal ideas that fostered a secular, materialist orientation to the world. In short, both elements of the dual reconstruction of conservative ideology played nicely to what was, and would continue to be, the ideological strength of conservatism: the capacity to picture a natural, spontaneous order (whether in American society or the world) and to blame the disruption of that order on liberal elites and their policies and ideas.

Three

The Growth of a Movement

Old Right and New

By the mid-1950s several waves of political reaction to the New Deal and its legacy had left American conservatism a significant political voice but still disorganized and powerless. The second act in the drama of postwar American conservatism was the steady growth of an organized conservative movement as both an independent entity and a dominating presence in the Republican party. I divide this process into two phases: from the late 1950s through the early 1970s the conservative movement became an effective political contender but failed to make its mark on American politics; from the mid-1970s into the early 1980s the movement, in the form of the New Right, reached full maturity and became for a time a dominant force in American politics.

Each phase raises distinct questions. In the earlier phase the central issues are why the movement grew and why, despite the mass of right-leaning discontents in the late 1960s, it failed to have more impact. In other words what were the sources of both its strengths and its weaknesses? Effective answers to these questions do not come from theories of status politics and the allied image of a radical Right, which have often framed discussion of the conservative movement of the 1950s and 1960s. I shall address the shortcomings of this approach later in the chapter.

The key to understanding the strengths of the conservative movement in this period lies instead in a more rounded perspective. Theorists of social movements sometimes distinguish members of a polity (those who have low-cost, routine access to government through established channels) from challengers (those who do not).[1] The great strength of the conservative movement was that it had characteristics of both groups, or more precisely, that it combined many of the resources of a member with the capacity to talk like a challenger. Even as it railed against a political and cultural establishment, it drew on significant established sources of power. This combination of insider resources—support from business and the upper middle class as well as solid roots within the Republican party—and a capacity to use antiestablishment rhetoric to talk to the growing range of discontents that grew out of the 1960s constituted the strengths of the conservative movement. Though paradoxical, this combination was certainly fruitful.

The weaknesses of the conservative movement in its earlier phase were of several distinct kinds. The movement failed to form solid attachments to the two most likely standard-bearers of their cause, Richard Nixon and George Wallace. Many of the discontents to which they spoke were politically ambiguous, and if they led substantial constituencies away from liberalism and the Democratic Party, they did not encourage them to embrace conservative Republicanism. Finally, the economic downturn that would ultimately break the association of Democrats and liberals with national prosperity and progress had not yet occurred.

In the later phase of the conservative movement, from the mid-1970s into the early 1980s, the central question inevitably is what accounts for the dramatic change in the movement's fortunes, that is, for its political ascendancy. Answering that question is the task of the remaining chapters of this book, but here I must first examine the relationship between the emergent New Right and the older conservative movement out of which it grew. Did the triumph of the Right result in part from its transformation in some important way? The most common image of the New Right as a neopopulist or right-wing populist revolt quite different from earlier conservatism, and as a result more effective, is quite misleading on this score. The leaders of the New Right were not newcomers to politics with a political agenda and strategy distinct from those of the old conservatism; they were men and women with deep roots in the conservative movement and a solid commitment to conservative ideology, whose greatest innovations involved reinvigorating established conservative principles and extending time-honored conservative strategies. Conservatism triumphed in the late 1970s and early 1980s not by changing but by staying mostly the same. What changed in multiple ways was the social context in which it acted.

The Old Right: Growth and Frustration

In the late 1950s conservatism was at a nadir.[2] Within the Republican party, where nearly two decades of conflict had sharply distinguished conservative and moderate camps, conservatives had been reduced to fruitless railing at the Eisenhower administration, which they deemed too liberal. Their longtime leader, Senator Robert Taft, had died in 1953; McCarthy had been discredited two years later; and the Democratic landslide in the 1958 midterm elections had swept much of a generation of conservative leadership out of office, though several moderate-to-liberal Republicans, most notably Governor Nelson Rockefeller of New York, managed to buck the tide.

Two palpable signs of the times came in 1960. In the spring, liberal Republican senator Clifford Case of New Jersey easily turned back a well-organized primary challenge from conservative Robert Morris, a former counsel for the communist-hunting Senate Internal Security Subcommittee. The *National Review* commented ruefully that Morris's loss might well mean that "a principled conservatism is not what the majority of the American people, or even, apparently, a majority of voting Republicans wants."[3] At the Republican convention that summer, Vice President Richard Nixon, the front-runner for the presidential nomination, who tilted toward conservatism without ever being one of the faithful, bent to pressure from the liberal wing of the Republican party in acceding to Rockefeller's demands that the party pursue civil rights legislation aggressively, use the government to stimulate the economy, and support a program of medical care for the aged.

More important, there was simply no independent conservative movement to speak of, no dense network of activists, ideas, and organizations dedicated to conservative goals. There was but a smattering of journals, political organizations, and intellectual societies struggling to preserve the faith. The *National Review*, along with *Human Events* and *Modern Age*, provided a recognized forum for conservative ideas. The Intercollegiate Society of Individualists (ISI, later renamed the Intercollegiate Studies Institute) disseminated antistatist ideas on college campuses—a belated response, said founder Frank Chodorov, to the Intercollegiate Society of Socialists of the early twentieth century.[4] Further to the right stood a collection of groups—collectively known to their many critics as the radical Right—who professed to see not just creeping collectivism at home and marauding communism abroad but also an actual communist conspiracy in control of major American institutions. The most prominent of these was the John Birch Society, founded in 1958 by Robert Welch. Others included a number of sectarian religious organizations, most of which were rooted in Christian fundamentalism: Carl McIntire's American Council of Christian Churches, Fred Schwarz's Christian Anti-Communism Crusade, Billy James Hargis's Christian Crusade, and Edgar Bundy's Church League of America.

Signs of the renewal to come were few. Out of the debacle of the 1958 elections emerged a new conservative Republican leader, Barry Goldwater. Goldwater had ridden the Eisenhower landslide into the Senate from Arizona in 1952 when he defeated then Senate majority leader Ernest McFarland. A delegate for Eisenhower, rather than Taft, at the 1952 Republican convention, he muted his criticism of the Republican administration throughout Eisenhower's first term. By 1957, however, Goldwater broke openly with the White House, declaring that it "aped New Deal antics" and that "the citizens of this country are tired of the New Deal now more than in 1952."[5] His outspokenness and his ability to win reelection in 1958 turned the rugged, handsome Goldwater into the new conservative standard-bearer. On a less conspicuous level, conservative activists, including John Ashbrook, William Rusher, and F. Clifton White, successfully won control of the Young Republican National Federation from more moderate forces, thereby establishing a base for what would be the Draft Goldwater movement.

The early 1960s witnessed an explosion of conservative activity. Its more sensational, but less important, element was the fast growth of the radical Right. The Birch Society and the major religious right-wing organizations together had raised only a few hundred thousand dollars a year in the late 1950s, but by 1964 they were gathering about $7 million a year.[6] The Birch Society claimed about fifty thousand members and public-opinion polls showed that at least 5 percent of the American public could be counted as supporters of its extremist position.[7] The insistence of these groups that communists directly controlled the government, the public schools, and the National Council of Churches received growing attention. This attention peaked in the mid-1960s, but the influence of the groups continued. The Christian Crusade and the Birch Society led the apparently grass-roots movement against sex education in public schools in the late 1960s, and the Birch Society itself played an important role in the movement against the Equal Rights Amendment in the 1970s.

Of much greater impact, however, was the growth of the less radical Right, of the conservative wing of the Republican party and the closely related conservative movement. Stung by the Nixon-Rockefeller agreement on the eve of the 1960 Republican convention (they called it the "surrender of Fifth Avenue" and the "Munich of the Republican party"), conservative Republicans managed to place Barry Goldwater's name in nomination. Knowing that conservatives were not yet strong enough to control the GOP, Goldwater withdrew his name but urged conservatives to "go to work to take this party back."[8]

Young conservative activists within the Republican party did just that. Not content to work solely within a Young Republican organization then gearing up to campaign for Nixon, they met at William F. Buckley's family home in September 1960 to form the Young Americans for Freedom. The organization sought to "mobilize support among American youth for conservative political candidates and legislation and to act as spokesmen for conservative opinion on key issues affecting young people."[9] Following Nixon's defeat in November, other Young Republican alumni, including Ashbrook, Rusher, and White, met in Chicago to launch what would become the Draft Goldwater movement.

Other signs of conservative revival abounded in 1961 and 1962. The New York Conservative party was founded; YAF held two successful mass rallies in New York City; and William F. Buckley, Jr., began his syndicated newspaper column. Between 1960 and 1964 the circulation of the *National Review* tripled to ninety thousand.[10] Noting the proliferation of conservative clubs on college campuses, conservative M. Stanton Evans proclaimed a "new wave" of campus revolt— not the radical revolt that marked the 1960s but a conservative one. These new campus conservatives, he predicted, would be the "opinion-makers—the people who in ten, fifteen, and twenty-five years will begin to assume positions of power in America."[11]

The Draft Goldwater movement went public in the summer of 1963 and a year later helped procure the Republican presidential nomination for their candidate, in what William Rusher describes as "the most important and truly seminal year for American conservatism since the founding of *National Review* in 1955. It laid the foundations for everything that followed."[12]

The glimmerings of success brought some friction within the conservative movement between the radical Right and less radical conservatives. In particular, the adamant claim of Birch Society head Welch that a literal communist conspiracy, led through most of the 1950s by none other than President Eisenhower, was taking control of American life did not sit well with more respectable conservatives who did not want their movement to appear as a lunatic fringe. The real problem, Buckley and other conservatives argued, was not a communist conspiracy but a liberal political culture, a set of widely shared beliefs that was leading America to ruin. The critique of the Birch Society escalated in the *National Review* from an attack on Welch alone in 1961 to a wholesale rejection of the society itself in 1965.

The growing split, however, should not obscure continuing commonalities and ties. Whether they identified it as a conspiracy or a culture, all conservatives had the same enemy—the liberal establishment. They supported the same causes, sponsored the same committees, got funds from the same sources, and shared leaders and ideas. ISI had Bircher trustees and contributors. *Human Events* for a time offered a joint subscription with *American Opinion*, the journal of the Birch Society. The radical rightist Carl McIntire joined YAF's first board of directors. Even after the break within the movement, certain connections continued. Scott Stanley, Jr., a YAF official in the early 1960s, went on to edit *American Opinion* for years until he left it in the early 1980s to edit *Conservative Digest*, a New Right journal. The active participation of Congressman Larry McDonald in the Birch Society did not dim his popularity among conservatives in the 1970s and early 1980s.[13]

Goldwater, of course, lost badly in the 1964 general election, and with his defeat another wave of political reaction in American politics appeared to have receded. The Goldwater debacle gave Democrats control of the presidency and better than two-to-one majorities in the

House and the Senate for the first time since the New Deal. Great Society legislation continued apace.

Appearances, however, were deceiving. The conservative movement itself continued to develop, hardly skipping a beat; and in the long run Goldwater even in defeat had a positive impact. His campaign gave conservatives a commanding voice in the Republican party that they would never wholly relinquish. It stimulated further conservative activism and initiated a new generation of conservative activists: leading conservatives immediately created the American Conservative Union to carry on the battle, while the membership of YAF grew to twenty-eight thousand by 1966.[14] The Goldwater campaign also provided the basis for direct mail as a means of fund-raising and communication for conservatives because it attracted a record number of individual contributors. Richard Viguerie, for one, began his direct-mail fund-raising empire with the names of 12,500 persons who had given fifty dollars or more to the Goldwater campaign.[15] Finally, Ronald Reagan launched his political career with a nationally televised speech for Goldwater—still known among conservatives as "The Speech." Reagan subsequently won the governorship of California in 1966, while Republicans made major gains in Congress and the statehouses.

By the mid-1960s, too, some conservatives, especially Draft Goldwater activists like White and Rusher, had developed a general strategy for how to build a conservative majority. They argued that under conservative auspices Republicans could offset Democratic gains in the Northeast by winning over Democrats and independents in the South and the West, adding these regions to bedrock GOP support in the Midwest and the Great Plains. The "bonding ingredient of the new coalition," as Rusher put it, looking back many years later, would be exasperation with the "social consequences of liberalism." "Hard-hats, blue-collar workers, and small farmers," once drawn to the Democratic party when the dominant issues involved conflict with employers and creditors, could be attracted to the GOP because of their anger at the growth of a welfare class and at the "upswing in drugs and pornography, the loosening of sexual restraints and much else."[16]

At the 1968 Republican convention, even though conservatives were not firmly in the saddle, the balance of political forces had shifted. Richard Nixon, again the front-runner, fought off a last-minute challenge, not from party liberals this time, but from Reagan and party conservatives. Nixon secured the nomination largely because prominent conservative senators like Goldwater, Strom Thurmond, and John Tower honored long-standing commitments to him and held southern and western delegations in line. The lesson was not lost on Nixon: The following year he remarked that if a Republican could not win with the party's right wing alone, neither could he win without it.[17]

By 1970 the American Conservative Union had sixty thousand members, and YAF had fifty thousand; the *National Review* and *Human Events* each boasted one hundred thousand subscribers. William Buckley's newspaper column had become one of the two or three most widely syndicated in the country, and his television debate program, *Firing Line*, flourished.[18] Also in 1970 James Buckley, William's older brother, won election to the U. S. Senate from New York, running on the Conservative party ticket in a three-person race.

By this point, too, the fate of the conservative movement had become caught up in the broader sweep of political change. The resurgent radicalism of the late 1960s—black rebellion, the student movement, the counterculture, the opposition to the war in Vietnam— shattered the easy consensus that had dominated American politics since the mid-1950s. Where once there was overwhelming agreement that American capitalism amended by a variety of liberal government programs was essentially just and progressive, voices from the left condemned the continuing concentration of wealth, misplaced priorities, and racial, class, and gender injustice. Where once economic growth appeared as the central precondition for a good society, dissenters now argued that the emphasis on growth was ruining the quality of everyday life. Where once American foreign policy was widely accepted as a high-minded effort to fight communism and spread the benefits of American society around the world, critics condemned the war in Vietnam as but one barbarous expression of an immoral, imperialistic foreign policy. The shattering of the American consensus and celebration from the left ironically created an even wider opening to the right. There emerged a backlash, partly patriotic, partly racial, partly concerned broadly with law, order, and morality, always complex and contradictory, which took the form of a protest vote against the Democratic party. In the 1968 presidential election Republican Richard Nixon and independent George Wallace together polled 57 percent of the popular vote.

Suddenly a potential conservative majority appeared within reach in America, and the political strategy of the conservative movement seemed suited to mobilizing it. To conservatives late-1960s radicalism was simply the logical extension of liberalism (not a bitter critique, as radicals saw their own actions), its ultimate harvest of violence and permissiveness. They felt sure that the popular backlash against radicalism could be turned ultimately against liberals as well as Democrats. A young conservative Nixon aide, Kevin Phillips, made these points effectively in his 1969 book *The Emerging Republican Majority.* (Phillips later said that he had almost substituted *conservative* for *Republican.*) American politics, he argued, was undergoing a major realignment along regional and ethnic lines comparable in magnitude to those of 1828, 1860, 1896, and 1932. Traditionally Democratic regions of the South and the West were moving into the Republican camp, as were the urban Catholics and other non-Yankee ethnic groups in the Northeast. The upheaval, Phillips argued, was partly a reaction to the "Negro socioeconomic Revolution," partly a creature of the growth of the Sun Belt and the "rootless, socially mobile" middle class that arose in its wake, and partly an expression of hostility to the liberal establishment among groups that had always opposed the established political elite. Whatever the causes, Republicans and conservatives had a great political opportunity and a clear way to exploit it—by appealing to the antielitist sentiments of the "silent majority" of Americans and to anger over what Dick Scammon and Ben Wattenberg a few years later referred to as the "social issue"—lawlessness, permissiveness, radicalism, and generally "the more personally frightening aspects of disruptive social change." [19]

By the late 1960s a strong, growing conservative movement faced increasingly favorable circumstances for taking political power and building a conservative majority. White southerners, Catholics, and blue-collar workers seemed poised to abandon the Democratic party in response to the conservative rhetoric of Nixon and Agnew or of Wallace. Yet the early 1970s did not bring a Republican realignment or a conservative majority. Republicans ruthlessly applied the social strategy in the 1970 midterm elections, appealing in the name of law and order to "middle America" against radicals, rioters, and "permissivists," but with little result. Democrats picked up twelve seats in the House and lost only three in the Senate, so that the new Congress was hardly less liberal than the previous one. In 1972 Nixon's landslide victory over McGovern brought all southern states into the Republican column for the first time and narrowed considerably class- and religion-based political cleavages. Nixon actually won a majority of blue-collar, low-income, and Catholic voters. His coattails, however, were quite short: Republicans won back only twelve seats in the House and actually lost two in the Senate.

Watergate doused conservative (and Republican) hopes. Nixon having resigned, and the GOP tarred with his disgrace, voters in 1974 elected the most Democratic Congress since the Goldwater debacle, and Republican party identification among the public hit an all-time low. President Ford chose Nelson Rockefeller, still the epitome of "eastern establishment" Republicanism to many conservatives, as his vice president. The political winds blew in a liberal direction: there was broad support for cutting defense spending; the Supreme Court had ruled unconstitutional all existing state laws restricting a woman's right to an abortion, and thirty-three of the necessary thirty-eight states had ratified the Equal Rights Amendment; government domestic spending continued to increase, and a new generation of regulatory agencies concerned with occupational health and safety, equal opportunity, and environmental protection was solidly in place; feminist, environmental, consumer, and many other liberal movements were taking wing.

What best explains the growth of the conservative movement in the 1960s, and what accounts for its limited impact? In other words, what were the sources of its strengths and weaknesses? To answer these questions effectively, one needs to move beyond the dominant line of social-scientific theorizing about American conservatism during this period. Most often sociologists, historians, and political scientists viewed the development of conservatism in terms of the growth of a radical Right, focusing in effect on the more extreme elements of the movement, such as the John Birch Society and the Christian Crusade, and they usually explained this radical Right as an expression of status politics.[20] In this way, they constructed a picture of the conservative movement that on balance obscured more than it clarified.

In particular, the status politics analysis of conservatism as the radical Right was misleading in four ways. First, it downplayed the most important and powerful elements of the conservative movement, from *National Review* intellectuals to YAF political activists to Draft Goldwater movement supporters, as well as the connections between these and the radical Right. Second, it treated the conservative movement not as a sustained organizational effort but as a series of discrete political eruptions, angry expressions of diffuse social discontent that had little structure or cumulative impact. Third, it pictured conservatism primarily as a political challenger operating outside established political institutions and cutting across established political allegiances. Finally, this analysis argued that as a political challenger conservatism drew its support from those groups whose status and power in American society were either increasing or decreasing rapidly as well as from people who occupied discrepant statuses (for example, those of high income and low education). These people experienced the strains associated with their uncertain or changing social status as resulting from broader threats to cherished values. They thus were receptive to conservative polemics about communist subversion, moral decay, and creeping collectivism.[21]

We have already seen how the first two are misleading. The radical Right did not stand alone but was one of the lesser parts of a broad conservative movement with which it shared political fortunes. Conservatism, in addition, was indeed a sustained movement to which ideology and organization were significant, not just an episodic eruption of jumbled discontent and diffuse malaise. The last two claims taken together are equally open to criticism. Conservatism was not primarily an outsider with tenuous access to political channels and resources and with its deepest roots in socially dislocated groups. On the contrary, it drew core support from the politically well-connected and the economically well-off.

Indeed, closer scrutiny reveals that the theory of status politics was not a very rigorous theory at all. It did not clearly specify who would, and who would not, be attracted to right-wing movements because in practice nearly everyone could be said to suffer status anxiety or dislocation. The contributors to *The New American Right* (1955) and its revised edition, *The Radical Right* (1963), found support for the Right everywhere—among upwardly mobile Catholic ethnics and downwardly mobile WASPs, among the newly wealthy and soured patricians, among the new elite of corporate executives and the declining elite of independent businessmen, among politically disgruntled Republicans and culturally alienated fundamentalists, and among the less educated in general.

In other words, the theory of status politics created a false unity out of the diversity of support that its own social-scientific literature showed that the conservative movement enjoyed. The Right raised a rallying banner for a variety of discontents, and different movement organizations attracted different combinations of support. Indeed, in their comprehensive study *The Politics of Unreason* Seymour Martin Lipset and Earl Raab conceded that right-wing movements have a "cafeteria kind of quality."[22]

A still closer look, nonetheless, reveals that common threads of another kind united the conservative movement from the McCarthy era through the 1960s. Although different movement organizations did reach out into different parts of society, they started from three common bases that assured them access to political channels and financial resources. First, they shared bedrock support among Republicans. Supporters of McCarthy in the early 1950s and the Birch Society in the early 1960s included a disproportionate number of Republicans, as did the membership of ISI and YAF and students at Christian Anti-Communism Crusade seminars. Goldwater delegates to the 1964 convention by and large were not outsiders or infiltrators with little loyalty to the party, as some maintained at the time. They had been active in the party longer and more intensively than other delegates and had contributed more money. The conservative movement thus had access to an established network of political loyalties and ties.[23]

Second, the conservative movement drew support from important elements of the business community. McCarthy rallied small businessmen and the more conservative elements of big business, especially from the Midwest and Texas and from family-owned independent companies. Birch Society founder Welch was a former executive in his family's candy manufacturing company and vice president of the National Association of Manufacturers. In the mid 1960s the society's national council was dominated by the executives of family-owned businesses. In the early 1960s the conservative movement enjoyed considerable financial support—estimated at about half their yearly total of fourteen million dollars by investigators Arnold Forster and Benjamin R. Epstein—from a range of businessmen, corporations, and business-related foundations. Certainly not all of the business community flocked to the conservative camp, but substantial elements did even before the conservative corporate mobilization of the 1970s.[24]

Third, with important qualifications the conservative movement had its greatest appeal among the upper middle class. Supporters of the Birch Society and other radical Right organizations in the 1960s were disproportionately affluent, well educated, and in professions or businesses. So were readers of the *National Review* and members of the Conservative party in New York. McCarthy, to be sure, got higher approval ratings among blue-collar workers than white-collar workers and among the less educated, but within particular occupational and educational levels he did better among those with higher incomes. Members of ISI and YAF in the 1960s were also partial exceptions to the rule, being drawn mainly from families of average income. Yet the conservative movement's center of gravity, compared to that of other movements with a quasi-conservative appeal, such as the Wallace movement, was clearly in the upper part of the social spectrum. In both the 1964 Democratic primaries and the 1968 general election presidential aspirant Wallace consistently drew his strongest support from blue-collar workers, the least educated, and the least affluent.[25]

Beyond this bedrock support the conservative movement also drew strength from the growth of the Sun Belt, the southern white backlash to civil rights, the drift of other groups away from the Democratic party, and a pervasive, growing dissatisfaction with major American institutions. After World War II the South and Southwest underwent a rapid process of industrialization, urbanization, and population growth. Although these changes were heavily subsidized by government spending on highways, water projects, and energy production as well as on the military and the aerospace industry, they created a culture that celebrated unfettered development, freewheeling investment, and individual enterprise—in general, unregulated capitalism. The transformation of the Sun Belt also created a class of nouveaux riches, extended affluence more broadly than before, and began to draw the disproportionate number of fundamentalists in the region back into the mainstream of American economic and, later, political life. In all these ways, it encouraged conservative political trends in the region.[26]

Certainly the conservative movement showed tangible strength in the Sun Belt. Independent Texas oilmen like H. L. Hunt and Clint Murchison were among McCarthy's strongest backers. The John Birch Society found its greatest support in urban and suburban areas in Texas and Southern California and in the faster-growing areas of the West. Conservative activists were able to dominate the Republican party in the late 1950s by mobilizing southern and western support to join core support in the Midwest against the party's moderate, predominantly eastern faction. Finally, the Sun Belt produced a number of prominent new conservative Republican leaders, including Goldwater and Texan John Tower.[27]

The national Democratic party's growing advocacy of civil rights legislation and an end to white supremacy in the South after World War II drove large numbers of southern whites out of the party, first in presidential elections and later gradually in lower-level races as well. The realignment had two distinct elements. The more immediate was a direct shift to the Republican party in the late 1940s and early 1950s among middle-class urban voters in the "rim" South—Virginia, Texas, Florida, North Carolina, Tennessee. This was a constituency with long-standing objections to the economic policies of the New Deal, a constituency that was already solidly Republican outside the South. Although these voters were less concerned about race, the Democratic turn to civil rights broke the thrall of the one-party South for them and left them free to pursue their economic interests. The immediate beneficiaries of their defection were moderate Republicans—Eisenhower in 1952 and 1956 and Nixon in 1960. The second kind of defection, indirect and less immediate, involved whites of all social strata in the Deep South, especially in the "black belts," those areas with high black populations. These voters supported Dixiecrat Strom Thurmond in 1948, tilted to Eisenhower in 1952, danced between the two major parties and various states' rights tickets in 1956 and 1960, went strongly for Goldwater in 1964, and then ran off with independent George Wallace in 1968. Nixon won them over (along with the rest of the South) in 1972, but Jimmy Carter brought them briefly back into the Democratic fold in 1976. This second element of realignment thus remained volatile throughout the 1950s, 1960s, and early 1970s, supporting the conservative movement's candidate in 1964 but manifesting no abiding political loyalties.[28]

The growing restiveness of traditionally Democratic working-class and white-ethnic constituencies in the Northeast and Midwest also provided a potential reservoir of conservative support. The strong support of Catholics for McCarthy in the early 1950s and the anger of so-called hard hats at campus unrest and antiwar demonstrations in the late 1960s were two manifestations of this, but survey data also showed a more gradual, less spectacular decline in class- and ethnic-based political cleavages.[29]

Finally, a broad public dissatisfaction with major institutions created an ethos in which an insurgent conservatism could flourish. From the 1930s through the early 1960s public confidence in government and other institutions generally increased. From the mid-1960s on, however, it plummeted. The decline perhaps was most noticeable with regard to government; more and more the public told pollsters that government leadership was unresponsive, corrupt, and subservient to special interests. Public trust in other major institutions, including business, the press, organized religion, the military, education, and unions, also declined.[30]

What gave the conservative movement the potential to address varied constituencies and broad discontent was not specifically its anticommunism, its enthusiasm for laissez-faire capitalism, or its preoccupation with the decay of social order but the common enemy it attacked on all these grounds: central to conservative ideology from McCarthyism on was an assault on the liberal, secular, insufficiently anticommunist elite or establishment associated with the New Deal and its legacy. This establishment was identified as both ideological (liberal) and regional (eastern); it was said to embrace Washington bureaucrats as well as the leadership of big business; it included the heads of the Democratic party as well as moderate Republicans. Its protean character helped it serve as an umbrella under which to gather diverse constituencies. The conservative attack on an eastern liberal establishment could appeal to the political animosities of midwestern and rural Republicans against the eastern urban kingmakers that dominated the GOP through the 1940s and 1950s, to generations-old regional hostilities of the West and South against the East, to the racial anger of southern whites against a federal government in pursuit of racial justice, to a host of divisions within the business world, to the class hostilities of workers against business, and to discontent with the leadership of major institutions.

Hence the strength of the conservative movement lay in a paradoxical combination of respectability and rebelliousness. It combined solid political and socioeconomic roots that gave it the resources and opportunities to make itself heard with a broad antiestablishment rhetoric that allowed it to appeal to a variety of discontents.

What, then, kept the conservative movement through the early 1970s from making a deeper impression on American politics? What were its weaknesses? To begin with, conservatives never effectively hitched their wagon to either of the two leaders capable at the time of leading them to power, Richard Nixon or George Wallace. Wallace they largely rejected out of hand: although Birchers flocked to the Wallace campaign, a *Human Events* poll of conservative leaders in 1968 found that they overwhelmingly opposed his candidacy for president. Why did conservatives oppose Wallace? Certainly Wallace was an enemy of liberalism and a symbol of a rising tide of reaction. Certainly, he took the correct conservative positions on Vietnam, crime in the streets, and the role of the federal government. Yet, conservatives argued, as governor of Alabama he had built a huge welfare state, and his presidential campaign supported Social Security and Medicare increases, public-works programs (if needed to overcome unemployment), and a range of labor legislation. Furthermore, his populist appeal coarsened, vulgarized, and distorted the conservative position. As Buckley put it in a column late in the 1968 presidential campaign: "What are we left with? The coarsening of distinctions, certainly. Polarization, just as certainly. But also the disintegrating penetration of Big Daddy Government, accelerated by the thumping dissent of the backwoods heckler."[31]

Nixon provoked more ambivalence. He garnered conservative support in his race for the presidency and ran on a basically conservative platform. Once in the White House, his rhetorical appeals to middle America and Agnew's attacks on liberals, student radicals, and the media warmed conservative hearts. Yet, at least in conservative eyes, Nixon's policies were too liberal. During his first term he enacted wage and price controls, proposed a modest guaranteed minimum income, and failed to curb the growth in government domestic spending. He also undertook détente with the Soviet Union and made his famous opening to the People's Republic of China. In August 1971 the *National Review* announced it was "suspending" its support for Nixon. Later that year Congressman John Ashbrook announced his candidacy to take the Republican presidential nomination away from Nixon in 1972. Ultimately most conservatives, with important exceptions, endorsed Nixon for reelection, but only as the lesser of two evils.[32]

The incompleteness of many of the regional, class, and ethnic realigning trends—of the revolt of middle America—in the 1960s and 1970s also limited the advance of conservatism. Although much of the West was solidly Republican and conservative, the South was in limbo, and workers and white ethnics were far from finding the Republican party and the conservative camp to be comfortable new homes. Writing in 1977, political scientist Everett C. Ladd, Jr., saw a still solidly Democratic middle America. "The protesting lower middle class may well be the natural constituency of the GOP," he remarked, "but, if so, these voters don't know it yet." Several years later, sociologist Jonathan Rieder made a similar observation about the 1970s. "Middle America was a mixture of discrete forces," he wrote, whose various discontents Republicans and conservatives could easily appeal to, but who could not easily be unified. In studying Jews and Italians of the Carnarsie neighborhood of Brooklyn, Rieder found one piece of middle America that was not so much a solidly conservative constituency as one that could be episodically and temporarily pushed to the right by antibusing controversies or bad economic conditions.[33]

Finally, however great the political and cultural backlash that buoyed Nixon, Wallace, and the conservative movement, one more pivotal issue, the state of the economy, had not yet become problematic: the economy through the early 1970s remained fundamentally sound. The gross national product, productivity, and real wages were still growing; unemployment and inflation were relatively low. Dissatisfaction with the economic state of the nation, however, has usually been the crucial factor in public openness to parties and movements that claim to offer political alternatives. Whatever else the conservative movement could feed on in its efforts to redirect American politics from the late 1950s to the early 1970s, it lacked the one essential ingredient for political success: a sick economy with a Democrat in the White House.

The New Right:
Conservatism Triumphant

The Rise of the New Right.   The early 1970s were the best and the
worst of times for conservatives—times of strengths and weaknesses, redolent of the possibility of long-sought political realignment but filled with disappointment. Unlike in the late 1950s, America had a conservative movement, but that movement seemed no
nearer to reorienting American politics. The tantalizing opportunities
and palpable frustrations of the early 1970s brought a new generation
of conservatives to political maturity and triggered a surge of conservative activism. Nixon's failure to be conservative enough, the
continuing liberal direction of American politics, the Watergate scandal, and, later, President Gerald Ford's naming of Nelson Rockefeller
as vice president all contributed to a growing conservative malaise.
In the eyes of direct-mail fund-raiser Richard Viguerie, the last of
these symbolized the dreadful state of affairs:

> Nelson Rockefeller! The liberal who attacked Barry Goldwater
> during the GOP primaries in 1964 so strongly it helped defeat
> Goldwater in November. The liberal who got Richard Nixon to
> agree to the infamous midnight Pact of Fifth Avenue in 1960,
> placing a liberal stamp on the GOP platform. Nelson Rockefel-
> ler—the high-flying, wild-spending leader of the Eastern Lib-
> eral Establishment.
>   As a conservative Republican, I could hardly have been more
> upset if Ford had selected Teddy Kennedy.[34]

Viguerie discovered that most Republicans were willing to accept the
Rockefeller nomination, and conservatives standing on their own
simply "didn't have the leadership or the clout" to stop it. More om-
inously, he decided that conservatives "might be close to losing the
entire battle to the left" unless something were done.[35]
    It was in this mood that new conservative leaders began to meet
in 1973 and 1974 to figure out how to shore up the fortunes of their
apparently sagging movement. The term *New Right* refers to these
leaders and the strategy and network of organizations they created.
They agreed that conservative failure lay not in a lack of opportunities but in a failure of leadership, organization, and effective outreach
to new constituencies. The established leadership of the conservative

movement, Viguerie proclaimed, "didn't know how to lead"; they "had no stomach for a hardnosed fight"; they were "defensive and defeatist." As a result, conservatives in the early 1970s had "no organized, continuing effort to exert a political influence on elections, on Capitol Hill, on the news media, and on the nation at large." They needed an autonomous, variegated network of organizations to make the conservative presence felt. By stressing independence, the New Right did not at all want a divorce from the Republican party but simply a more equitable relationship: its leaders wanted their own independent clout so as better to influence party and politics. Conservatives had also failed, these New Right activists reasoned, to reach out to the hard-hat, ethnic, and white southern constituencies that had supported Wallace and might be ripe for conversion to the Republican party and conservatism, and the movement needed new ways for doing so.[36]

The core leaders of the New Right included Richard Viguerie, the direct-mail fund-raiser; Howard Phillips, head of the Conservative Caucus; Paul Weyrich, head of the Committee for the Survival of a Free Congress (CSFC) and of Coalitions for America; John Terry Dolan, longtime head of the National Conservative Political Action Committee (NCPAC); and Jesse Helms, founder of the National Congressional Club. The Viguerie Company was the major New Right fund-raising organization; NCPAC and the Congressional Club became the movement's two largest political action committees; CSFC and the Conservative Caucus were pivotal organizations for lobbying, recruiting candidates, training activists, and all-purpose politicking; and Coalitions for America, including the Library Court, Kingston, and Stanton groups, was the umbrella for an array of single-issue organizations concerned with social, economic, and national-security questions. These leaders were at the heart of a dense and endlessly proliferating network of conservative organizations of every type.

Others mentioned as major New Right leaders or consistently topping lists of most-admired conservatives included Phyllis Schlafly, who spearheaded the drive against the Equal Rights Amendment; Edwin Feulner, Jr., head of the Heritage Foundation; Morton Blackwell, founder of the Committee for Responsible Youth Politics and director of the Leadership Institute; Patrick Buchanan, political columnist and for a time White House communications director in the second Reagan administration; and Congressmen Phillip Crane, Jack Kemp, and Larry McDonald. One might include as well the leading figures of the New Religious Right because they were tied so closely to the New Right, including Pat Robertson, Jerry Falwell, James Robison, Edward McAteer, and Robert Billings.[37]

The conservative network grew impressively in the latter half of the 1970s. By 1980 Viguerie's computer data banks held the names of about fifteen million conservative contributors, of whom about one-quarter were deemed reliable activists. NCPAC and the National Congressional Club became the two largest political action committees of any kind, followed in the top ten by several other conservative PACs, including the Fund for a Conservative Majority, Citizens for the Republic, Americans for an Effective Presidency, and CSFC. Coalitions for America served as a central forum for more than one hundred conservative organizations concerned with economic, social, and national-security issues. Beyond these were a vast range of organizations for policy-making (the Heritage Foundation), coordinating the efforts of conservative senators, congressmen, and their aides (the Senate Steering Committee, the House Republican Study Committee, the Madison Group), organizing conservative programs in state legislatures (the American Legislative Exchange Council), influencing the media (the National Journalism Center, Accuracy in Media), and pursuing conservative issues in the courts (the Pacific Legal Foundation, the National Legal Center for the Public Interest and its regional affiliates), as well as countless single-issue organizations. In some cases, New Right leaders simply worked with existing conservative organizations on an issue—for example, with the National Right to Work Committee to oppose labor unions. In others, they created organizations where none had existed before, such as Stop ERA. In still other cases, where existing single-issue groups steered clear of close ties to the conservative movement (the National Right to Life Committee on abortion and the National Rifle Association on gun control), New Right leaders added their own distinctive groups (the American Life Lobby and the Life Amendment Political Action Committee, Gun Owners of America).[38]

New Right leaders also made a systematic effort to reach out to new constituencies in several ways. First bucking the general conservative disdain for George Wallace, they established ties with the renegade Democrat. In 1973 Viguerie took on the job of retiring Wallace's 1972 campaign debt, and in the next few years he raised $7 million for the governor and came away with many million new names for his computers. In 1975 several conservatives sought to create a Reagan-Wallace third-party ticket, an effort that fell apart when Reagan's prospects for the Republican nomination seemed to improve the following year.[39]

Second, New Right leaders made a concerted effort to appeal to the social conservatism of traditionally Democratic or politically independent constituencies on a growing list of issues that the 1970s bountifully threw their way: abortion, the Equal Rights Amendment and feminism, drug use, pornography, school textbooks and curricula, busing, affirmative action, gay rights, and so on. "Conservatives cannot become the dominant political force in America," Viguerie insisted, "until we stress the issues of concern to ethnic and blue-collar Americans, born-again Christians, pro-life Catholics and Jews. Some of these are busing, abortion, pornography, education, traditional Biblical moral values and quotas." Weyrich argued that social or family issues would be to conservatives in the 1980s what Vietnam or the environment was to liberals in the late 1960s and early 1970s. Upon Reagan's 1980 victory and for several years thereafter New Right leaders emphasized the importance of the social agenda in putting Reagan in power and maintaining his support.[40]

Most important, the New Right sought to organize the growing political restlessness of evangelical Christians in the late 1970s. As television preachers and other evangelical leaders became politically active over abortion and what they regarded as government harassment of private Christian schools, New Right leaders helped channel their efforts. Howard Phillips recruited Edward McAteer, already active in the conservative Christian Freedom Foundation, as a field director of the Conservative Caucus and then helped him found the Religious Roundtable. Weyrich helped Robert J. Billings, long active in the Christian schools movement, found the National Christian Action Coalition to lobby for legislation relevant to these schools. McAteer and Billings in turn brought Phillips and Weyrich together with television evangelists James Robison, Pat Robertson, and Jerry Falwell. With New Right help, Falwell founded the Moral Majority in 1979. The New Right was also instrumental in starting the third major religious Right organization, Christian Voice, whose first Washington representative, Gary Jarmin, had been legislative director of American Conservative Union. "We are sort of the operations people," said Weyrich, summing up the New Right's role. "It has been our job to tell them, 'Okay, here is what to do.' "[41]

With heightened activism and organization, the New Right also showed signs of substantive political clout. The opposition to the ERA, led largely by Schlafly and Stop ERA, along with the John Birch Society and other older conservative groups, effectively blocked further progress to ratification after 1974. In 1976 conservatives, with the conspicuous exception of Goldwater and Clifton White, united around Ronald Reagan's candidacy for the Republican presidential nomination, and President Ford needed the full power of his office to eke out a narrow victory. In the late 1970s the Conservative Caucus, along with the American Conservative Union and the American Security Council (a right-wing organization founded in the 1950s), led the vigorous opposition to the Panama Canal treaty, which enjoyed bipartisan political support. In the 1978 midterm elections NCPAC backed the successful senatorial campaigns of several conservative Republican challengers, including Gordon Humphrey in New Hampshire and Roger Jepsen in Iowa. In the New Jersey Republican primary that year Jeff Bell, a young activist with the American Conservative Union, did what conservatives had failed to do eighteen years before—defeat Senator Clifford Case. Bell lost to Bill Bradley in the general election, but his success in the primary symbolized how far conservatism had come.

Reagan's victory in the 1980 elections completed the conservative ascent. Gone were the dour tones and long looks of 1974; "the greatest victory for conservatism since the American Revolution," crowed Phillips; "the most massive political victory" in the history of conservatism, exulted Dolan; "conservatives don't have to be ashamed of what they profess to believe in order to win elections," rejoiced Weyrich. It was "your victory," Reagan told the Conservative Political Action Conference in March 1981. In retrospect the 1970s appeared as a "conservative decade" to James C. Roberts, a former ACU political director and conservative historian of the period. Conservatism had "come to the climax of its long march," William Rusher concluded; whatever future elections might bring, it was "unmistakably on the playing field."[42]

What Was New about the New Right?   In coming of age, did conservatism, or some element of it, change? Did the secret of the New

Right's success lie in some qualitative transformation in the nature of right-wing politics? Many of the most influential studies of the New Right, most notably Alan Crawford's *Thunder on the Right* and the writings of Kevin Phillips, argued that it constituted a major rupture within the conservative movement. The New Right, it was alleged, comprised a cadre of political activists with roots outside the conservative movement, who departed from older conservatism by advocating collectivist economic positions and making other ideological innovations, attacking established elites (including big business) and invoking populist symbols, and noisily proclaiming themselves radicals while assailing other conservatives. It was, in short, neopopulist, not conservative. Kevin Phillips put it this way:

> Leaders of the overtly populist New Right—Richard Viguerie, Paul Weyrich, and Howard Phillips, among others—also waved the banner of radical conservatism, invoking the tactics of Andrew Jackson, inveighing against the *Fortune* 500, mobilizing single-issue movements, criticizing the institutionalized elites of both parties, and occasionally even acknowledging their roles as radicals, not as traditional conservatives.[43]

Although many New Right leaders themselves at times seemed to endorse this image, it was for the most part misleading and wrong. The most striking characteristic of the New Right was its continuity with the older conservative movement in leadership and ideology as well as to a large extent in strategy and rhetoric. In it the conservative movement had come of political age. Differences between the New Right and the Old Right were usually superficial.

New Right leaders, when in a more reflective mood, acknowledged as much. Thus Viguerie at a 1981 conference on the New Right said, "There's not a great deal 'new' about the New Right. Our views, our philosophy, our beliefs, are not that different, if at all, from the Old Right. It is our emphasis that is different at times."[44]

And Roberts, in his exhaustive work on the conservative movement in the 1970s, added:

> To the extent that *Old Right* and *New Right* have any meaning at all, it is only in purely chronological terms. . . . Such differences as exist between these two factions—and they are numerous enough—tend to be personal or to issue quite understandably out of a competition for fame and fortune.

On matters of principle and policy there is no *major* difference between these groups and individuals.[45]

Most of the leaders and core activists of the New Right had cut their political teeth in the conservative movement or the Republican party (or both).[46] Those who had not were recruited largely by those who had and came to similar political positions independent of the conservative movement. Viguerie was the first executive secretary of the Young Americans for Freedom in the early 1960s, before beginning his own direct-mail organization in 1965 with a list of Goldwater contributors. He subsequently raised funds for various conservative Republican candidates, including Phil Crane's initial run for Congress in 1969 and John Ashbrook's 1972 primary challenge to President Nixon, thus establishing himself as a major conservative fundraiser. Howard Phillips helped found the Young Americans for Freedom in 1960 while student body president at Harvard and joined its first board of directors. He spent the 1960s and early 1970s working in and around the Republican party, ending up as head of the Office of Economic Opportunity in the Nixon administration, where he was initially charged with dismantling the War on Poverty program. Weyrich, though the product of a blue-collar, union neighborhood, came from a Republican family and got his political training in the GOP as an aide to conservative Republican senators Gordon Allott of Colorado and Carl Curtis of Nevada. Dolan was a member of YAF and an organizer for Nixon in 1972.

Other New Right leaders had similar or even longer histories in conservative and Republican politics. Schlafly got her first job after graduate school in 1945 with the American Enterprise Association (later the American Enterprise Institute). Between 1952 and 1964 she ran unsuccessfully for Congress on the Republican ticket, served as a delegate to several Republican conventions, presided over the Illinois Federation of Republican Women, worked with a number of right-wing organizations, and published several anticommunist pamphlets. In 1964 she gained considerable fame for her pro-Goldwater book *A Choice, Not an Echo*. Subsequently she published several more books on the communist threat, lectured and spoke at conservative gatherings, and was elected vice president of the National Federation of Republican Women. After losing a bitter contest for presidency of that organization in 1967, she withdrew and began to publish the *Phyllis Schlafly Report* to keep in touch with those who supported her. These supporters became the core of Stop ERA and the Eagle Forum in the 1970s.

Phillip Crane began his political life in the Draft Goldwater movement in the early 1960s before winning election to the House of Representatives and serving a stint in the late 1970s as head of the American Conservative Union. Patrick Buchanan, who was a YAF member, worked in the Goldwater movement and subsequently became a speechwriter for Nixon and Agnew. Edwin Feulner of the Heritage Foundation joined ISI in his undergraduate days and did graduate work in the mid-1970s on an ISI Weaver Fellowship before becoming a personal assistant to Nixon's defense secretary, Melvin Laird, and working as an aide to Congressman Crane. Larry McDonald was a member of the John Birch Society (of which he became national director shortly before his death in 1983) before his election to Congress in 1974. Morton Blackwell began his political career as the youngest delegate at the 1964 Republican convention, where he supported Goldwater. He subsequently became executive director of the College Republican National Committee, an executive with the Viguerie Company, and editor of *Conservative Digest*, Viguerie's New Right monthly. Finally, Jack Kemp, a quarterback for the Buffalo Bills in the American Football League in the 1960s, supported Goldwater in 1964, served as an aide to Governor Reagan in California, and was a long-time member of ISI before winning election to Congress in 1970.

To be sure, not all prominent New Right figures grew up in the conservative movement and the Republican party, but even those who did not hardly represent departures from the conservative mold. They simply came to the same conservatism along a different route. As I shall show in Chapter 4, issues like abortion, pornography, school prayer, and the rights of Christian schools put a number of evangelical Christians on the road to the conservative movement, with indigenous conservative activists helping them along. Helms began his career in segregationist politics in North Carolina. In 1950 he worked on Willis Smith's successful primary campaign against incumbent senator Frank Graham, a campaign marked by racist and red-baiting tactics. He subsequently served as head of the North Carolina Bankers' Association and was elected to the Raleigh City Council before beginning a twelve-year stint in 1960 as a commentator on a Raleigh television station. Helms's commentaries were noted for

their uncompromising support of free enterprise (he had read libertarian economist Ludwig von Mises years before) and opposition to
civil rights and communism, which he tied closely together. He
switched to the Republican party in 1970 and ran successfully for the
U. S. Senate in 1972, a position to which he was reelected in 1978 and
1984.

The continuity in leadership between the New Right and the older
generations of the conservative movement stretched well below the
top ranks. The generation of conservative activists that came of age
in the 1970s was filled with alumni of YAF and ISI. Important former
YAF members included Robert Bauman, a former Republican congressman and head of the American Conservative Union before the
revelation of his homosexuality ruined his career; Jeffrey Bell, also an
important figure in ACU and a Reagan campaign advisor in the late
1970s; Anthony Dolan, a Reagan speechwriter; Lee Edwards, onetime editor of *Conservative Digest*; Kathleen Teague, head of the American Legislative Exchange Council; R. Emmett Tyrrell, Jr., editor of
the *American Spectator*, a conservative journal begun in 1967. ISI
alumni prominent on the Right have included Kemp and Feulner as
well as Richard Allen, Reagan's first national-security advisor; Paul
Craig Roberts, an assistant secretary of the treasury under Reagan
and a major proponent of supply-side economics; John F. Lehman,
who served many years as Reagan's secretary of the navy; and
Charles Heatherly, who edited *Mandate for Leadership*, the Heritage
Foundation's primer for the incoming Reagan administration, and in
the mid-1980s was acting head of the Small Business Administration.[47]

Just as important, the basic ideology of the New Right did not
change substantively: it combined a militant anticommunism with a
libertarian defense of pristine capitalism and a traditionalist concern
with moral and social order. In the 1980 volume *The New Right: We're
Ready to Lead*, for example, Viguerie evenhandedly condemned government intervention in the economy, the decay of traditional values,
and the advance of world communism. Just as telling were the heroes
and mentors Viguerie invoked, virtually all of whom were of the conservative movement. His first political heroes, he wrote, were "the
two Macs," Douglas MacArthur and Joseph McCarthy. He credited
William F. Buckley, Jr., and Barry Goldwater as the "two men more
responsible than any others for the strength and vitality of conservatism in American today," and for a definition of conservatism he

turned to the fusionism of Frank Meyer.[48] Surveying New Right writings, one finds no evidence for the claim that it was a neopopulist combination of statist economics with social conservatism. The label might well fit George Wallace, but the New Right's overtures to Wallace did not result in an abandonment of its economic libertarianism.

Moreover, the two most noteworthy ideological departures of the New Right, the emphasis on social issues and the adoption of supply-side economics, ended up simply reemphasizing or restating established conservative themes. The emphasis of New Right Leaders in the 1970s on social issues as a way of winning over blue-collar, Catholic, and evangelical constituencies certainly was new, but it largely reflected historical opportunities: the 1970s gave conservatives a cornucopia of social issues on which to build. Although some conservatives and many of Reagan's advisors disagreed with the strategy, because social issues are divisive and unpredictable, the general approach was one that conservative activists had employed with growing awareness at least since the Draft Goldwater movement.

Above all, the New Right's stance on social issues invoked the basic traditionalist themes that were incorporated into conservatism in the 1950s and 1960s. More precisely, by the 1970s an ideological division of labor had developed within conservatism that directed the traditionalist emphasis on moral order, community, and constraint to the social issues while the discussion of economic issues stressed mainly libertarian themes of individualism and freedom. A gender division inevitably developed as well, in which issues relating to what was considered the male world of work evoked libertarian rhetoric and those relating to what was seen as the female world of family evoked traditionalist rhetoric.

The March 1981 *Conservative Digest* provided an especially sharp example of this compartmentalization. In that issue articles on unions and big government struck a distinctly libertarian chord. A discussion of the National Right to Work Committee criticized the union shop ("compulsory unionism") as a restriction of "freedom of choice for millions of American workers." An account of the work of the Council for a Competitive Economy stressed that organization's effort "to put the 'free' back into a free economy." Both articles were effusive in their praise of individualism, opportunity, and self-fulfillment.[49]

In the same issue articles on abortion and the family echoed very different traditionalist themes. A critical discussion of the National Abortion Rights Action League expressed skepticism about the whole notion of free choice: "To hear the pro-abortion folks talk, you'd think choice is an absolute right. But it isn't. Underlying the whole concept of law is the idea of choice limitation. In no area of human activity is choice unlimited."[50] Another article stressed that the very existence of society requires restraining the pursuit of individual self-interest: "A society cannot exist without recognition of and adherence to a common good. The common good requires people to act out of motives larger than their own narrow self-interest. Unless people are capable of self-restraints upon their appetites and desires, the common good cannot be maintained."[51] The family and the traditional nurturant role of women in it, the article continued, are essential to cultivating these self-restraints.

In short, the New Right's emphasis on social issues did not introduce a new concern into conservative ideology and certainly not one that was incompatible with established themes. Granted that on issues like abortion and the Equal Rights Amendment one could find in the New Right, as one observer put it, a strong "critique of market rationality, individualism, and the prevalence of career convenience over nurturant ties of kin and community"; this critique still did not imply a new and explosive philosophical incompatibility. As I showed in Chapter 2, such traditionalist themes had been central to conservative ideology for a generation. If they seemed to contradict the libertarian themes of the Right, the contradictions were time-honored, and conservatives had considerable experience managing them.[52]

A second unique feature of the ideology of the New Right was the adoption of supply-side economics.[53] Developed by a small but enthusiastic group of economists in the mid-1970s and propagated in *The Public Interest* and the *Wall Street Journal*, this theory caught the imagination of New Right intellectuals, and of Ronald Reagan and Jack Kemp in particular. Its basic argument was that high marginal tax rates are a major cause of economic stagnation and hence that tax cuts are the key to economic prosperity. Cutting marginal tax rates, supply-siders argued, stimulates investment, work, and creativity and thus promotes economic growth. A sufficient cut could produce enough economic stimulus actually to increase government revenues by greatly expanding the tax base. This was the message of the so-called Laffer curve: a large tax base and low rates will yield as much revenue as a smaller tax base and higher rates.

Supply-side economics reoriented conservative and Republican economic thinking in two ways. First, it made reducing the size of government more palatable by emphasizing cutting taxes before dealing with the more arduous problems of cutting spending and balancing the budget, which had traditionally preoccupied the Right. Second, it conveyed a rosy optimism by arguing that the economic problems wrought by big government could be solved with little pain or dislocation. Previously conservatives and Republicans had usually offered tight money, balanced budgets, a degree of austerity, and other painful remedies for the nation's economic ills.[54] Supply-siders, by contrast, were sure that tax cuts would so stimulate the economy that no one would suffer: there was, after all, a "free lunch." In both these ways supply-side economics, when taken up by Reagan, Kemp, and others, offered what seemed a more positive and appealing statement of the conservative economic position to an American public concern about unemployment, inflation, and economic stagnation and less than sanguine about the capacity of the Democratic party to deal with those problems. If the 1980 election, as many observers have argued, was largely a plebiscite on how well the Carter administration had handled the economy, the presence of a cheery supply-side alternative made the judgment all the more easy. As Thomas E. Cavanagh and James L. Sundquist noted in 1985:

> The Republican Party is no longer the party of austerity, the party of balanced budgets and tight money. . . . The adoption of supply-side economics has given it a new rhetoric of growth and opportunity, and its politics have given priority to tax reduction for both individuals and corporations with an almost casual disregard for deficits far larger than those for which it used to castigate the Democrats.[55]

In no sense, however, was supply-side economics a substantive departure from conservative ideology; indeed, it echoed the deepest of conservative themes. In justifying tax cuts, it provided an especially forceful restatement of the classic libertarian defense of pristine capitalism by emphasizing that individual creativity and productivity, not rational planning, are still the essence of capitalism; that entrepreneurship and competition still energize the system even in an age of large corporations; and that the state is largely an impediment to economic health, not its prerequisite. At the same time it also lent itself to the incorporation of traditionalist themes and to the construction of a moral, as well as a utilitarian, case for capitalism. In *Wealth and Poverty,* the 1980 volume that became a bible for the new Reagan administration, George Gilder argued that capitalism is not only economically productive but morally good as well: its creative impulse is fundamentally altruistic and divinely inspired.[56]

In light of the continuities of leadership and ideology on the Right, neither the invocation of populist and radical rhetoric nor occasional political infighting constitute evidence for a fissure between the New Right and the Old Right. To be sure, New Right leaders occasionally boldly proclaimed themselves radicals, not conservatives, as in Weyrich's often-quoted statement: "We are radicals who want to change the existing power structure. We are not conservatives in the sense that conservative means accepting the status quo." But the conservative movement, since its earliest days in the 1950s, had never been conservative in this sense; its goal had been to undo the legacy of the New Deal. The very first issue of the *National Review* in 1955 in fact referred to its readership as "radical conservatives." Other New Right leaders, like Jack Kemp, spoke spiritedly about a "new conservatism." The newness, however, usually meant greater optimism or activism, a new effort to appeal to traditionally Democratic constituencies, not any major change in ideology or agenda.[57]

The New Right leaders also used populist rhetoric, attacking the establishment and the elite in the name of the people. In the mid-1980s they founded the American Populist Institute and the Populist Conservative Tax Coalition, and there was much talk about a populist-conservative third party. But all this was just rhetoric, and even as rhetoric it was hardly new. As John Judis pointed out, "populist conservatism" was not an alternative to an older conservatism, but simply a "new way to market it." Although in his 1983 book *The Establishment vs. the People* Viguerie took broad aim at the power and corruption of America's elites, attacking big business and banks as well as big government, unions, and media, he offered no program for radical decentralization of power in general or for dealing with the concentrated power of business in particular. Indeed, big business in his view sinned not by being capitalist or big but by being liberal—seeking government subsidies and regulation, supporting sex and violence on television, and trading with the Soviet Union. Accordingly, Viguerie's proposals for change were standard conservative pleas for less government domestic spending, more law, order, and morality, and a tougher foreign policy. His populist rhetoric, moreover, was hardly new. As I have shown, ever since the days of Joe McCarthy and Whittaker Chambers conservatives have inveighed in the name of the people against the establishment, though less because it was an establishment than because it was liberal.[58]

Finally, the rise of the New Right certainly caused conflict within the conservative movement itself. Older conservative organizations initially feared that the creations of Viguerie and other New Right activists would siphon off scarce resources rather than expanding them. New Right leaders criticized some older conservatives for failures of leadership and organization. More strikingly, they beat a steady tattoo of criticism of the Reagan administration for failing to appoint enough movement conservatives to government positions and to pursue the conservative agenda aggressively. None of these conflicts, however, reflected a basic split over ideology and policy, which is why they never led to outright schism. Despite often feeling the barbs of New Right criticism, Buckley could still praise the New Right as the "front-line troops of the conservative movement" and as "brilliant technicians" exerting "the kind of lobbying pressure we haven't seen in years." And the venerable *National Review,* while disagreeing with New Right criticism of Reagan, could still acknowledge that such criticism valuably focused attention on the unfinished elements of the conservative agenda. The *National Review* and *Human Events,* another older conservative publication, ran large congratulatory ads in the tenth-anniversary issue of the New Right's *Conservative Digest* in 1985. Even Barry Goldwater, who clashed bitterly with those in the New Right over the nomination of Sandra Day O'Connor to the United States Supreme Court (he supported his fellow Arizonan, they opposed her as too liberal) and a host of other issues never totally lost their affection. The Heritage Foundation honored the retiring senator at a 1985 dinner, during which Feulner declared him to be "the main contributor to the whole political movement which led to the election of Ronald Reagan."[59]

All in all, what was new about the New Right was much less significant than what was old. Its leadership, ideology, strategy, and even rhetoric was largely of a piece with those of the Old Right.

Those who claimed otherwise either misread what the New Right said or invoked a faulty image of the history of the conservative movement.

The conservative movement that had emerged haltingly in the late 1950s and early 1960s with a reconstructed ideology and the beginnings of political organization and had become an effective political contender by the early 1970s strode confidently into power in the early 1980s. The secret to its transformation from contender to victor cannot lie in internal changes since in fact it had changed little in the 1970s. Nor can the secret lie simply in growing public discontent or social upheaval, of which the late 1960s certainly had more than the late 1970s. It lies instead in broader changes that crystallized existing conservative-leaning discontents into the palpable form of activists, money, and votes, matters that the remaining chapters address.

Part Two

Taking Power

Four

The Rise of the
New Religious Right

The triumph of conservatism in the late 1970s and early 1980s was closely tied to three phenomena: the rise of the New Religious Right, the conservative mobilization of big business, and the revival of the Republican party. Each of these, in turn, was part of a set of broader changes in American society: respectively, the emergence of social issues and the reassertion of evangelical Christianity, the changing nature of American capitalism (at least as perceived by capitalists themselves), and the complicated interplay of economic voting, realignment, and dealignment in electoral politics. These do not exhaust the factors that account for the rise of the Right, but from any perspective they are the most important.

The term *New Religious Right* refers to a set of organizations that emerged in the late 1970s, the Moral Majority (later renamed the Liberty Federation), the Religious Roundtable, and the Christian Voice; their leaders, including Pat Robertson, Jerry Falwell, and Ed McAteer; and the movement that these leaders and organizations fostered. Though this movement made a broad, religiously based conservative appeal, its deepest roots and most lasting impact were among white evangelical and fundamentalist Christians.

The New Religious Right took typically conservative stands on all issues, but its distinctive emphasis was a moral traditionalism characteristic of evangelicals and fundamentalists since the early twentieth century. Its leaders decried American weakness in the face of the Soviet Union and the decline of free enterprise, but underlying this they saw America afflicted by what Jerry Falwell has called a "tide of permissiveness and decay" brought about by a denial of God. Once man replaces God at the center of life, they argued, all moral absolutes disappear, existence loses all meaning, and human life all respect. Human beings become preoccupied with self-gratification in the present, and society breaks down in a chaos of "divorce, broken homes, abortion, juvenile delinquency, promiscuity, and drug addiction." Moreover, once human beings no longer believe that God controls their affairs, they turn to the "superstate" instead. The New Religious Right especially blamed this drift into amorality and godlessness on an "ungodly minority" of "secular humanists" who run government, education, and the media.[1]

Why did the New Religious Right emerge? Sociological theories explain why groups mobilize in numerous ways, but usually they rely on some combination of three causes: an increase in a group's grievances; an increase in a group's resources, organization, and opportunities for collective action; and heightened mobilizing efforts by social-movement professionals or entrepreneurs outside the group.[2] Sociologists have usually applied these factors to understanding social movements to the left of the political spectrum, but they can be applied as well to the right. Indeed, each helps to explain the rise of the New Religious Right.

I have already noted in Chapter 3 the role of movement entrepreneurs in the crystallization of the New Religious Right. New Right leaders Howard Phillips and Paul Weyrich played a pivotal role in founding the major organizations of the New Religious Right and in recruiting and training its leaders. The New Religious Right, however, was not simply a creature of the conservative movement. It grew as well from the dense organizational infrastructure of an evangelical and fundamentalist subculture that had been growing for several decades. The electronic ministries, the superchurches, and the network of independent fundamentalist churches provided the means through which the movement could mobilize leaders, followers, and their resources around long-standing evangelical and fundamentalist discontents with a secularized, hedonistic, and permissive society.

At the same time, these discontents, if they did not actually increase, at least became more politically salient because of the emergence of the so-called social issues in the 1970s and early 1980s—issues like abortion, the Equal Rights Amendment, drug use, sexuality, the nature of the family, and the content of public education. These issues became more important for a variety of reasons: the partial transformation of America into a postindustrial society and the emergence of postmaterialist values; complicated and contradictory changes in gender roles; and growing polarization of Americans between the religiously devout and the irreligious.

Whatever led to the rise of the social issues, it is important to get an accurate gauge of their impact. In the early 1970s it was common to regard the social issues as harbingers of "a broad new sociopolitical period in American history" and "a basic redrawing of the political agenda," as the authors of one influential book put it.[3] With the benefit of hindsight we can see that they were no such thing. They did, however, have a more modest impact: they gave certain general themes of the Right's moral traditionalism concrete political application and thus helped stimulate a new wave of conservative political activism in general and the rise of the New Religious Right in particular. The combination of the emergence of the social issues and the growth of the evangelical/fundamentalist world produced the New Religious Right.

The Social Issues

The 1960s first made America aware of the so-called social issues and introduced the argument that these issues would become the new basis for political alliances and conflicts. The term has embraced quite a range of issues having to do with social order, civil liberty, morality, sexuality, race, gender roles, family, education, and quality of life. The emphasis shifted substantially from the late 1960s and early 1970s, when the important social issues focused on blacks (racial inequality, civil unrest, civil rights, busing, affirmative action) and youth (premarital sex, marijuana use, political dissent), to the late 1970s and early 1980s, when the issues of gender, the family, education, and the relationship between church and state rose to prominence. Of the latter, those having to do with women's rights, especially abortion and the Equals Rights Amendment (ERA), were most important.

Why the Social Issues Emerged   Many theories can help to explain the emergence of the social issues, but two have been especially prominent—one emphasizing the transition of America from an industrial to a postindustrial society, the other stressing uneven changes in gender roles. To these I will here add a third, which focuses on changing patterns of religious affiliation.

The first approach examines how postindustrialism has transformed American politics.[4] According to this theory, the central features of a postindustrial society include growing affluence, greater education, and an expanding tertiary sector embracing government, universities, communications, and other service and information functions. Increasing affluence mutes the economic issues that once divided a conservative upper middle class from a liberal working class, and a broad consensus develops on an expanded role for government in economic life. With economic issues put aside, noneconomic issues, on which the lower socioeconomic strata have traditionally been more conservative than the higher strata, become prominent.

Postindustrialism reinforces this division on social issues by partially transforming both classes. The growth of education and the expansion of the tertiary sector create a so-called New Class of college-educated professionals, whose work emphasizes trained intelligence and creativity and thus changes the upper middle class from primarily business and managerial to professional. This New Class is concerned with postmaterialist values like self-fulfillment, quality of life, and personal freedom and is open to cultural change. Hence its members are likely to be especially liberal on social issues. At the same time, growing affluence gives large segments of the working class a foothold on economic security and intensifies their opposition to further social change, thus making its members even more conservative on social issues. In this way Postindustrialism, according to this theory, creates a new kind of class struggle—what pollster Louis Harris once called "Karl Marx upside down"—in which the upper middle class becomes the proponent of change and the working class the defender of the status quo.[5]

A second and very different kind of argument roots the rise of the social issues in the partial and often contradictory transformation of gender roles in America.[6] This transformation, some feminists argue, has been due partly to various long-term trends: the increasing percentage of women in the paid work force; skyrocketing divorce rates and sharp increases in the number of female-headed households; later marriage age and smaller families; and changing sexual mores along with an enhanced capacity to control reproduction. It has also been due to the emergence in the 1970s of a women's movement that criticized the traditional role of wife and mother as oppressive and asserted women's needs for economic independence from men, for control over their own bodies, and for equal rights generally.

The net effect of these changes has been to weaken the traditional place of women without fully establishing a new one. On the one hand, for example, increasing marital instability reduces the security of the housewife role, and the growing tendency of middle-class women in particular to choose paid work outside the home diminishes its status. On the other hand, women in the paid labor force still face barriers to equal status with men—occupational segregation and income inequality, a workplace geared to the needs of traditional families, and a persistence of the gender division of labor at home.

Both the magnitude of the changes and their unevenness provoke political conflict and make a series of family- and gender-related issues important in American politics. Specific issues like abortion rights and the Equal Rights Amendment often take on broader meaning, symbolizing the woman emancipated from her traditional roles, focused more on education and work than on marriage and childbearing, sexually active without being married, and financially independent of men.

These issues, the argument continues, often pit against each other groups of women with different visions of women's ideal place. If women with college educations, good professional jobs, and independent incomes (or prospects of acquiring them) flock to the women's movement and embrace abortion rights and the ERA as ways of furthering their independence, housewives with less education, few good employment prospects, and little personal income resist abortion and the ERA as destructive of women's protected place in the family and provide an attentive audience for antifeminist movements and their appeal to reinforce the traditional role of women.

In one view, then, social issues pit the middle class against the working class; in the other, they pit professional women against housewives. Both images of the social divisions in which the social issues are rooted contain some truth, but they do not complete the picture. In fact, different social issues are class-linked to varying degrees, and each of the measures of socioeconomic position (income, education, occupation, relationship to the production process) bears a unique relationship to the social issues. The professional/housewife division may fit contending groups of activists on issues like abortion and the ERA, but that line of conflict is much less visible on these same issues among the general population.[7]

Indeed, the factor that most strikingly distinguishes the opposing sides on the social issues is neither of these but rather religiosity or religious involvement. The more often people attend religious services, the more importance they give to religion, and the more involved they are in church-based activities, the more likely they are to take conservative stands on abortion, ERA, or the other social issues. A national study of abortion activists in 1980, for example, found that 86 percent of pro-life activists attended church at least once a week, whereas only 9 percent of pro-choice activists did. Similarly, a California study found that 80 percent of pro-choice activists never attended church, whereas only 2 percent of pro-life activists never did so.[8]

Similar results emerge from surveys of the general population. To be sure, other factors ostensibly distinguish conservatives and liberals polled on the social issues. The social conservatives generally tend to be less educated, less affluent, of lower occupational status, older, rural, and from the South and Midwest. These differences, however, do not show up consistently from study to study; they are often quite small; and, most important, they are often reduced significantly or wiped out in multivariate analysis. By contrast, the effects of religiosity (typically measured by church attendance) are found in virtually every study, are usually quite large, and are rarely wiped out in multivariate analysis. When the variable of religiosity is controlled, the effects of most other variables usually are reduced significantly, but controlling for these other variables does not diminish the impact of religiosity as much.[9]

Religiosity has an impact even within specific denominations. Opposition to abortion, for example, increases with religiosity for Catholics and for liberal, moderate, conservative, and fundamentalist Protestants alike. The differences are more marked for Catholics than for Protestants, and for the more conservative Protestants than the less conservative ones, but they are present across the board.

Thus the influence of religiosity on attitudes toward ERA and abortion cannot be understood purely or primarily in terms of differences in church doctrines. If doctrine were the major factor, one would expect a socialization effect: in liberal churches the more religious would be more accepting of abortion and ERA than the less religious; in conservative churches the opposite would happen. This, however, is not the case: religiosity has a conservative effect no matter what the denomination or its doctrines (though the magnitude of the effect varies). Clearly religiosity itself is important.

This finding suggests a third explanation of the rise of the social issues, one centered on the growing polarization of the United States between the more religious and the less religious, the traditional and the secular, the churched and the unchurched. This polarization, in turn, reflects several related changes in America's religious landscape.[10]

Since at least the 1950s boundary lines between the various religious denominations, particularly within Protestantism, have become more fluid because rising levels of education and higher rates of geographical mobility along with declining generational continuity in denominational affiliation have helped to erode the distinctive class, ethnic, and regional identities that previously unified specific denominations. At the same time, the religious world has become increasingly polarized as the ranks of the religiously unaffiliated, at one end, and those of the more theologically conservative churches, at the other, have swelled while those of the moderate and liberal "mainline" Protestant churches have declined. The once low-status conservative churches have flourished because of a growing ability to hold onto their more affluent members as well because of relatively high birth rates. The higher status liberal and moderate churches have declined because of relatively low birth rates, less influx of the upwardly mobile from the conservative churches, and, above all, a loss of higher-status members to the ranks of the religiously unaffiliated. Finally, the growth of religious nonaffiliation reflects the development of so-called religious individualism, the tendency to treat religion as largely a matter of personal choice and belief independent of any institutional or community commitment.

The fluidity of the religious world has reduced the relative importance of denominational differences while its polarization has diminished the religious center and the spiritual consensus for which it was the base. These factors have led to the increased importance of traditionalist/secularist cleavages (i.e., differences in religiosity) within denominations and in society at large and have made religiosity a major axis of conflict. It is not surprising, then, that issues on which public opinion divides along this axis should become more politically salient.

What the Social Issues Have and Have Not Done.   However one explains the rise of the social issues, one needs to have a clear sense of how much they have risen, that is, how politically important they have become. In fact, the social issues, despite predictions and claims to the contrary, have never become the dominant focus of American politics; they have not played a central role in shaping the voting behavior and political allegiance of the electorate at large, nor were they crucial in moving American politics to the right in the early 1980s. Their influence must be seen as more limited: the social issues gave immediate political currency to certain basic issues of values addressed by the traditionalist element of conservatism. As a result, they played a big role in the mobilization of cadres of conservative activists and contributors, and they provided the terrain for the politicization of evangelical Christians and the rise of the New Religious Right.

Rather than becoming increasingly important for Americans over the course of the 1970s, the social issues receded in importance in the public mind. At one point in 1970 more than half of the American public identified one or another social issue as the most important problem facing the United States whereas only 10 percent identified economic issues. By 1979, however, the figures were reversed: nearly 70 percent identified economic issues as important whereas less than 10 percent chose social issues. In addition, public opinion on such issues as abortion and women's rights, despite the influence of powerful, contending social movements, did not become firmer or more polarized in the 1970s, nor did these issues consistently have a large or growing impact on whether Americans called themselves liberal or conservative, or Democratic or Republican, or on how they voted. Moreover, to the extent that social issues influenced political behavior and allegiances in the 1970s and early 1980s, it is unlikely that they did so in a conservative direction. Public opinion on many social issues remained relatively liberal, and one study of single-issue voting found that issues like abortion, affirmative action, the environment, and gun control moved more persons to vote in a liberal direction than in a conservative one.[11]

Conservatism on social issues certainly was not central to electing Ronald Reagan to the presidency in 1980. Reagan's campaigns in the primary and general elections did not stress them, and voters did not often mention them in exit polls as a reason they voted for Reagan. More important, voters who switched to Reagan in 1980 (after voting Democratic or not at all in 1976) were not consistently more conservative than traditional Republicans on social issues like ERA and abortion or more liberal on economic issues like government domestic spending. They were more conservative on social issues than those who did not switch to Reagan, but they differed even more on economic issues and more strikingly still in their opinions of President Carter and his administration. Ultimately the 1980 election was a plebiscite on an unpopular incumbent, not an ideological contest.[12] (I shall return to the character of the 1980 election in Chapter 6).

The social issues, in short, are not the key to American politics and the successes of conservatism in the 1970s and 1980s, but they did play a significant narrower role. Issues like abortion and the ERA evoked broader themes that fit nicely with the traditionalism of the Right. Consider two examples. First, surveys of the general population suggest that the abortion issue involves basic beliefs about freedom and constraint. Those who oppose abortion are also very likely to disapprove of premarital, extramarital, and homosexual sex and to oppose looser divorce laws, provision of birth control information to teenagers without parental consent, sex education classes in public schools, voluntary sterilization, and the legalization of marijuana, euthanasia, and suicide. This seems like quite a disparate list, but there is a clear common theme here—opposition to too much freedom from constraints imposed by traditional roles and norms, too much emphasis on individual self-determination and self-fulfillment, and too much play for personal drives and whims. This opposition implies a worldview in which individual freedom on a range of personal matters is perceived negatively as mere license and in which constraint and order are inherently valued. The antiabortion position thus invokes a worldview that resonates with the traditionalism of the conservative movement, preoccupied as it is with the decay of the social bond.[13]

Second, studies of pro- and anti-ERA women activists suggest that underlying their angry political conflict in the 1970s and early 1980s are very different assumptions about the conditions under which women can survive and prosper in a male-dominated world and about the role of the family. Pro-ERA activists implicitly assumed that what women need is equal access to education, jobs, and other resources that would allow them to be economically independent of men. Traditional family roles, which limit such access, appear from this perspective as inimical to the interests of women. Anti-ERA activists, however, saw things differently. They believed that the only effective safeguards for women in a male world are the privileges and protections that they can claim from men within the family. From this perspective the family, when it works, requires men to support women and thus protects women from having to compete in a working world dominated by men and male values. Consequently, as a survey of ERA activists in Massachusetts showed, pro- and anti-ERA activists differed most sharply precisely on the value to women of those things that most directly attacked traditional family roles—abortion, government-funded day care, paternity leave, and increased sexual freedom. Anti-ERA activists interviewed in North Carolina were quick to accuse pro-ERA activists and feminists of being traitors to the female sex for wanting to require women to give up their family-based privileges and to compete on equal terms in the male-dominated world of work. The anti-ERA position thus tended to invoke a worldview in which the protection of the family from attack and the affirmation of traditional gender roles is central. This perspective, too, resonates with the broader defense of traditional institutions that is central to conservative traditionalism.[14]

One result of the resonance of the social issues with the traditionalist element of conservatism was that these issues helped to mobilize a new cohort of conservative leaders, activists, and contributors. Evidence of this is abundant. Certainly the opposition to abortion and the ERA constituted two of the largest, most active countermovements of the 1970s and early 1980s. To some extent they mobilized persons already active in the conservative movement or in some conservative causes, but they also attracted some with no such background. Antiabortion activists typically were new to conservative politics. A study of committed antiabortion activists in California found that they had virtually no prior political experience. "They were not members of the League of Women voters, they had no ties with professional associations or labor unions, they were not active in local party politics, and many of them had not even voted in previous elections," writes sociologist Kristin Luker of this group. Many of the antiabortion activists in a North Dakota study had had previous political experience, but in local Democratic party politics or on liberal causes. Anti-ERA activists often had prior experience in conservative Republican politics, the John Birch Society, or other right-wing groups, but the movement attracted political novices as well, especially in its later years.[15]

Similarly, social issues seem to have played an important role in the dramatic movement of ministers of the Southern Baptist Convention into the Republican party, about which I shall have more to say shortly. Over half of those ministers who switched political affiliation from Democratic to Republican in the early 1980s cited a social issue as the most important problem facing America whereas only a third of those who still called themselves Democrats did.[16]

Finally, social issues have been of special interest to the more religiously active contributors to right-wing political action committees and to supporters of Pat Robertson. In a survey of religious and secular contributors to a range of political action committees in the early 1980s, religious right-wing contributors were more likely than others to cite the social issues as the most important set of problems facing the country. Thirty percent named social issues—far from a majority, but as many as mentioned any other set of issues—in comparison to 5 percent of secular conservative contributors, 11 percent of religious liberal contributors, and 7 percent of secular liberal contributors. The religious conservatives also proved more conservative on social issues than on others and differed from other groups on these issues more than on any others. Similar findings emerge from a study of contributors to Pat Robertson's presidential campaign in late 1986 and early 1987. In comparison to other Republican contributors, Robertson supporters were more likely to be new to politics and the GOP. They were also more likely to cite a social issue (especially abortion, pornography, and school prayer) as the most important national problem or as the most important influence on their vote and to take conservative stands on these issues.[17]

The great importance of social issues like abortion to a cohort of conservative leaders, activists, and contributors helps explain why social issues seem so important in America's move to the right while actually having little impact on how most Americans vote and think about politics. Because social issues have special significance for many of those most active in the conservative movement, they are disproportionately visible and contentious; thus they get disproportionate attention from politicians and the media. But even if they do not have a direct impact on the general public, they may have an indirect one: without influencing how the average person votes, they may help mobilize the activists who get people out to vote and help shape who they vote for.

The second effect of the broader moral resonances of the social issues was to provide fertile political terrain for the rise of the New Religious Right. Several of its founding fathers gave them great importance. Recounting the issues that led him to work with the Conservative Caucus and later to found the Religious Roundtable, Ed McAteer stressed busing, issues having to do with public-school curricula, and the 1973 Supreme Court decision on abortion. Among the many issues that Moral Majority founder Jerry Falwell listed as having drawn him into politics were abortion, pornography, the rights of Christian schools, and school prayer. Among the general population, as well, opposition to abortion and the ERA and support for school prayer increased markedly with religious fundamentalism while conservatism on other issues did not. Social conservatism, moreover, had the greatest impact on presidential voting among the most fundamentalist segment of the population.[18]

Yet if the conservative position on the social issues was strong among the more religious, why did these issues lead to the rise of a religious Right that was rooted primarily in evangelicalism and fundamentalism? The answer to this question and the key to the interface between the social issues and the New Religious Right lie in the transformation of the evangelical and fundamentalist world.

The Rebirth of Evangelicalism

Who are the evangelicals? Historian George Marsden defines evangelical Christians as "people professing complete confidence in the Bible and preoccupied with the message of God's salvation of sinners through the death of Jesus Christ." As evangelicals stirred politically in the late 1970s, survey researchers eager to examine them and their beliefs hastened to adopt some variant of this definition. The Gallup Poll settled on three criteria: evangelicals are those who (1) claim a born-again experience, "a turning point in your life when you committed yourself to Christ"; (2) have encouraged others to believe in Christ or accept him as a personal savior; and (3) believe that the Bible is not merely divinely inspired but the actual word of God and to be understood literally. By this operational definition 19 percent of Americans were evangelicals at the beginning of the 1980s. Other studies using somewhat different criteria (or different ways of measuring the same criteria) categorize from 15 percent to 25 percent of Americans as evangelical.[19]

Evangelicals are overwhelmingly Protestant—indeed some definitions restrict the term to Protestants—and Protestant evangelicals are overwhelmingly Baptist. Evangelicals are also disproportionately from the South and are more likely to be women. They tend to be slightly older than nonevangelicals and to score slightly lower on measures of income, occupational status, and education. The more successful evangelicals often hold business or managerial posts rather than professional ones. Surveys disagree over whether they are more likely to be black. My concern here, however, is with white evangelicals.[20]

Not surprisingly, evangelicals tend to be more involved with religious matters than other Americans: they are more likely to belong to a church, to do religious volunteer work, to tithe, and to regard their church involvement as meaningful. They also attend church and read the Bible more often. Beyond this, the term *evangelical* denotes a diversity of religious traditions, not one unified denomination, with differing degrees of emphasis on born-again experience and differing political traditions.[21]

This basic profile of evangelicals—relatively low in socioeconomic status, rural, southern, older, religious, and, among the more affluent, holding business and managerial positions—with an adjustment here or there also characterizes the audience for religious media programs and, superficially at least, those who take conservative positions on specific social issues or on some combination of them. Take away low socioeconomic status, and the profile fits as well contributors to conservative political action committees.[22]

The political emergence of evangelicals in the late 1970s and early 1980s—or, more properly, their reemergence—must be put in historical context. What was originally known as evangelical Christianity in America began to develop with the first Great Awakening in the mid-eighteenth century and came into its own with the second Great Awakening in the early nineteenth century. In finished form it emphasized religious experience and feeling, rather than formal teaching and intellect, and relatively unstructured religious relationships, rather than a formal church organization. More important, it offered a relatively democratic, optimistic notion of salvation. Orthodox Calvinism had portrayed a stern God who predestined only the elect for salvation while consigning all others to hell. Evangelical Christianity, in contrast, offered a loving God eager to offer salvation to all who chose to repent their sins and open themselves to him. It thus stimulated large-scale revivalism, its lasting trademark. It also put great faith in the power of free will and was optimistic about triumphing over humanity's sinful nature. It viewed the United States as God's chosen nation with a special destiny to renew the world. Finally, evangelicalism linked the cultural and material progress of humanity to its spiritual perfection rather than seeing them as antithetical. It considered biblical and scientific views of the world, supernatural and natural explanations of events, as complementary rather than mutually exclusive.[23]

Nineteenth-century evangelicalism was rooted in the less formal, less established Baptist and Methodist churches, the two largest Protestant denominations of that era, but it had a strong presence in most other denominations as well. Just as America in the first three quarters of the 1800s was a solidly Protestant country, so American Protestantism was solidly evangelical. This easy domination reinforced evangelical confidence and optimism. As Marsden put it: "In 1870 almost all American Protestants thought of America as a Christian nation. . . . Protestant evangelicals considered their faith to be the normative American creed. Viewed from their dominant perspective, the nineteenth century had been marked by successive advances of evangelicalism, the American nation, and the kingdom of God."[24]

The evangelical emphasis on revivalism and individual salvation did not preclude an equally strong emphasis on social reform. Indeed, the two were seen to go hand in hand. The quest for individual salvation led inevitably to the effort to transform society in accordance with Christian values. Evangelical churches were at the forefront of both the abolition and the temperance movements, and evangelical women began America's first women's rights movement. Politically, the more heavily evangelical churches, in common with all less established, lower-status churches, tended to support Jeffersonianism and Jacksonianism. Their concern with moral and social reform, along with some anti-Catholic nativism, led northern Baptists and Methodists from the 1840s on first into the Whig party and then into the Republican party, a shift completed by the Civil War.[25]

The sweeping social change of the late nineteenth and early twentieth centuries transformed evangelicalism. By the end of the 1920s, when the transformation was complete, it had largely given way to something called fundamentalism, at once its continuation and its negation. Industrialization and urbanization radically changed the way a majority of Americans lived and created a new, more imposing set of social problems that called into question existing social institutions and more and more urgently demanded social action. Mass immigration from eastern and southern Europe increased the non-Protestant minority and Americans' consciousness of religious diversity. The continuing advance of science popularized ideas like the Darwinian theory of evolution that seemed incompatible with traditional religious beliefs.[26]

These changes, which some observers call collectively *modernity*, led to a series of debates within Protestantism as some sought to adjust to the changes and others to resist. Where once evangelicals had uniformly taken an optimistic view of the world, now they split more and more between *postmillennialists* and *premillennialists*. The former foresaw continuing spiritual and cultural progress through human effort leading to the millennium, at the end of which Christ would reappear on earth. The latter predicted increasing sin, strife, and cataclysm interrupted only by the return of Christ, who himself would cleanse the world and establish the millennium. Where once evangelicals had supported both individual salvation and social reform, now they divided between those who stressed the social sources of human ills and hence the centrality of social reform and those who emphasized personal sinfulness and personal salvation as the exclusive way to help humanity. Where once evangelicals had assumed the naturalistic explanations of science to be compatible with the supernatural explanations of the Bible, they increasingly split between those who argued that interpretations of the Bible had to be adjusted in the light of modern scholarship, science, and historical conditions and those who argued all the more adamantly in reaction that the Bible was not simply the guide for everyday life but that its every word was divinely inspired and hence it was infallible.

Initially, these differences were but several distinct bases for debate and disagreement within the major Protestant denominations. In the first two decades of the twentieth century, however, they became the mutually reinforcing bases for major theological polarization focused on the issue of how to interpret the Bible. The optimistic, postmillennial spirit of evangelicalism found its way into an increasingly secular modernist camp that stressed the social gospel and social reform, a more flexible, ecumenical approach to religious belief, and, above all, reinterpretation of the Bible in the light of science and current events especially by downplaying its supernatural elements. The religious fervor of evangelicalism was expressed in the fundamentalist camp that emerged in reaction to the modernists. It emphasized individual salvation, doctrinal purity, and a traditional reading of the Bible. With important exceptions, it tended to a premillennial worldview in which the world was headed ineluctably downhill. The growth of the modernist camp was exemplified in the founding of the Federal Council of Churches in 1908; the emergence of a fundamentalist coalition was signaled by the publication of *The Fundamentals* (from whence the name) in twelve volumes from 1910 to 1915 and the founding of the World's Christian Fundamentals Association in 1919.

Until the late 1910s this growing schism remained largely theological and within the confines of the major Protestant denominations. After World War I, however, it became more and more politicized, and theological fundamentalism and modernism became more closely aligned respectively with political conservatism and liberalism. In fundamentalist eyes the rise of a secular modernism ceased to be merely a theological issue. It came to be seen as integral to a broader cultural crisis in which the survival of civilization itself was in question, a crisis exemplified in World War I, the Bolshevik revolution, rising crime rates, and the rampant hedonism of an increasingly consumer-oriented society. The battle for the Bible rapidly became a battle for civilization from the fundamentalist perspective. The war in particular made important elements of the once apolitical fundamentalist coalition superpatriotic, anticommunist, and ultra-conservative.

Fundamentalists and modernists battled in the 1920s on two

fronts, within various denominations and in the broader society. The latter struggle focused on the teaching of the theory of evolution in public schools and climaxed in the Scopes trial in 1925 in Dayton, Tennessee. On both fronts fundamentalism suffered defeats, losing its hold on a substantial segment of the educated urban public. As the 1920s ended, fundamentalism, and with it much of the once dominant evangelical tradition, had become a beleaguered minority culture.

The two phrases most often used to describe the broad transformation of American evangelicalism from the last decades of the 1880s through the 1920s are *the Great Reversal* and *the Second Disestablishment*. The Great Reversal refers to the separation of evangelicalism and social reform. Evangelical beliefs, religious fervor, and the quest for individual salvation, once the source of reform movements, became more and more indifferent or even hostile to them. The reform tradition, in turn, became more and more secular. The Second Disestablishment refers to the transformation of evangelical Protestantism from the dominant religious outlook in America to a marginal status, from a set of beliefs and practices that once had appealed to broad strata of the population to one relegated to a distinctly lower-class to lower middle-class, rural, aged, and southern constituency.

After its defeat the fundamentalist impulse expressed itself in two distinct ways. One, which retained the name fundamentalist, involved the formation of independent churches split off from the modernist-dominated major Protestant denominations. These churches stressed an ultraconservative approach to the Bible and religious doctrine and the necessity of radical separation from a sinful world. Many of them joined to form the American Council of Christian Churches (ACCC) in 1941.[27] From the independent church movement as well ultimately came a series of ultraconservative political groups, which formed in effect a fundamentalist adjunct to the ongoing conservative reaction to the New Deal. A precursor was Gerald B. Winrod's Defenders of the Christian Faith, founded in 1925. Winrod initially focused his preaching on the evils of evolution and the virtues of Prohibition, but in the 1930s, the New Deal became his main target as his rhetoric became more blatantly anti-Semitic and profascist.

Of much greater importance were Carl McIntire and the array of churches and political organizations associated with him. McIntire joined with the conservative faction that broke off from the Presbyterian Church in the U.S.A. in the 1920s and later formed the Ortho-dox Presbyterian Church. He subsequently split with this group and formed his own Bible Presbyterian Church in 1937. He was a seminal figure in the ACCC and later founded the International Council of Christian Churches and the Twentieth-Century Reformation. After World War II McIntire preached ardently against communism, even supporting the use of nuclear weapons against the Soviet Union; and the ACCC worked together with a number of congressional commit-tees investigating domestic communist subversion. McIntire's special targets were the National Council of Churches and the World Council of Churches, successors to the Federal Council of Churches. He iden-tified them with the whore of Babylon envisioned in the Book of Rev-elation and argued that they were central to the communist appa-ratus in America. The other organizations of the fundamentalist Right in the 1950s and 1960s were allied with McIntire and either the ACCC or ICCC: Billy James Hargis and The Christian Crusade, Edgar C. Bundy and the Church League of America, and Verne P. Kaub and the American Council of Christian Laymen. (McIntire also recruited Dr. Fred C. Schwarz, who founded the Christian Anti-Communism Crusade, but that organization often went its own way.)

The important fact about this old religious Right, in comparison to the New Religious Right, was that it consisted of narrowly sectarian groups with limited political appeal. Whatever their support among the hard line fundamentalists of the ACCC, they did not speak for the second, and larger, manifestation of the fundamentalist impulse, the more moderate group that began to call itself neoevangelical or simply evangelical. This group, represented by the National Associa-tion of Evangelicals (NAE), founded in 1941, while sharing much of the worldview of the more ardent fundamentalists, did not stress the need for absolute separation or doctrinal purity. The NAE sought to speak for and to supporters within the major denominations as well as those outside. Although it was politically very conservative, it re-jected the activism and the extremism of the ACCC and hence caught some of the broad criticism that the ACCC leveled at America's churches. The distance of the ACCC from the NAE is measured by the difference between the conspiracy-mongering, strident, sectarian McIntire and the more nationalistic, appealing, and ecumenical Billy Graham, who rose to prominence in the late 1940s and for several decades was America's leading evangelist.

Both evangelicals and fundamentalists evangelized widely and worked at building an infrastructure of cultural organizations in the decades after World War II. Evangelical radio and television programs and youth organizations proliferated and met with great success. Billy Graham's mass crusades brought evangelical ideas back into the public light. Evangelical Bible institutes, colleges, seminaries, journals, and publishing houses flourished.

Meanwhile the evangelical and fundamentalist Protestant churches were growing, and they continued to do so even as the mainline churches started losing their members in the late 1960s and early 1970s. Between 1970 and 1980 the United Presbyterian Church lost 21 percent of its members; the Episcopal Church, 15 percent; the United Church of Christ, 11 percent; and the United Methodist Church, 10 percent. At the same time the Southern Baptist Convention grew by 16 percent and the Assemblies of God by 70 percent. The membership of the more conservative evangelical churches was becoming more middle-class as they began to hold their more affluent members and attract new ones. By the mid-1970s evangelicalism and fundamentalism were no longer a marginal religious force in retreat. They were growing in organization, followers, and resources.[28]

Two developments especially emblematic of this growth were the *superchurch* and the *electronic ministry,* especially important since they are the most direct links between the growth of the evangelical subculture and the rise of the New Religious Right. By 1980 the two dozen largest churches in America were nearly all evangelical. The unpretentious, low-ceilinged evangelical or fundamentalist meeting hall had begun to give way to the superchurch with thousands of members, multiple buildings covering many acres, and a world of activities that constituted an entire Christian community. Carol Flake's description of W. A. Criswell's First Baptist Church of Dallas, whose twenty three thousand members in 1983 made it the largest Southern Baptist congregation in America, conveys a sense of the enormity of a superchurch:

> The church itself was well equipped for fitness-building, with its own Nautilus machines, sauna, twin gymnasiums, skating rink, bowling alleys, and racquetball courts. . . . The multitudinous ministries of the church included "21 choirs, a mission center, an academy with a kindergarten-through-twelfth-grade enrollment of over six hundred, the Criswell Center for Biblical

Studies with over 275 students pursuing two degrees of religious certitude, an FM radio station, and a Fellowship of Christian Truckers. . . .' The annual budget of the church is $8 million.[29]

Or consider the relatively small (six thousand members) Northside Baptist Church in Charlotte, North Carolina. In 1984, thirty years after its founding, it could boast of having moved from a small frame building to a two-acre site with a 105,000-square-foot main complex (topped by a seventy-five foot spire), a sports center, a youth center, and a child-care center. In addition to religious services and Sunday school, the church offered a Christian academy from kindergarten through twelfth grade, an array of youth activities, a full sports program, day care, and a program for senior citizens. Pastor Jack Hudson preached not only to his flock but also to a wider audience on twenty-six radio stations throughout the Carolinas and beyond.[30]

More spectacular still was the growth of the so-called electronic church. Part of the defeat of fundamentalism in the 1920s was a series of agreements between the major broadcasting networks and the Federal Council of Churches to give free time only to the mainline churches for nondenominational programming. Shut out of radio, the evangelicals ultimately regrouped, forming the National Religious Broadcasters in 1944. They remained marginal in broadcasting, however, until the 1970s, when television evangelism burst into prominence. The growth was due partly to a ruling by the Federal Communications Commission that paid religious broadcasts could fulfill a station's public-service requirement, partly to the new cable technology that made airtime more available and cheaper, and partly to the development of computerized mailing that allowed for large-scale fund-raising. The result was a new kind of religious broadcasting stressing evangelical themes (personal salvation through Jesus Christ, biblical inerrancy, the evils of the dominant secular-humanist culture) and sustaining itself through on-the-air fund-raising.[31]

By the 1980s evangelicals virtually monopolized religious airtime. The audience for religious broadcasting, estimated at about ten million in 1970, was several times that by 1984. One study estimated that about sixty-one million Americans had at least some exposure to it. The highest ratings went to Pat Robertson, whose "700 Club" reached 16.3 million viewers per month and whose Christian Broadcasting Network was the fifth largest cable network of any kind, with thirty million subscribers. In all some two hundred local television stations and more than eleven hundred radio stations had a religious format. Religious broadcasters spent between $1 billion and $2 billion for airtime, up from about $50 million in the early 1970s.[32]

When New Right operatives Howard Phillips and Paul Weyrich set out in the mid-1970s to mobilize evangelical Christians for the conservative movement, they naturally turned to the television evangelists and the ministers of the superchurches. Each of the major organizations of the New Religious Right was initially associated with a major television preacher: the Moral Majority with Jerry Falwell; Christian Voice with Pat Robertson; and the Religious Roundtable with James Robison. The Moral Majority's first board of directors included the ministers of five of America's largest churches: Falwell of the Thomas Road Baptist Church in Lynchburg, Virginia; Greg Dixon of the Indianapolis Baptist Temple, Charles Stanley of the First Baptist Church in Atlanta; D. James Kennedy of Coral Ridge Presbyterian Church in Fort Lauderdale, Florida; and Tim LaHaye of the Scott Memorial Baptist Church in San Diego.[33]

As the evangelical subculture prospered, its growing societal presence did not translate immediately into political clout. Its values stressed individual salvation and the futility of attempting to improve the world through social action. Surveys from the 1950s to the early 1970s found that evangelicals typically participated less in politics and were less likely to condone the participation of their churches. Across all religious denominations and tendencies, theologically and politically liberal clergy were more politically active (and more likely to approve of political activity) than conservative clergy.[34]

Sometime in the mid-1970s this situation changed dramatically. From then on, surveys consistently showed evangelicals to be more politically active and supportive of church involvement in politics than nonevangelicals. They were more likely to be registered and to vote, to write to an elected representative, or to work on a political campaign. They were also more likely to approve of a religious organization's making public statements on political issues, lobbying for legislation, or supporting candidates for public office. The shift occurred among the clergy as well as the laity. Evangelical clergy became more likely to preach on controversial political issues than their nonevangelical counterparts. By the early 1980s Southern Baptist ministers had matched or surpassed ministers from more liberal denominations in their approval of taking public stances on issues and candidates, and among them supporters of the Moral Majority were more active than its opponents.[35]

What happened was that one time-honored evangelical attitude toward politics had given way to another of even older lineage. For most of the twentieth century evangelicals had stressed separating the church from a corrupt political order. In the 1970s they reverted to the nineteenth-century view that the church should infuse the political order with Christian values, though in a way quite different from that of much nineteenth-century evangelical politics.[36]

Consider the case of Jerry Falwell, for example. In 1965 Falwell preached a classic separationist sermon, entitled "Ministers and Marchers," in which he declared:

> We have a message of redeeming grace through a crucified and risen Lord. Nowhere are we told to reform the externals. We are not told to wage war against bootleggers, liquor stores, gamblers, murderers, prostitutes, racketeers, prejudiced persons or institutions, or any other existing evil as such. The gospel does not clean up the outside but rather regenerates the inside.

"Preachers," he added, "are not called to be politicians, but soul-winners."[37] Falwell, of course, was aiming his remarks primarily at Martin Luther King and other ministers, black and white, who marched in the civil rights movement, but he unmistakably meant his point more broadly as well.

Falwell's strictures against politics seemed categorical, but as issues changed, so did his position. As abortion and other social issues surfaced, Falwell was politicized. He preached against abortion, homosexuality, pornography, and the ERA. In 1976 he began a series of "I Love America" rallies at state capitols around the country. In 1977 and 1978 he associated himself with Anita Bryant's antigay campaign in Florida and with Stop ERA. Finally, in 1979 he founded the Moral Majority.[38]

Falwell's political course is emblematic of that of the evangelical Right, moving from specific issues to broad political organization. Conflicts over the ERA, gay-rights initiatives, the content of school textbooks, and the tax status and rights of private Christian schools abounded in the 1970s. At the end of the decade three major organizations emerged to attempt to build a broad political movement out of the ferment. Early in 1979 several antigay, antipornography, pro-family groups in California banded together as the Christian Voice. It attracted several well-known evangelicals to its policy board and received crucial support from television evangelist Pat Robertson, who featured it on "The 700 Club." Although drawing clerical and lay membership from a range of Protestant denominations as well as the Roman Catholic church, its core leadership came from a number of independent fundamentalist churches. Falwell's Moral Majority (renamed Liberty Federation in the mid-1980s) drew its leadership from conservative clergy of many denominations but had its roots in the independent Baptist churches. It kicked off its fund-raising by using the computer mailing lists of Falwell's "Old Time Gospel Hour" television show. The Religious Roundtable (later known simply as the Roundtable), the last of the three to emerge, intentionally recruited not just from the independent churches but from evangelicals and theologically conservative congregations within the mainline denominations as well. Its board of directors constituted a who's who of secular and religious conservative leaders and drew representation from major evangelical organizations, such as the National Association of Evangelicals and the National Religious Broadcasters.[39]

The first political efforts of these organizations involved lobbying on a range of specific issues, through both mass mail campaigns ("grass roots" lobbying) and direct contact with members of Congress. The Christian Voice focused its efforts on opposing the SALT II nuclear-weapons treaty and protesting the efforts of the Internal Revenue Service to challenge the tax-exempt status of Christian schools that it accused of racial segregation. It also began to publish a "morality rating" of members of Congress based on their stands on a variety of economic, social, and national-security issues. The Moral Majority supported school prayer legislation and the Family Protection Act while opposing legislation on domestic violence.

The 1980s dawned with a large Washington for Jesus rally in April, a strong Moral Majority presence at the Republican convention in July, and the Roundtable's "National Affairs Briefing" in Dallas in August, at which evangelicals enthusiastically cheered Ronald Reagan. New Religious Right organizations used their strong base in local churches to register evangelical voters and get them to the polls on election day. Working with the secular New Right, they threw their support behind Reagan and other conservative candidates and targeted a number of liberal senators and congressmen.

Reagan's surprisingly easy victory in November simply confirmed what the activism of the previous year had shown: the New Religious Right had come into its own in American politics. It was widely touted as the new decisive political force, and its leaders were media celebrities. Falwell graced the cover of the September 15 issue of *Newsweek*, whose lead story trumpeted "A Tide of Born-Again Politics." Tens of millions of born-again Christians, it seemed, were marching lockstep to the right with the Moral Majority, the Christian Voice, and the Roundtable at their head.[40]

But how big was this tide really? How influential was the New Religious Right in the evangelical world and in American politics? Caught by surprise after years of ignoring evangelical Christians, the media initially saw it as massive: Falwell had twenty-five million to fifty million television viewers in his thrall and was leading them straight into the arms of the conservative movement. Social scientists, more detached and reflective, were less sure, at first playing down the importance of the New Religious Right but later giving it more credence.

Analysis by sociologists and political scientists in the early 1980s ridiculed the role of Falwell and company as a matter of the evangelical tail wagging the Republican dog. Public-opinion polls showed that relatively few Americans had even heard of the Moral Majority and that of those who had, a plurality was hostile. Even in white middle-class neighborhoods in Dallas—the heart of the Bible Belt and home of the Southern Baptist Convention, the Roundtable, and the James Robison Evangelistic Association—only 16 percent of those who had heard of the organization were favorable toward it, whereas 31 percent were unfavorable and the rest neutral. National polls showed similar results. In addition, a closer look at the electronic church in the early 1980s revealed much smaller audiences than the movement claimed, especially for the most political of the so-called televangelists; no single religious program had anywhere near tens of millions of viewers. Arbitron ratings in 1980 showed about twenty million viewers for all the syndicated religious programs (no higher than five years earlier), with the highest ratings going to relatively apolitical preachers like Oral Roberts (2.7 million weekly viewers) and Rex Humbard (2.4 million). Falwell ranked sixth with a mere 1.5 million.[41]

Studies of the political beliefs of evangelicals themselves had similar implications. The 1980 Gallup Poll found that the 19 percent of Americans defined as evangelical by its criteria were not markedly more conservative on most issues than other Americans. Evangelicals and nonevangelicals were about equally likely to favor a tax cut (63 percent and 62 percent), an increase in defense spending (65 percent, 61 percent), and a decrease in welfare spending (56 percent and 62 percent). Evangelicals were more likely to favor a ban on all abortions (43 percent and 31 percent) and to oppose the ERA (44 percent and 30 percent), but even here the majority seemed to take relatively liberal stances. Only on issues like school prayer did large differences emerge, with 84 percent of evangelicals favoring the idea and 56 percent of nonevangelicals. Furthermore, although more aware and active politically in the late 1970s, evangelicals were still deeply split about their relationship to politics. Some of the sharpest criticism of Falwell and the Moral Majority came from fellow fundamentalists who insisted on strict separation from the secular world and noninvolvement in politics. Bob Jones II, of the fundamentalist Bob Jones University in South Carolina, condemned Falwell as "the most dangerous man in America" and described his political activities as "spiritual fornication." Others rejected involvement in politics as "a mere cosmetic treatment of the deeper problem of sin." From a different direction, many politically moderate or even radical evangelicals criticized the stridency and conservative direction of the New Religious Right.[42]

A survey of Southern Baptist Ministers in 1980–1981 seemed not only to confirm the limits of the New Religious Right's political base but also to suggest a degree of social marginality. The ministers of America's largest and most conservative major Protestant denomination split down the middle on their attitude toward the Moral Majority, with 46 percent approving and 47 percent disapproving. Support fell along established theological lines, with 64 percent of self-described fundamentalists approving, 46 percent of conservatives, and only 16 percent of moderates. These data seemed to corroborate the claim that even in a relatively conservative denomination the New Religious Right could not gain general assent. Further analysis by political scientist James Guth showed that supporters of the Moral

Majority tended to be less educated than its opponents, from less affluent churches, and less active in the life of the Southern Baptist Convention. They were, it seemed, a marginal group unlikely to have much long-term influence, even though the fundamentalist conservative wing had won the presidency of the SBC in the late 1970s after years of moderate control.[43]

A closer look at the role of the New Religious Right in the 1980 and 1982 elections called into question its independent impact. Certainly, many candidates targeted by the New Religious Right (and the New Right) lost in 1980, but the year was bad for incumbents in general as Americans expressed their dissatisfaction with economic conditions and their disaffection with the Democratic party. Studies in several states where incumbents met unexpected defeat concluded that the efforts of the New Religious Right had little unique effect. Analysis of postelection surveys, moreover, showed that Jimmy Carter lost no more of the evangelical white Protestant vote than of the nonevangelical white Protestant vote and that voters switching to Reagan were not disproportionately born-again, religious, or favorable to the Moral Majority. Those evangelicals who did switch their votes, moreover, were simply returning to their long-standing Republican voting pattern in presidential elections after being lured away in 1976 by Jimmy Carter. In the 1982 elections the result was even clearer: the New Religious Right, like its ally the New Right, failed broadly in its electoral efforts.[44]

The combination of a limited, or even marginal, base of support among evangelicals themselves and no clear evidence of independent political impact seemed to justify dismissing the New Religious Right. But in the mid-1980s equally persuasive, if not more persuasive, evidence emerged to support the very opposite conclusion. For one thing, evangelicals continued to flock to the Republican party. The figure of 63 percent of white born-again Christians that the CBS News/*New York Times* exit poll reported voting for Reagan in 1980 may not have been out of the ordinary, but in 1984 Reagan got 80 percent of that vote. The seventeen-point shift was the largest for any identified social category and twice the shift for the electorate as a whole. Analysis of the National Election Studies, the postelection surveys carried out by the Institute for Social Research at the University of Michigan, showed that whereas Reagan had not done significantly better among white evangelicals than white nonevangelicals in 1980, he did so in 1984. Evangelical support for Republican congressional candidates also increased between 1982 and 1986 at a rate substantially greater than for the general electorate. The same polls showed that evangelicals were shifting party identification in similar numbers: in 1980 Democrats held a 40–37 percent edge over Republicans in party allegiance of born-again Christians, but by 1984 the Republicans enjoyed a 45–29 percent margin. The shift again was one of the largest for any social category and much greater than for nonevangelicals, culminating what appears to be a longer-term shift in evangelical political loyalties.[45]

At the same time, assessments of the electronic church in the mid-1980s showed its viewership to be larger and more skewed to political preachers than previously believed. In 1985 the biggest audience (more than sixteen million monthly viewers) went to Pat Robertson, who had joined Jerry Falwell as a major luminary of the New Religious Right and was already conspicuously testing the political waters for a run for the presidency in 1988. Falwell still ranked sixth, but the latest figures gave him 5.6 million viewers. In between were at least two other highly political preachers, Jimmy Swaggart and Jim Bakker. (Oral Roberts and Robert Schuller rounded out the top six.) The major television evangelicals, including Roberts, Swaggart, Bakker, and Rex Humbard united in support of Robertson's potential candidacy; and even his major rival Falwell seemed restive about his early endorsement of Vice President George Bush.[46]

In addition, Ronald Reagan endeared himself deeply to the evangelical subculture in a way that no politician had done for decades. His writings on abortion became prominently displayed staples in Christian bookstores, and his speeches to enthusiastic audiences from central evangelical organizations like the National Religious Broadcasters became a yearly event.[47]

Perhaps the most striking evidence of the strength of the New Religious Right, however, was the continuing shift to the right within the Southern Baptist Convention. By 1984 the fundamentalist/conservative faction had maintained its control of the SBC for six years, and at the 1984 meetings it elected as SBC president Charles Stanley, a founder of the Moral Majority and member of the Roundtable. The SBC voted against ordination of women, the right to an abortion (even in the case of rape or incest), and what it called "secular humanism" (the tendency to "dilute biblical principle in public life"). At the same time, a second survey of SBC ministers showed a broad-based move into the Republican party. In 1980, 41 percent had called themselves Democrats, 29 percent Republicans, and 31 percent independents, roughly mirroring the South and the nation as a whole. In 1984 only 26 percent were Democrats and 8 percent independents whereas 66 percent were Republicans, a much greater shift than among the general public in the region or the nation. The shift in part reflected conversions among older clergy, but it also resulted from the emergence of a newer generation of SBC ministers, more conservative and politically active and less reluctant to call themselves Republicans than their elders. By 1986 conservative fundamentalists had maintained their control of the SBC long enough to begin to assert control over the independent boards that run some of the more liberal seminaries and organizations, including the Baptist Press Service and the Baptist Joint Committee on Public Affairs. In short, by the mid-1980s within the Southern Baptist Convention the rise of the New Religious Right no longer seemed a transitory rearguard action by marginal elements. It was broadly based and well ensconced.[48]

It seems clear that even if evangelicals had remained diverse in their opinions on the issues and split on their stance toward political involvement itself, and even if the organizations of the New Religious Right on closer scrutiny had failed to have an independent impact on elections and to get substantial public support and affection, a big change nonetheless had occurred. Evangelical religious leaders, churches, cultural organizations, and many evangelicals themselves had developed strong ties to the conservative movement and the Republican party.

What explains the rise of the New Religious Right is not only long-standing evangelical discontents newly crystallized in the social issues but an increased capacity to mobilize around those discontents. This argument presumes a theory of resource mobilization, which focuses on how social conditions make building a social movement more or less easy. As sociologist Robert Liebman put it, "Social movement organizations do not appear spontaneously. They are nurtured by shifts in the cultural environment which provoke changes in the mood of potential participants and by alterations in the political environment which provide opportunities for collective action. They develop through deliberate efforts to organize participants and accumulate resources." Above all, social-movement mobilization is most likely in groups with "extensive internal organization and high participation." Recruitment into a movement is "facilitated by an existing structure of ties."[49]

In other words, the rise of the New Religious Right was due to conditions that made evangelical Christians, long a discontented group, more open to mobilization. The civil rights movement, Vietnam, and Watergate progressively blurred the line between morality and politics in the late 1960s and early 1970s and legitimated raising moral issues in a political context. In the 1976 presidential campaign Jimmy Carter, himself a born-again Christian, stressed the need to return morality to government and appealed in particular to evangelicals, who voted for him in substantial numbers. In the wake of Carter's victory there was increasing talk of an imminent religious revival in American life. All of these changes gave evangelicals greater sense of political legitimacy and entitlement, of having the right and the obligation to express their moral concerns politically. Carter, however, did not give their concerns high priority, nor did he appoint a significant number of evangelicals to public office. As evangelical discontent with Carter increased in the late 1970s, evangelical leadership became more open to the organizing efforts of New Right leaders.[50]

At the same time, the growing membership, affluence, and organizational infrastructure of the evangelical world gave evangelicals more resources and an expanded network of churches and schools through which movement leadership could mobilize support. The New Religious Right flourished, above all because it had deep roots in this infrastructure. These roots are most apparent in the Moral Majority, the most successful of the original New Religious Right organizations in terms of recruiting members, raising money, and obtaining public recognition. As I have shown, its original board members were all ministers of major evangelical churches, and it used the computerized mailing list of Falwell's "Old-Time Gospel Hour" to raise funds. More important, it drew heavily on a network of independent Baptist churches, especially the aggressively expansionist Baptist Bible Fellowship (BBF). Nearly all the original chairmen of the Moral Majority's state affiliates were independent Baptist pastors, most of them with the BBF. The Moral Majority succeeded in recruit-

ing members from the ranks of the BBF through national pastors'
conferences and the Christian schools movement and by supporting
the growth of new churches.[51]

The Explosive Combination

The rise of the social issues and the long-term proliferation of evangelical and fundamentalist religious institutions together provided
fertile soil for the growth of the New Religious Right. Neither factor
alone was sufficient. The reconstruction of the evangelical and fundamentalist worlds had proceeded from the 1940s through the 1960s
without producing any but the most marginal of political movements. The social issues raised broader moral questions of interest to
the more traditionally religious, but they stimulated widely focused
conservative political movements and a political realignment among
evangelicals only. A politically undermobilized group with the infrastructure necessary for mobilization together with new political issues of special importance to them created an explosive combination
ignited by the organizing efforts of conservative movement entrepreneurs, the leaders of the New Right.

As a result, the New Religious Right never fully expanded its political influence beyond its evangelical and fundamentalist base despite the wide appeal of the social issues on which it played. Between
1980 and 1984 evangelicals were more likely than nonevangelicals to
transfer political loyalties to the Republican party. According to the
National Election Studies, among evangelicals a positive image of the
Moral Majority was associated with a greater likelihood of party shift.
The correlation, however, did not hold for nonevangelicals. Similarly,
the presidential candidacy of Pat Robertson in 1988 ignited little support outside his evangelical base: in the so-called Super Tuesday Republican primaries in southern and border states, according to the
CBS News/*New York Times* poll, Robertson won a plurality (45 percent)
of the "white fundamentalist or evangelical Christian" vote but only
about 6 percent of the vote among the rest of the Republican electorate.[52]

A further result was that the full political impact of the social issues
was felt not among religious persons in general, as sociological evidence would lead one to expect, but more narrowly among evangelicals and fundamentalists. The opposition to the ERA and abortion

rights certainly mobilized activists from a variety of religious backgrounds, but the anti-ERA movement mobilized fundamentalist women more fully than others, especially after the mid-1970s. Phyllis Schlafly may have begun the movement after the early 1970s with her cadre of already committed conservative Republican activists, and she may indeed have successfully reached out to housewives, who wrote letters and made phone calls to state legislators in their spare time. But in the late 1970s and early 1980s women from fundamentalist churches predominated in anti-ERA demonstrations at the capitals of states that had not ratified the amendment. Social scientist Jane J. Mansbridge suggests the following explanation:

> Many of these fundamentalist women were full-time homemakers. But unlike most homemakers, their church activities had given them experience speaking in public and approaching strangers. . . . These skills and the evangelical enthusiasm that gave them life made it relatively easy for such women to enter the political arena. Moreover, the churches were already organized. They had preexisting meeting places, buses, and claims on their members' time and money.[53]

Similarly, given the strong relationship between social conservatism and religiosity, one might expect that religious persons would have been especially likely to shift their political loyalties to the Republican party in the early 1980s. In fact, however, according to the National Election Studies of 1980 and 1984, church attendance had a major impact on political realignment only among evangelicals, not among nonevangelicals. Evangelicals who frequently attended church moved sharply toward the Republican party (from a 39–34 percent Democratic edge in party identification in 1980 to a 31–46 percent Republican lead in 1984) whereas those who attended infrequently actually drifted slightly away from the GOP (their 41–25 percent Democratic plurality in 1980 increased to 42–21 percent in 1984). In contrast, among nonevangelicals frequency of church attendance made little difference as both frequent and infrequent attenders moved slightly toward the GOP (among the former, from a 32–31 percent Democratic edge to a 34–38 percent Republican edge; among the latter from a wide 39–24 percent Democratic lead to a narrower 40–32 percent.)[54]

In short, only among evangelicals, where conservative political organizations could draw on previously untapped religious and cultural networks, did religiously based conservatism have significant political consequences. If the social issues created a new political terrain, only the evangelical-based New Religious Right managed to make a stand there. It thus became the primary conduit through which social issues had a palpable impact on American politics. Together the social issues and the New Religious Right embody one set of trends important to the triumph of conservatism in America.

Five

The Mobilization of
Corporate Conservatism

Chapter 4 examined one set of developments central to the triumph of conservatism. The politicization of evangelical Christians and the emergence of the New Religious Right provided conservatives with a new mass constituency and a new cohort of activists responsive in particular to the social issues and the traditionalist themes they evoked. Here I turn to a second set of developments on a different political terrain. The political mobilization of big business in the mid-1970s gave conservatives greater access to money and channels of political influence. These helped turn conservative personnel into political leaders and advisers, and conservative ideas, especially economic ones, into public policy.

The rise of corporate conservatism has played a central role in many accounts of America's move to the right. In *The New Class War* (1982) Frances Fox Piven and Richard A. Cloward discussed Ronald Reagan's election as the culmination of a decade-long corporate mobilization against government entitlement programs, whose expansion during the 1960s and early 1970s had tended to "limit profits by enlarging the bargaining power of workers with employers." Thomas Ferguson and Joel Rogers, in *Right Turn* (1986), similarly focused on how the "center of gravity of American big business" moved to the right in the 1970s, emphasizing the pivotal role of "capital-intensive industries, investment banks, and internationally oriented commercial banks" in shaping American politics. Joseph G. Peschek, *Policy-Planning Organizations* (1987), talked about a "political mobilization of business and allied elites to redefine the terms of political debate and redirect the ends and content of policy."[1]

Perhaps the most extensive argument of this kind appears in Thomas Byrne Edsall's *New Politics of Inequality* (1984):

> This book attempts to describe a major shift in the balance of power in the United States over the past decade. . . . In recent years there has been a significant erosion of the power of those on the bottom half of the economic spectrum, an erosion of the power not only of the poor but of those in the working and middle classes. At the same time, there has been a sharp increase in the power of economic elites, of those who fall in the top fifteen percent of the income distribution.

Edsall goes on to argue that the growing economic crisis of the 1970s provided the opportunity for "newly ascendant representatives of the interests of the business community and the affluent to win approval of a sea change in economic policy, especially regressive tax reforms and cuts in domestic spending."[2] He examines the growing skew of upper middle-class political loyalties to the Republican party, the Republicans' growing financial and organizational edge over the Democrats, the conflict and polarization within the Democratic party, and the declining clout of organized labor; but above all he looks at the political mobilization of big business and its systematic effort to reshape the American political agenda.

Big business indeed worked successfully from the mid-1970s on to support policies it deemed in its interests: cutting tax rates on profits and investment income, defeating labor law reform, preventing the creation of a consumer protection agency, limiting the growth of government domestic spending, and promoting deregulation of specific industries. The immediate reasons for business mobilization are not hard to figure out: by the mid-1970s corporate leaders perceived a political crisis against a backdrop of economic stagnation. Even as economic growth sputtered and profits dropped, popular demands on government seemed to escalate. Businessmen felt powerless in the face of growing pressure for government to act in ways they found inimical to their interests. Perhaps neither political problems nor economic doldrums alone would have moved business to act, but together they certainly did.

In a broader sense the political mobilization of big business raises a number of questions for political sociologists. Indeed, Alan Wolfe's judgment is largely warranted: "The triumph of the right destroyed every existing theory of the state and class offered by the sociological tradition."[3] Since the late 1960s political sociologists have generally assumed that capitalists are a ruling class that has dominated American politics throughout the twentieth century; this implies either that capitalists by the 1970s were already sufficiently active and organized politically to pursue their class interests effectively or that those interests were routinely ensured by a relatively autonomous state. Political mobilization, however, implies heightened, better-coordinated, and better-organized political activity, a change that would be redundant from the one perspective and unnecessary from the other. Moreover, even the most important corporate executives conveyed a sense of powerlessness in the mid-1970s that ill suited the leaders of a ruling class. Sociological theories of a capitalist ruling class, in addition, believe that capitalist problems yield statist solutions. Faced with economic crisis or social unrest, the capitalist class or the capitalist state seeks to expand the role of government to meet those problems either through liberal social-welfare and regulatory policies or corporatist efforts at planning. Yet the political mobilization of big business sought to reduce the economic role of government, and it had no time for any of the much discussed variants of industrial policy that would have given government a more systematic role in organizing and subsidizing investment, research and development, manpower training, and infrastructure.

All these anomalies are enough to make one revive the pluralist theories of the state that once dominated sociology. Those theories stress that business is only one among many interest groups capable of making a mark on politics. If the theory is correct, it is not hard to understand why business might at some point find itself outfought and hence in need of mobilization to protect its interests. An important axiom of pluralism, however, is that other groups effectively shape policy, and business often fails to do so because businessmen are disorganized and, more important, because they lack the capacity to organize as a class. Rather than organizing to shape the policy agenda to fit a broad class interest, business is able to organize only by individual industries to procure legislation of limited, short-term benefit. That is, businessmen act politically as an interest group rather than in a hegemonic manner. But perhaps the most important feature of the political mobilization of big business in the 1970s and early 1980s was precisely its hegemonic nature. Business organized across a broad front to seek a reorientation of American politics. Pluralist theories, in short, hardly do any better than others at characterizing the relationship between the capitalist class and the state.

The apparent irrelevance of major theories of the state—or, more precisely, of their images of big business as a political actor—prompts us to look more closely at the political mobilization of big business in the 1970s and 1980s. Why did big business mobilize and why in so resolutely a conservative a direction? What has been the character of this mobilization? What implications do the answers to all these questions have for theories of the state?

Why Big Business Mobilized

Big business mobilized politically in the first instance in response to an epochal decline in economic growth. In the late 1960s and the 1970s, the American economy got progressively sicker by almost every indicator of economic health. From 1948 to 1966 real net national income per hour of work—a measure comparable to the per capita gross national product—increased by an average annual rate of 2.9 percent; from 1966 to 1973 it rose only 2.0 percent a year, and by the late 1970s, it was growing by only about 0.6 percent a year. The annual inflation rate, which had averaged around 2 percent from the early 1950s through 1965, began edging upward in the late 1960s, staying above 4 percent for most of the 1970s and hitting double digits at several points in the decade. Unemployment rose at the same time, with each succeeding cyclical trough and peak since the late 1960s being higher than the last. Real spendable hourly income, after rising 2.1 percent annually from 1948 to 1966, slowed to 1 percent from 1966 to 1973 and then began to drop. Annual net investment in plant and equipment slumped through the 1970s, and productivity growth fell to almost zero. Finally, and most relevant for the discussion here, corporate profits declined from a postwar high of 13.7 percent in 1965 to an annual average of about 8 percent in the early 1970s.[4]

Quantitative measures, however, do not capture the full nature of the change because the decline of economic growth was closely tied to the decay of the social arrangements abroad and at home that had once sustained growth.[5] Internationally the geopolitical and economic hegemony that the United States had exercised in the two decades after World War II became increasingly tenuous. The growth of revolutionary and other anti-Western forces in the Third World, of Soviet military power and world influence, and of the independence of America's Western allies all contributed to the decline of American geopolitical clout, evident in a series of events from the Vietnam War to the Iran hostage crisis. The gradual recovery of other industrial capitalist economies in the decades following World War II, the growth of industrial enclaves in the Third World, and in some cases the growing organization of resource-producing countries all helped undermine American access to world markets and cheap raw materials, with the result that U.S. dominance of the world economy waned even as its integration into that economy increased. America's share of the world gross national product fell from 40 percent in 1950 to 23 percent by 1970, and its share of world trade fell from 20 to 11 percent over the same period; after 1969 the U.S. terms of trade (the ratio of the price of U.S. exports to the price of imports) began to fall after rising throughout the 1950s and 1960s. In the postwar decades, and even more so in the 1970s, the American economy became internationalized: imports had made up less than 5 percent of all goods manufactured in the United States in 1960; by 1980 that share had more than quadrupled (21 percent). In the same period exports as a percentage of manufactured goods nearly tripled.[6] Where once America's international position had provided American business with an ample cushion, by the 1970s more and more companies, even large ones, felt ever growing competitive pressures from abroad.

Domestically the arrangements of class compromise that had helped to ensure social peace and economic prosperity became increasingly counterproductive and difficult to maintain. After World War II business and labor developed what Samuel Bowles has called a limited "capital-labor accord."[7] This is not to say that harmony prevailed. On the contrary, businessmen immediately after the war bitterly fought unions and successfully supported such antiunion legislation as the Taft-Hartley Act; strike activity among workers remained high in the late 1940s and early 1950s. Gradually, however, in those core industries dominated by a few large corporations, business and labor reached an agreement that limited the scope of their conflict. Labor accepted the logic of profitability as the principle for organizing production and the prerogatives of management within the workplace. Business, in turn, recognized unions and conceded better pay and working conditions.

Broad support gradually developed as well for a growing government role in managing the business cycle and for a limited set of social welfare programs, an arrangement often called the Keynesian welfare state. The 1960s and early 1970s in particular witnessed a marked expansion of income maintenance programs. Spending on social security pensions, unemployment compensation, public housing, and aid to dependent children and the disabled increased; new programs were added, including food stamps and other nutrition programs, Medicaid and Medicare, job training, and energy assistance.[8] Much of the government expansion in the early 1960s at least had the support of major corporate leaders.[9] Both the capital-labor accord and expanded social-welfare programs served the interests of capitalism. Détente in the workplace gave business surer control over its work force and a greater capacity to make the work process more efficient. Better pay for workers in core industries and government income maintenance programs helped prop up aggregate demand and mitigate chronic capitalist problems of overproduction.

With time, however, these domestic arrangements created as many problems as they solved. Because once social-welfare programs were in place beneficiaries claimed their services as a basic right, the programs persisted and proliferated even when economic growth, and hence tax revenues, declined. Moreover, along with the capital-labor accord, they helped to increase the bargaining power of workers and limit the capacity of business to control labor costs. Real wages increased sharply from the early 1950s through the mid-1960s; even after they leveled off, several indicators of the leverage of labor vis-à-vis capital continued to rise. The cost of losing one's job—measured by the average number of weeks' earnings lost by a laid-off worker—declined markedly in the late 1960s and early 1970s. The ratio of job quittings to job firings rose at about the same time (after declining in the late 1940s and the 1950s), as did the percentage of union workers involved in strikes (which had also declined in the 1950s and early 1960s). Perhaps most important, increases in the unemployment rate during cyclical downturns had a progressively less depressing effect on the growth of real wages for each business cycle from the late 1950s into the early 1980s.[10] These statistics strongly suggest that a set of arrangements that had suited capitalism for a time after World War II by assuring harmony in the workplace and pumping up aggregate demand had become more and more problematic by the 1970s because they created intractable government expenses and made labor costs hard to cut. In the eyes of business, at least, problems of profitability and productivity had become more important than those of social peace and overproduction.

The point here is not to explain definitively the economic stagnation of the United States that began in the late 1960s. No doubt there were numerous causes, and as many explanations as people making them. Rather, the point is that affluence, empire, and the Keynesian welfare state fit together closely for a time and characterized a whole period of American life. Just as they flourished together, they fell together. The problem was profoundly *structural*.

Thus the first reason why big business mobilized politically beginning in the early 1970s was not simply that the economy turned sour but, more important, that a whole set of social arrangements had ceased to work economically and politically. In other words, its concerns were more than narrowly economic. To be sure, in the early 1970s big business was preoccupied both with restoring international competitiveness and with cutting labor costs and controlling unions. The Business Roundtable, which became the premier corporate lobbying group, developed from groups absorbed in both; one of big business's major political campaigns was against the Labor Law Reform Bill of 1978.[11] Its central concern, nevertheless, lay elsewhere, with a political system spun out of control.

Many corporate executives believed their main problems came not from international competition or labor but from government and a democratic political system. In 1974 and 1975 Leonard Silk and David Vogel were allowed to attend a series of seminars for several hundred corporate executives sponsored by the Conference Board, a policy discussion group for businessmen.[12] The pervasive sense they record among these men, who by any standard were among the most powerful in the world, is a feeling of political impotence and a political system out of *their* control.

The focal point of these feelings was the new regulatory agencies that had emerged in the late 1960s and the 1970s, ones whose authority spread across business as a whole rather than being limited

to a few industries; these included the Environmental Protection
Agency, the Occupational Safety and Health Administration, the
Consumer Product Safety Commission, and the Equal Employment
Opportunity Commission. Although an agency like OSHA inspected
only a few percent of all workplaces each year and imposed tiny fines
even in cases of serious violations, these new agencies increased business's sense of being overregulated. "My industry is regulated up to
its neck," complained one executive; "You are regulated up to your
knees. And the tide is coming in." This preoccupation with government regulation also is conveyed in Michael Useem's interviews with
executives in the mid-1970s and in the argument made by Murray
Weidenbaum, the first chairman of Reagan's Council of Economic Advisers, that the new regulatory agencies constituted a second managerial revolution, a transfer of power from corporate managers to federal   bureaucrats.   The   term   *regulated   industry*   had   become
anachronistic, Weidenbaum asserted, because "every industry in the
United States is feeling the rising power of government regulation in
each major aspect of its day-to-day operations."[13]

High business taxes, chronic government deficits, expanding income maintenance programs, and other features of government also
drew the fire of corporate executives, but most important was the fear
embracing all of these specific complaints that a "rising tide of entitlement" was engulfing America and threatening the viability of capitalist enterprise. Encouraged partly by business itself Americans had
come to expect an ever-increasing standard of living and ever-
growing security. When they could not get what they believed they
deserved from the market, they demanded it from government. In
the view of many executives, this behavior created a vicious cycle:
displeased with the capacity of the private sector to deliver, people
turned to government to do more. As government spending and regulation increased, the rate of private investment fell, and the private
sector could deliver even less. This downward spiral looked all the
more ominous against the backdrop of generally sluggish economic
growth. Silk and Vogel summarize the view of executives as follows:
"For executives, the central drama of contemporary American politics
is the rapidly growing role of the state in attempting to supplement
the economic wants of citizens that are unmet in the marketplace.
This, in their view, represents the gravest threat to the survival of the
free enterprise system."[14]

This political crisis led some executives to conclude that the problem lay with democracy itself. "One man, one vote has undermined the power of business in all capitalist countries since World War II," noted one. "Can we still afford one man, one vote?" worried another; "We are tumbling on the brink." In this view while the market disciplined the average person by requiring direct payment for all goods and services, the democratic polity promoted individual and collective irresponsibility by not demanding a quid pro quo.[15]

Beneath the political crisis executives saw a more fundamental ideological one. Public approval and understanding of business was at a low ebb. The root cause, they believed, was a "failure of communication": the media, universities, and businessmen themselves had not communicated to the people the importance of capitalist enterprise and private profit to their lives and well-being. As a result, the public sought government programs and policies inimical to capitalism less out of hostility than out of ignorance. Executives, Silk and Vogel note, regarded this ideological problem, more than any other, "as the basic threat to the enterprise system." As one businessman put it, "We have been successful in selling products, but not ourselves."[16]

Big business, in short, mobilized beginning in the mid-1970s in response to a crisis it saw as political and ideological as much as economic. This understanding of the crisis is crucial to the nature of the political mobilization. Big business did not just see an economic crisis to which individual corporations might respond with their own resources, or a narrow political one that required discrete, limited political responses. It saw instead a political system veering out of its control, and more important, it construed this political crisis in the broadest terms possible—not just as a matter of one or two bad policies, or even of a bad program or regime, but as a deeper crisis of how politics and the role of the state were understood to begin with. It saw a broad crisis requiring a broad response.

Realizing how big business understood its economic, political, and ideological situation in the mid-1970s takes us a long way toward understanding not only why it mobilized but also why it did so in such a hegemonic way—a matter to which I shall return in the next section. But it does not help as much in answering two other questions. First, if capitalists really were the ruling class, why did they feel so powerless and why did they feel the need to mobilize to enact

their political will? Certainly, no ruling class is omnipotent or immune to economic and political dislocation, but the notion of a ruling
class surely implies a routine for dealing with such things. Political
mobilization, however, implies recourse to extraordinary means,
the marshaling of resources and people usually devoted to other en-
deavors.

Second, why did business mobilize behind a conservative agenda?
That is, why did they reject not only liberal programs but also corporatist ones? There was nothing inevitable about a conservative
antistatist response to the various crises that big business faced. One
could plausibly argue that corporate interests might have been served
through industrial policy and new forms of planning, as most radical
and Marxist thinkers did in the 1970s. Indeed, in the mid-1970s *Business Week* took up the idea of government-guided reindustrialization
and expressed the need for a new social contract between business,
labor, and government. Furthermore, the executives observed by Silk
and Vogel seemed irritated as much by the chaos and inefficiency of
government as by anything else about it. These executives, however,
nearly to a man, rejected any kind of planning.[17] I shall take up both
these issues later in the chapter; but now let us turn to an examination of the political mobilization itself.

What Big Business Did

Big business mobilized politically beginning in the mid-1970s. That
is, businessmen sought to influence the political process by expend-
ing greater resources, increasing their level of political organization,
and establishing new conduits of influence. They threw their whole-
hearted support behind a conservative economic agenda, hoping to
reduce the role of government in the economy, including many activities usually viewed as helpful to business. Most important, big business mobilized in a hegemonic way. Businesssmen routinely have organized themselves as interest groups, each drawing support from
specific industries or fractions of capital and each seeking specific
legislation or government action in the interests of its specific constituency. Corporations thus have often divided and clashed politically along basic lines: domestically oriented companies versus internationally oriented, labor-intensive versus capital-intensive, new
versus old, smaller versus larger, fast-growing versus slow-growing,

rising industries versus declining ones, and so on. Such interest-group or class-fraction cleavages certainly did not disappear and re-mained important in the politics of the 1970s and early 1980s. The major political actions of big business, however, were characterized on the one hand by broad-based support that cut across conventional divisions in the business world and on the other hand by an effort not only to influence specific pieces of legislation but also to shape policy discussion and formation generally in a way congenial to big business. As Edsall put it, "During the 1970s, business refined its ability to act as a class, submerging competitive instincts in favor of joint, cooperative action."[18] Let us look more closely at several ele-ments of the political mobilization with an eye especially to docu-menting its hegemonic nature.

Lobbying the Government: The Business Roundtable. Both critics and supporters of the idea that capitalists constitute a ruling class agree that historically, in the direct lobbying of Congress and federal agencies, big business has acted as a set of disparate interest groups seeking specific economic advantages, not as a unified class seeking to shape coherently the broader framework of politics. Those orga-nizations that had traditionally sought to do more, like the National Association of Manufacturers and the Chambers of Commerce, were generally dismissed as too skewed to smaller businesses or as ineffec-tive. Grant McConnell made the general point in his classic *Private Power and American Democracy* and concluded that a ruling class or power elite did not exist. Others, like G. William Domhoff, who ar-gued that big business does constitute a ruling class, usually con-ceded the fragmented nature of business lobbying and located uni-fied class influence elsewhere—in policy planning bodies or in the state itself.[19]

The historical fragmentation of business lobbying makes all the more interesting the emergence in 1972 and 1973 of the Business Roundtable, an organization that represented the vast majority of large corporations, sought to be a lobbyist for big business as a whole, and combined lobbying on discrete issues with broad-gauged policy-making. Swimming against the predominant political tide to-ward single-issue groups, as Thomas Ferguson and Joel Rogers noted in 1979, the Roundtable "is distinguishing itself as a single group with multiple issues making a unified attempt to control the agenda of national legislative politics. Massive, centralized and tightly coordinated, this legislative intervention represents a sharp break with the practice of more than a generation of formal Big Business organizations."[20]

The Roundtable emerged from the unification of three more narrowly focused business groups: the Construction Users Anti-Inflation Roundtable, concerned with cutting labor costs and union power in the construction industry; the Labor Law Study Group, formed to oppose organized labor's efforts to repeal right-to-work laws; and the March Group, an informal gathering of top corporate executives concerned about the declining international competitiveness of American industry. Its membership consisted exclusively of chief executive officers of major corporations. By 1975 160 companies were represented, including the ten largest and seventy of the top one hundred on the *Fortune* 500 list; by the early 1980s more than two hundred corporations participated. Its budget of a few million dollars and its staff of less than a dozen belied its real strength, for it could call on the personnel and resources of its member corporations.

The Roundtable's most visible and innovative activity was using corporate chief executives to lobby congressmen on specific issues rather than relying on paid lobbyists of lesser stature. Supporting this lobbying effort were a series of task forces, each of which developed position papers on specific issues of broad impact on business, monitored legislation, and publicized its position. The Roundtable played a major role in the 1970s opposing a consumer protection agency, labor law reform, and new antitrust legislation and supporting corporate tax cuts and natural-gas price deregulation. It also sought to shape public opinion by sponsoring a series of articles on free enterprise and productivity and by supporting the efforts of the Joint Council on Economic Education to promote economics courses in primary and secondary schools.[21]

To be sure, the Roundtable spoke effectively for big business only where there was some consensus, such as on reducing the power of unions or limiting the reach of government regulation. It had more trouble speaking on issues like protectionism and free trade or trade with Communist nations, where big business has been split. Nonetheless, unity was more apparent than disunity.

Elections: From Pragmatism to Ideology.   The 1970s also witnessed the transformation of the forms and goals of big-business financing of candidates for public office. Corporate campaign contributions became both more ideological and more carefully coordinated. The campaign reform laws of the early 1970s seemed to threaten the capacity of businessmen and others to funnel large amounts of money to specific candidates by placing strict limits on the amount individuals could contribute to any given candidate and by requiring public disclosure of major contributions. Rather than democratizing the political process by limiting the impact of big money on elections, however, these laws encouraged greater rationalization and coordination of campaign contributions. Political action committees flourished, and like-minded PACs showed a distinct ability to work together.[22]

Big business adapted readily to the new political world. In 1974 labor PACs still outnumbered corporate PACs by 201 to 89. Within two years corporate PACs outnumbered labor PACs by almost two to one (433 to 224), and by 1984 by more than four to one (1,682 to 394). In 1972 labor PAC expenditures roughly matched those of corporate and trade association PACs ($8.5 million to $8 million); by 1982 the former managed less than half the expenditures of the latter ($35 million to $84.9 million). Business PAC activity, moreover, was concentrated among the largest corporations. In 1978, for example, half of all active corporate PACs came from the 1,300 largest corporations, and the larger the corporation, the more likely that it had a PAC and the more that PAC was apt to spend. Seventy of the one hundred largest corporations and 202 of the top five hundred had PACs, as opposed to only 34 of the second five hundred. The PACs of the ten largest industrial corporations spent about seventy thousand dollars each, while those near the bottom of the top 500 spent about six thousand dollars each.[23]

More important than the simple fact of big business's adjustment to the world of PACs was a change in how its money was spent. Until the mid-1970s business contributions had been primarily pragmatic, to gain access for a particular company to entrenched incumbents of whatever political persuasion. This practice implies a narrow concern with securing specific advantages for particular companies with little attention to broader issues of ideology and policy. By the end of the 1970s, however, important business leaders were urging their colleagues to contribute on the basis of ideology, favoring those candidates, whether challengers or incumbents, who were most favorable to the interests of business as a whole. In the 1978 elections, for example, Donald Kendall, chairman of the Business Roundtable, and

Clark MacGregor, senior vice president of United Technologies, circulated a letter calling on businesses to support probusiness candidates and forsake those who were antibusiness.[24]

Such exhortations reflected and encouraged a trend already under way to shift support from incumbents regardless of their politics to ideologically suitable challengers. In 1972 incumbents in House races received six times as much money from business as did challengers; in 1976 only 3.9 times as much; and in 1980 just 1.9 times as much. The change occurred not in races where Republican incumbents faced Democratic challengers but in ones where Democratic incumbents faced Republican challengers. Because both pragmatism and ideology favored Republican incumbents, they received more than twenty times as much as their opponents in both 1976 and 1980. Democratic incumbents, in contrast, got progressively less support, averaging 3.98 times as much as their opponents in 1972, 2.14 times as much in 1976, and actually less than their opponents in 1980. Since campaign money is especially crucial to challengers, this change in corporate giving undoubtedly contributed to Republican gains in the late 1970s.[25]

This ideologization of business campaign contributions still left individual companies pursuing a range of strategies, some giving primarily to ideological conservatives, some primarily to incumbents, some doing both. In the 1980 elections, for example, Coors Industries lay at one extreme, giving only 4 percent of its contributions to incumbents; most of its donations went to candidates supported by a half-dozen conservative ideological PACs. McDonnell Douglas lay at the other extreme, with 93 percent of its contributions going to incumbents and its average donation going to candidates who received no conservative PAC money.[26]

Differences in contribution strategies, however, did not follow the more obvious lines of cleavage within big business. Some observers have fixed support for conservatism within distinct fractions or segments of American capital, the most common distinctions being centrality and region. According to the first, smaller, labor-intensive, domestically oriented firms with the fewest ties to other businesses (in the form of interlocking directorates) were most likely to support right-wing politics, whereas larger, capital-intensive, multinational corporations closely interlocked with other corporations took a moderately liberal stance. According to the second, companies located in the Sun Belt, as opposed to those in the Northeast and Midwest, provided the solid base for corporate conservatism.[27] Whatever the historical relevance of these categories for explaining political differences among capitalists, they tell us little about corporate conservatism in the 1970s and early 1980s generally and about the ideologization of campaign contributions in particular. A study of corporate contributions to congressional candidates in the 1980 elections found no relationship between most measures of either centrality or region and the likelihood of contributing to conservative candidates. A study of the 1982 elections also found that centrality had no effect but that Sun Belt companies were slightly more likely than those in the Northeast and Midwest to support conservatives. In both studies the combined class-fraction variables explained only a small amount of the variance in corporate contributions.[28]

Just as important, different contribution strategies rarely led big business to divide its support sharply in any given electoral contest. In the 1980 elections, for example, in nearly three-quarters of all contested congressional and senatorial races 90 percent or more of corporate donations went to one of the two candidates; in another fifth of all races one candidate got between 67 percent and 90 percent. In less than 10 percent of the races, then, did corporate contributions come even close to splitting evenly between the two major candidates.[29]

This lack of conflict may have reflected a spontaneous process through which pragmatic PACs happened to choose mostly those incumbents not facing conservative challengers and ideological PACs chose only those conservative challengers not facing powerful incumbents. But it probably also indicates the extent to which corporations sought to coordinate and plan their PAC contributions to maximize their impact. In the 1982 midterm elections, for example, the Reagan White House, the Republican National Committee, and the Republican congressional campaign committees met directly with corporate PACs and drew on extensive GOP polling data to direct PAC money into crucial races. The last-minute infusion of such money saved perhaps two dozen GOP congressional seats that tracking polls had shown to be especially vulnerable. These meetings between Republican campaign officials and corporate givers were organized in part by two influential corporate figures, William Timmons, head of a major corporate lobbying firm, and McGregor of United Technologies.

Other groups that provided information coordinating the contributions of corporate PACs include the Business-Industry PAC (started by the National Association of Manufacturers in the 1960s), the National Association for Association PACs, and the National Association of Business PACs. A survey after the 1986 elections showed that 45 percent of major corporations communicated at least monthly with the Business-Industry PAC and 42 percent with the U.S. Chambers of Commerce.[30]

Shaping the Political Culture: Advocacy Advertising.   Big business also stepped up its efforts to shape the assumptions underlying political discussion of economic issues. Corporations and corporate foundations supported public-television series that extolled free enterprise, including Milton Friedman's "Free to Choose" and Ben Wattenberg's "In Search of the Real America." They produced films and other educational materials for classroom use; for example, millions of secondary school students saw the "American Enterprise" film series funded by Phillips Petroleum. They endowed several dozen professorships of private enterprise at leading colleges and universities.

The most interesting and symptomatic trend, however, was the rise of advocacy advertising. Unlike conventional advertising that pushes either a product or a corporate image, advocacy advertising sells political beliefs and thus appeals to the public as citizens rather than as consumers. It clearly aims not at providing direct benefits to the sponsoring company but at procuring a political climate conducive to business as a whole. By the late 1970s a substantial number of major corporations and trade associations were spending hundreds of millions of dollars on advocacy advertising, which by one estimate took up one-third of the advertising dollars of major corporate advertisers. SmithKline Beckman regularly bought space in the print media to allow selected intellectuals to discuss important issues. Mobil Oil used its regular advertising slots to stake out its stance on innumerable topics. W. R. Grace and Company pushed tax reform; Dresser Industries opposed divestment in South Africa; and Tiffany and Company decried the decline of religion.[31]

Perhaps most ambitious of all, Union Carbide sought not simply to make its political preferences clear but to show that the public in general agreed with it. To this end it commissioned a survey in 1979 of one thousand adult Americans by Roger Seasonwein Associates and took out considerable advertising space to publicize the results. One such ad, which appeared in numerous newspapers and magazines, announced in boldface type, "AMERICANS REJECT NO-GROWTH FUTURE," adding in smaller print, "see technology and business as forces for growth." Right above these claims were the supporting survey data: a vast majority of respondents had told the pollsters they wanted the economy to grow in the next five years, and solid pluralities identified technology and major corporations as helping growth but saw business and individual taxes, government spending, and government regulations as hindering it. These findings were enough for Union Carbide to jump to the conclusion that the American public shared its own prescriptions for promoting growth, which it proceeded to lay out in the remainder of the ad: less government spending and regulation, lower business taxes. To be sure, the actual survey, which Union Carbide made available on request, showed a much less wholeheartedly procapitalist public. In response to other questions not mentioned in the ad, a majority of those surveyed opposed cuts in government social welfare spending and regulation even in the name of economic growth and expressed considerable skepticism at business's need for higher profits or more incentives to invest. Nonetheless, Union Carbide's idiosyncratic presentation of the survey results effectively conveyed the sense that its views were not simply self-interested but were those of the public at large. What was good for Union Carbide was good for the American people.[32]

Making Policy: The Rise of the Conservative Think Tank.   The most important element of the big-business mobilization was the flow of corporate money to expand existing conservative research organizations and create a host of new ones. These organizations constitute the conservative wing of a network of policy-oriented research and discussion organizations that some sociologists argue are the major way in which big business influences major government policies in the United States. The conventional sociological analysis, however, has focused on the moderate and liberal elements of this network, such as the Council on Foreign Relations, the Committee on Economic Development, the Brookings Institution, and the Trilateral Commission and has treated the conservative ones as peripheral. In the 1970s and early 1980s corporate money flowed precisely into this periphery, and it became marginal no longer. This is not to say that

policy-planning organizations spoke with one voice during this period. They disagreed sharply on both foreign policy (over whether
the central threat to the United States was international economic
instability and inequality or growing Soviet military might) and domestic policy (over whether industrial policy or free-market measures
offered the appropriate solutions to America's economic problems).
The point is that the more conservative organizations predominated,
and virtually all the groups moved to the right at least somewhat.[33]

The sentiment underlying this flow of money was epitomized in *A
Time for Truth* (1978), by William Simon, former secretary of the treasury and head of the Olin Foundation, who played as great a role as
any in eliciting and coordinating the contributions. After arguing at
considerable length how government spending, taxes, and regulation threatened capitalism and economic liberty, Simon issued a clarion call for business to fight back. The root trouble, he asserted, citing
the writings of neoconservative Irving Kristol in particular, was that
a "New Class" of government bureaucrats, intellectuals, journalists,
and foundation heads hostile to capitalism had taken power in America and were using that power to undermine business. Political and
cultural power had become at odds with economic power. Businessmen had allowed this to happen because they had retreated from
politics, because they had become "more concerned with short-range
respectability than with long-range survival." Worse still, they had
contributed to their own demise by allowing their money to fund this
New Class. Simon concluded that what businessmen needed to do,
above all, was not lobby more energetically for specific legislation or
spend more to elect suitable political leaders but support the growth
of a "counterintelligentsia" in the foundations, universities, and media that would regain ideological dominance for business. Accordingly, he issued a series of marching orders to his peers: businessmen
must shift their funding to foundations willing to support conservative scholars and research; they must "cease the mindless subsidizing
of colleges and universities whose departments of economics, government, politics and history are hostile to capitalism"; and they
must shift their support "from the media which serve as megaphones
for anticapitalist opinion . . . to media which are either pro-freedom
or . . . at least professionally capable of a fair and accurate treatment
of procapitalist ideas, values, and arguments." Simon aptly captured
a broader sentiment among big business, and well before his book

was published, it was doing what he bid, in particular pouring money into conservative policy-making bodies.[34]

The American Enterprise Institute, long the flagship of conservative think tanks, saw its budget increase tenfold, from $0.9 million in 1970 to $10.6 million in 1983, thanks to corporate largesse and the fund-raising efforts of neoconservative intellectuals like Kristol. (During the same period the budget of the more liberal Brookings Institution only doubled, from $5.5 million to $11.9 million.) By the late 1970s AEI had forty-five full-time scholars in residence and many more adjunct scholars at various universities. It funded, in addition to research, four journals and a monthly television show. Among its six hundred corporate sponsors were the Lilly Endowment, the Smith Richardson Foundation, the Ford Motor Company, Reader's Digest, the Potlatch Corporation, and the Weyerhauser Foundation. Its board of trustees, headed by a vice chairman of Mobil, consisted almost entirely of corporate representatives; and a special development committee for raising a multimillion-dollar endowment included the chairmen or former chairmen of Citicorp, General Electric, General Motors, and Chase Manhattan Bank. To be sure, the mid-1980s saw AEI facing a fiscal crisis due to overexpansion and stagnant revenues. This was certainly not due, however, to a change of political heart among its business supporters but rather to internal mismanagement and external competition from more activist, more conservative organizations.[35]

The Hoover Institution at Stanford University, on the verge of bankruptcy in the early 1960s, had an annual budget of $8.4 million by 1983 (up from $1.9 million in 1970). About 40 percent of that money came from corporations and business-related foundations (much of the remainder coming from Stanford itself), and its board of overseers included David Packard of Hewlett-Packard and top officers of Standard Oil of California and the Sun Company. A third venerable conservative think tank, the Center for Strategic and International Studies at Georgetown University, was spending $8 million a year by the early 1980s.[36]

Joining these established think tanks were a host of new ones, the largest, most famous, and most activist of which is the Heritage Foundation. Started in 1973 with several hundred thousand dollars from industrialist Joseph Coors, Heritage had an annual budget of $10.6 million by 1983. Its biggest contributors included the Scaife family, Coors, and nearly one hundred corporations and foundations, though it also relied heavily on direct mail. The list of those who gave one hundred thousand dollars or more to the Heritage Ten campaign, which raised more than $35 million for the Heritage Foundation in the mid 1980s, shows the diversity of business support that even this most conservative of think tanks received, drawing together major corporations with owner-controlled companies, rich individual businessmen, and longtime supporters of right-wing causes. Included were Chase Manhattan Bank, Dow Chemical, Mobil Corporation, Pfizer, Reader's Digest, and SmithKline Beckman; Coors Industries, Mesa Petroleum, Mr. and Mrs. Joseph Coors, and Lewis E. Lehrman; Carthage Foundation, J. M. Foundation, Samuel Roberts Noble Foundation, John M. Olin Foundation, J. Howard Pew Freedom Trust, and the Sarah Scaife Foundation.[37]

A wide range of corporations and foundations supported a growing network of conservative think tanks and policy centers.[38] Perhaps the most active, innovative, and central were the Mellon-Scaife, Olin, and Smith Richardson foundations. The Scaife family trusts (the Sarah Scaife Foundation, the Allegheny and Carthage foundations, and the Trust for Sarah Mellon Scaife's Grandchildren), based in Gulf Oil, Alcoa, and Mellon Bank money, were probably the largest single donors to conservative causes, and their contributions were fairly representative. For years these trusts had given money primarily to population control and the arts, causes favored by Sarah Scaife. Beginning in 1973, however, when Richard Mellon Scaife (Sarah's son) effectively took charge of them, they turned their attention to conservative causes, providing support to the tune of about $10 million to $12 million a year. By 1980 the Scaifes had given more than $5 million each to the American Enterprise Institute, the Georgetown University Center for Strategic and International Studies, and the National Strategy Information Center, as well as $4.1 million to the Hoover Institution and $2.6 million to the Heritage Foundation (of which they, not Coors, were the major benefactor). They supported Friedman's and Wattenberg's public-television shows; conservative foreign-policy groups, such as the Committee on the Present Danger and the Committee for the Free World; conservative journals, such as *The Public Interest* and *The American Spectator*; a series of procorporate legal foundations, including the Pacific Legal Foundation and the National Legal Center for the Public Interest and six of its regional affiliates; and a host of lesser think tanks.[39]

Beginning in 1977 the John M. Olin Foundation, founded by the former head of the Olin Corporation, spent about $5 million a year to support "scholarship in the philosophy of a free society and the economics of a free market." The foundation supported AEI, Hoover, and Heritage; it underwrote Friedman's and Wattenberg's shows; it helped start a number of university centers for the study of economics and law, the Center for the Study of Religion and Society, and several probusiness legal foundations; and it funded a range of conservative publications, including *The New Criterion* and *The American Spectator.* Its director, William Simon, as I noted earlier, played a central role in the mobilization of big business.[40]

The Smith Richardson Foundation, founded in 1935 by H. Smith Richardson with money from the Richardson-Vicks Company, had done mostly routine philanthropy until 1973 when son Randy Richardson took over and directed its money more exclusively to conservative causes. Three years later, on the recommendation of Kristol, the Foundation hired Leslie Lenkowsky as director of research. Lenkowsky was instrumental in directing much of the foundation's yearly budget of $3 million to the support of supply-side economic theory, which became central to the ideology of the Reagan administration. The Smith Richardson Foundation provided a grant to Jude Wanniski, a *Wall Street Journal* editorial writer, which, along with an appointment at the American Enterprise Institute, helped him write *The Way the World Works.* It also subsidized Kristol's journal, *The Public Interest,* which published several of Wanniski's early articles and other seminal supply-side pieces. In addition, the foundation helped underwrite two other supply-side books, George Gilder's *Wealth and Poverty* and Bruce Bartlett's *Reaganomics: Supply-Side Economics in Action,* and gave grants for studying supply-side economics to Hoover, Heritage, and other conservative think tanks. As Wanniski once remarked, "The Smith Richardson Foundation has been the source of financing in the supply-side revolution." Together with Scaife and Olin, the foundation also helped establish in the late 1970s a series of free-enterprise centers, including the Washington University Center for the Study of American Business, the University of Chicago Center for the Study of the Economy and the State, and the University of Rochester Center for Research in Government Policy and Business.[41]

Together Scaife, Olin, and Richardson also contributed more than three hundred thousand dollars to found the Institute for Educational Affairs (IEA). The brainchild of Kristol and Simon, who sought to coordinate more effectively the production of conservative ideas, IEA acted as a clearinghouse for channeling corporate money into suitable conservative intellectual projects. By 1982 it had 145 corporate donors and had dispensed several million dollars in grants. It specialized in funding alternative conservative newspapers and journals on college campuses and providing internships for promising young journalists who might then move on to careers at conservative newspapers and publications.[42]

The development of conservative policy-making organizations embodied all the salient features of the political mobilization of big business: the simple expansion of political activity; its resolutely conservative, antistatist cast; and, most important, its hegemonic quality in regard to both its base of support and its goals. Support for conservative think tanks crossed most lines of intraclass cleavage. The corporations and corporate foundations that funded think tanks represented a cross-section of American business and did not fit the stereotype of the smaller, labor-intensive, domestically oriented, peripheral Sun Belt company. The rise of conservative think tanks also reflected an effort to go beyond influencing specific pieces of legislation to shaping the broader agenda of politics as well. These organizations were not mere talking shops; they were conduits for channeling personnel and ideas into the Reagan administration. Some, like AEI, provided the broad justifications for conservative ideas; others, especially Heritage, offered proposals for specific policies. Each year Heritage produced dozens of brief reports focused on public-policy issues for distribution to members of Congress and their staffs, executive-branch officials, and the press. Perhaps the most important collection of these reports was *Mandate for Leadership: Policy Management in a Conservative Administration* (1981), which provided major guidance to each department and agency in the early years of the Reagan administration. The conservative policy-making network was also the source of the two works that especially inspired conservative cadres within the administration, George Gilder's *Wealth and Poverty* and Charles Murray's *Losing Ground:* the Smith Richardson Foundation, as I have noted, funded Gilder, and the Manhattan Institute and the Olin Foundation supported and publicized Murray.[43]

In addition, the major think tanks provided a great many high-level appointees to the Reagan administration. In Reagan's first term alone, fifty came from Hoover, thirty-six from Heritage, thirty-four from AEI, and eighteen from the Center for Strategic and International Studies. Murray Weidenbaum, the first chairman of the Council of Economic Advisors; Martin Anderson, Reagan's first chief domestic-policy adviser; Jeanne Kirkpatrick, ambassador to the United Nations; James C. Miller III, Reagan's second budget head; James Watt, secretary of the interior; and William Bennett, head of the National Endowment for the Humanities and later secretary of education, as well as many others, all had close ties to conservative policy groups. The Heritage Foundation in 1982 began to publish its *Annual Guide to Public Policy Experts,* which served as a kind of directory of potential conservative appointees.[44]

Of course, many of Reagan's top advisers came with more conventional credentials as corporate executives with ties to more moderate policy groups like the Council on Foreign Relations and the Committee on Economic Development.[45] The conservative organizations, however, provided a leavening of more ideologically committed conservatives. In the absence of these organizations the ideas of supply-side economics, so important in justifying across-the-board tax cuts and in making tax breaks for business acceptable to the public, would probably have remained the half-articulated insights of a few true believers; these true believers would have remained an isolated group discussing their ideas in obscure places rather than moving into positions of considerable influence—for example, David Stockman as budget director and Norman Ture and Paul Craig Roberts as assistant secretaries of the treasury. The whole dynamic of the early Reagan years, pitting conservative activists against more conventional and cautious advisers (so nicely chronicled in Stockman's *The Triumph of Politics*), would have been absent.

Conservative think tanks thus provided an effective interface between the world of big business and the world of conservative ideologues, making the former more ideological than otherwise and the latter more influential.[46] The result was what Sidney Blumenthal has called a "whole new species" of "Counter-Establishment intellectual-politico": "In the past, Republican Administrations had been staffed almost completely by big businessmen and party professionals. While these groups were still represented, they were now joined by the Counter-Establishment ideologues, whose network provided a ready reservoir of closely connected and intensely committed appointees."[47]

Implications for Theories of the State

The political mobilization of big business, as mentioned earlier, challenged the images of the capital class as a political actor in most theories of the state. Let us now examine these images more closely.

Pluralism.   Pluralist theories argue that capitalists are not a ruling class and that their political power is limited for any of three reasons. First, there is a diversity of autonomous potential bases of effective power in American society. Certainly ownership and control of property are one such base, but so may be control of the state apparatus itself, of the military, of ideas or expertise, of organized labor, or of any other major social resource. As a result, many groups have the capacity to act politically in a successful way. Each does so, however, only on a limited range of issues of special relevance to its own interests. Consequently, there exists not one monolithic power structure but many power structures: on each issue of public policy a distinct hierarchy of powerful interests comes into play. This point has been made countless times, but William Spinrad put it best in 1965:

> People try to exercise power when a particular decision is salient and/or required. This obviously means that different groups in the community will be more involved in different kinds of decisions. Many groups possess appropriate resources, internal decision-making mechanisms, access to those who make the necessary formal decisions, widely accepted legitimacy and values, means for communicating to and mobilizing large publics.[48]

Second, within the pluralist political universe the balance of power has shifted from those who control property to those who control technical intelligence and the flow of ideas. Daniel Bell spoke in the late 1950s and early 1960s of a dual revolution, "a change in the mode of access to power insofar as inheritance alone is no longer all determining" and "a change in the nature of power-holding itself insofar as technical skill rather than property, and political position rather than wealth have become the basis on which power is wielded." These changes implied on the one hand the break-up of the capitalist-based ruling class and on the other hand the emergence of a new constituency, "the technical and professional intelligentsia."[49]

Third, even if ownership of productive property might give capitalists a high "potential for control," in Robert Dahl's phrase, they have a very "low potential for unity." That is, they lack any basis for classwide unity and any clear sense of common interests and common political strategies. "Businessmen are decreasingly a coherent and self-sufficient autonomous elite," wrote Ivar Berg and Mayer Zald in the late 1970s. "Increasingly, business leaders are differentiated by their heterogeneous interests and find it difficult to weld themselves into a solidified group." This lack of class cohesion may be seen as the result of historically specific conditions—for example, the long-term decline of the family-owned, family-run company—or as one instance of the more general rule that classes rarely act in a unified fashion unless established modes of gaining wealth and privilege are directly challenged. Either way, lack of class unity means that capitalists typically act politically as a cacophony of discrete interest groups that often come into conflict with each other and, more important, are likely to seek short-term economic gains from government rather than shape long-term public policy. Indeed, one pluralist writer in the mid-1960s concluded that "it is questionable whether most of the businessmen involved [in political activities] have any conscious conception of affecting public policy."[50]

In the pluralist view, then, both external and internal factors prevent the capitalist class from being a ruling class. Externally the power of other organized groups balances or even overwhelms that of capitalists. Internally capitalists simply lack the organizational capacity for hegemonic action, even though they may have the resources.

Pluralism in a sometimes premeditated, often inadvertent way has dominated most writing on the political mobilization of big business. Certainly, those like Simon and Kristol, who played a central role in coordinating this mobilization, struck pluralist chords in arguing that until the mid-1970s capitalists had failed to exert a unified, broad influence on politics and that in the absence of a hegemonic business presence the power to shape the political agenda had passed to the so-called New Class. Corporate executives too were pluralists, though in a more inchoate way. The corporate leaders whose sentiments Silk and Vogel captured chafed at their own political impotence, and they were sure that real power lay elsewhere, in the hands of bureaucrats, congressmen, journalists, or intellectuals. They blamed their political vulnerability as much on their own failure to organize or even think about their long-term interests as on the hostile or ignorant actions of the New Class.

Less obviously, many liberal to radical accounts of the political mobilization also assume a pluralist status quo ante, perhaps despite themselves. Even as they seek to document the overwhelming political clout of big business in contemporary politics, they tacitly point to an earlier time when business had markedly less political influence. To talk, as Edsall does, about "newly ascendant representatives of the interests of the business community" necessarily suggests that not long ago representatives of business interests were *not* ascendant. To present the American state as an arena of class war and then to talk about a corporate assault on the welfare state in the Reagan years, as Piven and Cloward do, implies that big business had been losing that war. To picture top corporate executives as only recently developing an interest in politics, as Blumenthal suggests, certainly implies prior political quiescence.[51]

The pluralist image of the capitalist class as political actor, in short, reigns supreme among the assumptions of those who study the role of big business in the rise of the Right. It does so because it captures the surface appearances of the phenomenon. Businessmen themselves, after all, sounded besieged in the mid-1970s; and an entrenched ruling class, confident of its power, would hardly need to mobilize.

Good reasons exist, nonetheless, for challenging the validity of the pluralist image of the role of big business in American politics. One reason, which I shall elaborate when examining instrumentalist theories of American politics, is simply that there is evidence that big business since the earliest years of the twentieth century has at least sought to be a ruling class, that it has actively worked to shape basic state policy, and that it has sometimes succeeded. Pluralism sees only a narrow interest-group orientation in business politics because it looks in the wrong places. A second reason for questioning pluralism is that however accurate its picture of previous decades, it has trouble accounting for the political action of business in the late 1970s and early 1980s. If businessmen before the mid-1970s lacked the capacity to organize as a class or to develop a coherent sense of long-term class interest, how did they suddenly develop this capacity? How can hegemonic activity emerge so fully developed where only interest-group politics had prevailed for so long?

The most likely way to answer these questions is to assert that the internal structure of big business changed so as to facilitate political unity. This is the argument Michael Useem makes in *The Inner Circle* (1984). Useem's emphasis on the rise of business political activity and the fact that he pays little attention to this activity before the mid-1970s again convey the tacit notion that pluralism once characterized American politics, and not so long ago. Indeed, Useem argues that the pluralist picture of the corporate community as "relatively disorganized and incapable of advancing its joint interests in the political arena" fits big business as a whole. It does not fit an "inner circle" of executives, those at the pinnacle of corporate power, however. These men, he asserts, are quite organized, cohesive, and class-conscious. The rising capacity of big business as a whole to act in a hegemonic way reflects the growing cohesiveness of this inner circle, which in turn reflects a growing structure of intercorporate ties. Big business has gained the capacity to act hegemonically since the mid-1970s because the concentration of business activity, the degree to which any given firm is owned by others, and the number of companies sharing common directors have increased substantially, creating the basis for a cohesive inner circle of top corporate executives.[52]

Useem's actual data, however, do not suggest a sea change in the period before the mid-1970s. He concedes that the extent of interlocking directorates in the United States did not grow between 1904 and 1974. Business concentration certainly had grown, but more so in earlier decades than in the years leading up to 1975. So had the percentage of all corporate stock owned by financial institutions, but again this growth was relatively small in the late 1960s and early 1970s; financial institutions owned 23 percent of all stock in 1958, 33 percent in 1974. Taken together, these data might imply an incremental increase in the basis for big-business unity but hardly a qualitative change.[53]

The pluralist image of big business thus remains only partly convincing because it cannot explain where business suddenly found the capacity to mobilize. The idea that big business was disorganized and powerless until the mid-1970s may be superficially appealing, but it makes the political mobilization seem all the more implausible.

Ruling-Class Theories.   If pluralist theories, when closely scrutinized, provide less guidance than expected at first glance, perhaps
we ought to return to Marxist and other radical theories of the state,
which picture capitalists as a ruling class. Here we find two very different images of how this class rules. Some theories argue that capitalists constitute a passive ruling class that does not actually govern;
others assert that they constitute an active ruling class that does indeed effectively govern. These two images are imbedded in what
sometimes are called *structuralist* and *instrumentalist* theories of the
state. Although these terms do not provide an accurate or exhaustive
way of categorizing ruling-class theories, they do accurately denote
two distinct ways of viewing the political role of the capitalist ruling
class.[54]

Structuralist theories typically argue that the ruling class usually
does not play an active role in maintaining its own domination. Instead, the state, acting on its own, defines and secures the class interests of capitalists; in Nicos Poulantzas's words, "The State is precisely the factor of cohesion of a social formation and the factor of
reproduction of the conditions of production of a system that itself
determines the domination of one class over the others." The state
performs in this way not primarily because capitalists occupy positions of political leadership or exert overwhelming pressure from outside but because it is subject to various structural constraints:

> The direct participation of members of the capitalist class in the
> State apparatus and in the government . . . is not the impor-
> tant side of the matter. The relation between the bourgeois class
> and the State is an objective relation. This means that if the func-
> tion of the State in a determinate social formation and the inter-
> ests of the dominant class in this formation coincide, it is by
> reason of the system itself.

Indeed, the capitalist state best serves the interests of the capitalist
class precisely when "the members of this class do not participate
directly in the State apparatus," when they are not "the politically
governing class." The reason is that the capitalist class is highly fractionated and often fails to form a coherent sense of its long-term class
interests; it thus lacks hegemonic capacity on its own. Only to the
extent that the state is "relatively autonomous from the diverse fractions of this class" can it effectively "organize the hegemony of the

whole of this class."[55] In short, the state independently provides hegemonic capacity for the capitalist class. Although structuralism would certainly deny the pluralist image of politics as a field for the play of diverse interests it shares the pluralist image of the capitalist class as divided and lacking in direction.

Instrumentalist theories, in contrast, argue that capitalists organized as a class have actively governed, playing a crucial role in shaping state policies and hence in fulfilling their own long-term interests. The most sophisticated versions of this theory are found in the work of G. William Domhoff.[56] (That Domhoff dislikes the label *instrumentalist* does not affect the substantive point I am making here.) They contend that the capitalist class decisively influences state policies not in the everyday world of interest-group politics, in which a pluralist reality more or less prevails, but through a network of private policy-making bodies external to the state. These organizations bring together leading members of the capitalist class, encourage a sense of class interest, formulate general state policies that serve that interest, train government policymakers, and serve as conduits for channeling ruling-class ideas and personnel into government. Through this policy formation process, the capitalist class determines the framework of government policy-making and public discussion on major issues in accordance with its long-term class interest, a process distinct from the everyday jockeying of interest-group politics, in which individual capitalists and trade associations pursue their short-term interests by trying to influence specific policies or pieces of legislation.[57]

The policy formation process, to be sure, does not make the capitalist class all-powerful, all-knowing, or totally unified. The capitalist class often responds to pressures from below—the threat of class conflict and social unrest—rather than acting on its own initiative; and it often finds its proposals modified or effectively opposed by other groups. A clear sense of its long-term class interest is not imposed on the state through the policy formation process; rather, that class interest is constructed through the policy formation process itself and always remains somewhat tenuous. Finally, capitalists never unanimously share the formulation of class interest that emerges from the policy formation process. Sharp disagreements often arise both within and outside this process.

According to this version of instrumentalist theory, the state does not act independently of direct capitalist *class* influence. This class influence occurs, however, not through the channels of everyday politics but through a special set of policy-making bodies that lie outside the state. Capitalists do effectively act politically on their long-term interests, but their organization, class consciousness, and farsightedness emerge only through the policy formation process. The important question, then, is not who controls the state or how the state is constrained to guarantee capitalist interests but rather through what routinized *processes* are the class interests of capital effectively formulated and transmitted to the state.

From this perspective capitalists did not suddenly gain a hegemonic capacity in the 1970s. Throughout the twentieth century they had had a broad class outlook and had acted on this basis through a changing array of policy formation groups: the National Civic Federation, the American Association for Labor Legislation, the Brookings Institution, the Twentieth Century Fund, the Committee on Economic Development, and the Council on Foreign Relations. What preceded the corporate conservatism of the 1970s was not an ideological and programmatic void but a distinct outlook and set of policies sometimes called corporate liberalism. Through various policy-making bodies leading capitalists had played a major role since the Progressive Era in shaping liberal reforms often conventionally viewed as anticapitalist—regulatory agencies, social insurance (Social Security, workmen's compensation, unemployment compensation), and the right to collective bargaining. These reforms in turn had helped corporate capitalism stabilize and prosper by blunting radical political movements and redirecting their energy into more conventional channels, by preempting more radical or disruptive alternative policies (as Social Security quashed the Townsend Plan), by routinizing labor-management relations and competition between capitalists, and by propping up consumer demand. Domhoff's account of the Social Security Act of 1935 can serve as a general description of the role of corporate capitalists in shaping liberal domestic legislation:

> The development of the Social Security Act can be summarized as follows: There was considerable distress and discontent bubbling up from the lower levels within the depression-ridden society. This was producing expensive solutions such as the Townsend Plan to give every oldster $200 a month, and the economic

system in general was being criticized. The moderate members of the power elite, with the help of academic experts, decided to accommodate these demands on the basis of plans developed by such elite-backed organizations as the American Association for Labor Legislation. These moderates carried their plans to a Congress that was more in sympathy with the less moderate NAM [National Association of Manufacturers] members of the power elite. Within Congress these moderate and conservative views reached a compromise that became the Social Security Act. While it is certainly true that many people benefited from the measure . . . it is also true that the result from the point of view of the power elite was a restabilization of the system. It put a floor under consumer demand, raised people's expectations for the future and directed political energies back into conventional channels.[58]

Like pluralist theories, ruling-class theories of the state reveal important deficiencies when confronted with the political mobilization of big business, though for different reasons. First, all such theories, whether structuralist or instrumentalist, assume that capitalist problems yield statist solutions. In the words of one influential summary, "The reproduction of favorable conditions for accumulation depends more and more upon the active intervention of the state."[59] From this viewpoint the capitalist response to the crisis of the 1970s should have been support for more, rather than less, state intervention in the economy, although not in the form of Keynesianism and social-welfare programs (liberalism) but as efforts to control production directly through selective investment in infrastructure, manpower training, and research and development (industrial policy) and through formal or quasi-formal economic decision-making processes that bring together government, big business, and organized labor (corporatism).[60] Such an analysis is certainly ill-equipped to deal with a capitalist class and a capitalist state that espoused an antistatist ideology, sought to cut government regulation and domestic programs, and, above all, resisted industrial policy and corporatism.

Second, structuralist theories, with their image of a passive capitalist class and a relatively autonomous state, are at best irrelevant to understanding capitalist class politics in America in the 1970s and early 1980s. They do no better than pluralist theories in explaining how an allegedly fractionated class managed the high degree of coordination, broad-based support, and classwide rationality evident in the political mobilization of big business.

Instrumentalist theories have significant advantages. Because they assume a degree of hegemonic action on the part of big business throughout the twentieth century, they have less trouble coming to terms with the active hegemonic character of the political mobilization of the 1970s and 1980s. They do not have to explain how a disorganized class suddenly organized. Useem's data on the high degree of business concentration, intercorporate ownership, and interlocking directorates through much of the twentieth century better fit the instrumentalist image of long-term classwide unity than the premise that this unity emerged only in the 1970s. These data describe a longstanding social infrastructure in which long-term political unity could develop.

The instrumentalist view also argues that the policy formation network is the major conduit for the influence of the capitalist class on the state. This notion implies that any shift in the political role of big business should make itself felt, above all, in changes in the network. As I have shown, such a transformation did occur with the political mobilization of big business in the 1970s. Business money flowed to conservative think tanks, and a new kind of organization, combining policy-making with lobbying, like the Business Roundtable, emerged.

If the instrumentalist approach accurately captures the capacity of big business for broad-based political action and identifies the forms such action would take, it still has a hard time explaining both why capitalists, if a ruling class, would have to mobilize and why their mobilization took a conservative direction. Domhoff pictures a capitalist class often under attack in the twentieth century but rarely out of control. Although subject to crisis and conflict, businessmen had developed fairly routine ways of coping. From this perspective it is hard to understand why even the most centrally located corporate executives felt so powerless in the early 1970s and why big business in general did not merely take the political initiative but transformed the ways in which it acted politically. More important, Domhoff and others have pictured a capitalist class at least reconciled, and perhaps even committed, to a growing liberal state. Time after time, from the Progressive Era on, business-dominated policy-making bodies responded to conflict and crisis with proposals for liberal or liberal-seeming programs. To be sure some capitalists resisted these proposals vehemently, but the conservative wing of the capitalist class and the conservative organizations of the policy network consistently appear peripheral in Domhoff's work. Even *Who Rules America Now?* published in 1983, does little to upgrade the importance of conservative think tanks and other such influences.

Why Mobilization? Why Conservatism?

All three available images of the capitalist class as political actor—passive and not dominant (pluralism), passive and dominant (structuralism), and active and dominant (instrumentalism)—have been found wanting. The passive images of the capitalist class make it difficult to understand how capitalists suddenly developed the capacity to act in a classwide, hegemonic way. The active image fails to explain why capitalists had to mobilize in a concerted way; and the assumption that capitalists had reconciled themselves to liberal domestic policies and state intervention in general conflicts with how easily businessmen rejected liberalism in the 1970s and does not shed light on why they embraced conservatism rather than industrial policy and corporatism. In these ways the political mobilization of big business creates problems for most theories of the state.

Two assumptions can take us a long way toward resolving those problems. First, different government policies are best for capitalist interests at different historical moments. Second, capitalists have demonstrated a substantial capacity for hegemonic action, but the degree to which that capacity has been realized has depended on the nature of those policies. At issue here is not so much whether capitalists are really a ruling class—a question of political impact—but the extent to which they are capable of acting in a unified, mobilized way—a question of political organization.

The policies that serve capitalist interests vary over time. They depend on the specific problems and contradictions that capital faces and the specific resources available for resolving these at a given historical moment. The class interests of capitalists and the political strategies they pursue may depend on whether the economy is growing or stagnant, whether class conflict is intense or relative social peace prevails, and whether a society is rising or falling within the capitalist world system. Big business accepted the domestic liberalism of the 1950s and 1960s because America's dominance of the world economy made the costs of liberal programs easy to bear and because at the time a capital-labor accord and a Keynesian welfare state may well have helped promote economic growth. Once growth sputtered and America's international economic preeminence faded, it began to seem as though these arrangements produced more costs than benefits, and corporate support for liberalism fell away quickly.

If big business embraces liberal or conservative policies depending on specific historical circumstances, it does so with different degrees of unity, mobilization, and enthusiasm in each case. Corporate commitment to, and enthusiasm for, liberal policies, even when they are historically relevant, is always likely to be less than for conservative policies, for two reasons. First, liberalism usually involves a trade-off for capitalists. It can be argued that liberal reforms shore up capitalism: social-insurance programs buttress consumer demand and mitigate social unrest; unions routinize capital-labor relations and dampen conflict in the workplace; regulatory agencies limit ruinous competition and help capitalists rationalize the accumulation process. They do so, however, usually at the cost of a transfer of resources, power, or legitimacy away from individual capitalists to other groups. Social-insurance programs partially insulate workers from capital-dominated labor markets; unions, even at their meekest, require some degree of power sharing in the workplace; and regulatory agencies give government some role in the production process. Liberal reforms often have significant material costs and usually provide institutional room for oppositional movements even as they blunt these movements. They generate a political culture that admits some of the shortcomings of capitalism and (within limits) legitimates criticism and opposition. Capitalism thrives, but capitalist activity and capitalists themselves lose some of their sanctity and status. In short, liberalism is a double-edged sword that is unlikely to inspire unified, active support among capitalists. Conservatism, in contrast, does not involve contradictions of this kind. Policies that call for less regulation, fewer entitlements, and weaker unions obviously transfer resources, power, or legitimacy to capitalists. Under historical circumstances in which they also serve the broader needs of the capitalist system they do not carry the same costs for capitalists as liberal policies do. Conservatism is thus *not* a double-edged sword, and capitalists consequently are more likely to embrace it wholeheartedly.

Second, as David Vogel has argued, American corporate executives, to an extent unknown in other capitalist countries, have mistrusted government even as some of the most illustrious of them have shaped legislation giving government more power.[61] This gut distrust of government, which has characterized American capitalists at virtually all times, is due partly to lack of bureaucratic state institutions before, and in the early stages of, industrial capitalism and partly to the early advent of political democracy in America. In European capitalist countries, where an independent, competent state apparatus well insulated from popular pressures predated industrial capitalism, capitalists learned to use the state directly to serve their interests. In the United States capitalists disdained the incompetence of the state or feared its democratic potential. Although some of the inner circle of corporate capitalists ultimately did help mold the liberal state and although this state served the broad class interests of capitalists, individual capitalists by and large reconciled themselves to it only grudgingly, if at all. Perhaps that is why the shaping of the liberal state occurred through informal policy-making bodies rather than directly.

Because liberalism imposes short-run costs in exchange for long-term stability and because of the deeply ingrained antistatism of American capitalists, liberal reforms rarely gained enthusiastic business support even though major corporate figures were instrumental in crafting those reforms. Typically business divided sharply on such measures, coming to support them only gradually at best. The support of more than a cadre of influential, centrally placed corporate leaders was not necessary, however, because other constituencies were already available to push for liberal reforms.[62]

In contrast, conservative policies both required and encouraged broad-based capitalist mobilization. They required mobilization because business is the natural constituency for such policies; they encouraged it because such policies involve no conflict between short-term and long-term interests and because they coincided with the instinctive reaction of the capitalist class. A basic asymmetry exists, therefore, between corporate liberalism and corporate conservatism as regards capitalist mobilization.

Big business, in short, moved from corporate liberalism to corporate conservatism because changing social conditions made the latter more unambiguously in their interests. This shift also involved a significant mobilization of resources, energy, and enthusiasm on the part of an already organized capitalist class because conservatism requires none of the trade-offs for big business that liberalism, even when historically appropriate, demands. Finally, conservatism triumphed over corporatism because of the deep antistatist bias of American business.

The image of big business as a political actor that emerges here is ultimately betwixt and between. The relationship between big business and the state is more variable and subject to historical contingency than is implied by the notion of a ruling class. The capacity of big business to organize itself broadly, to address basic issues of policy, and to bring its influence to bear on American politics is much greater than implied by pluralism. Social reality, or at least this piece of it, is more complicated than the theories about it.[63]

Just as important as what happened and why are the consequences. Here the parallels between corporate conservatism and the New Religious Right as political phenomena are worth noting. In each case linkages to the conservative movement and to conservative ideology were nothing new. In the 1950s conservative ideologues and political activists enjoyed the financial support of a number of corporations and individual businessmen and the political allegiance of a cadre of fundamentalist preachers. But in each case the relationship was limited. Big business generally joined in the liberal consensus of the day, and most of the evangelical and fundamentalist world remained removed from politics; the conservative activists in both instances formed a small sectarian group. In the 1970s these linkages broadened and deepened: New Right political activists, on the one side, recruited a new generation of less sectarian evangelical leaders and established organizations that helped mobilize a substantial part of the evangelical community. On the other side, big business mobilized around a conservative agenda. These linkages help explain why the fortunes of the conservative movement changed dramatically for the better in the mid-1970s. The strengthened relationship with a religious Right meant a new popular constituency with whom conservative themes resonated, and the increased support of big business meant access for conservative ideas to those networks that have always provided the routes for ideas to power.

Six

The New Republican Edge

Gains without Realignment

The New Religious Right and corporate conservatism represented a strengthening and deepening of preexisting ties between conservatism and evangelical-fundamentalist Christianity, in the one instance, and conservatism and big business, in the other, during the 1970s and 1980s, reflecting broader changes in American society. In the case of the relationship between conservatism and the Republican party, what changed was not so much the strength of the connection as one of the elements linked: the Republican party made significant gains in the late 1970s and early 1980s, and this resurgence of course redounded to the benefit of the conservative movement. The important questions are what kind of gains were made and what changes in the American electorate made these gains possible.

The standard way of approaching these questions has been to rephrase them somewhat: did American politics undergo an electoral realignment during the Reagan years? To answer yes is to say that the Reagan victories reflected shifts in fundamental political and ideological allegiances: voters elected and reelected Ronald Reagan out of a newly developed preference for Republicans and conservatives. To answer no is to say they reflected a range of short-term judgments by voters about individual leaders, specific issues, and immediate social conditions that had little relationship to long-term allegiances. Above all, in this view the 1980 and 1984 votes were a plebiscite on the state of the economy: voters first rejected President Carter because of high inflation, high unemployment, and stagnant growth and then reelected President Reagan because inflation had subsided, unemployment was stable, and the economy was growing. Their economic judgments, moreover, occurred in a context of dealignment, of weakening loyalties to any political party.

However one answers the realignment question, the more important point is that it tends to frame discussion of contemporary American politics in a way that obscures more than it illuminates. It encourages seeing the broader political landscape in all-or-nothing terms, as either totally transformed or remaining essentially unchanged. It encourages viewing specific electoral races in dichotomous terms, either as ideologically charged affairs in which voters choose between distinct political visions and policy alternatives or as more mundane referenda on the state of the economy or judgments on the personal merits of particular candidates. Above all, it does not allow an understanding of the gains the Republican party made.

The reality of electoral politics in the Reagan era cannot be explained simply as either realignment or economic voting; it was neither a sea change nor business as usual. On the one hand, no grand realignment on the models of the elections of 1860, 1896, or 1932 occurred. On the other hand, neither did the Reagan elections reflect mere economic voting and other short-term political judgments that left the political landscape unchanged. In fact, the Reagan era was a mosaic, manifesting elements of realignment and economic voting, as well as dealignment, and the Republican party benefited systematically at least in the short-term from all three. If no overall realignment took place, there was still some selective realignment, notably in the South and among evangelicals. If economic voting was a dominant feature of the 1980 and 1984 elections, it sometimes involved judgments not only about specific candidates but also about the greater ability of Republicans to create economic prosperity. Finally, if dealignment, the general decline of stable political loyalties, was prevalent, it too worked to the advantage of a Republican party well equipped to win swing votes in close races.

A similar political mosaic emerged in specific elections. Political and ideological loyalties, economic judgments, and independent preferences for individual candidates combined to determine electoral outcomes. Moving from an overview of the general political scene to close scrutiny of a specific political contest can shed light on the complicated way in which different pieces of political reality fit together. In the 1984 U.S. Senate race in North Carolina incumbent Republican senator Jesse Helms fought off a challenge from Democratic governor Jim Hunt. This race is worth studying for several reasons. It took place in the South, the region that most clearly underwent a political realignment, and in a state that gave the Republicans in 1984 their greatest electoral gains—a solid win for Reagan, victories in the senatorial and gubernatorial races, and a gain of three House seats. It was the most expensive Senate battle ever waged and one of the most bitter. It concerned the fate of Jesse Helms, the most conservative member of the Senate and a leader of the New Right. Although Helms won, the race had initially appeared to be in his opponent's pocket. One can argue that aside from the presidential races it was the most important electoral contest of the early 1980s.

The Broad View: Selective Realignment, Economic Voting, and Dealignment

Oversimplified Images. Even though neither classic realignment nor simple economic voting captures the electoral reality of the Reagan years, both are compelling images that need to be examined closely to get a more accurate picture of what happened. The idea that the Reagan era represented a political sea change got its appeal from the historical observation that American politics had gone through a series of relatively stable, inertial "party systems"—beginning respectively in 1800, 1828, 1860, 1896, and 1932—punctuated by "critical realignments" at intervals of twenty-eight to thirty-six years. In this view, accumulated social strains and crises periodically shatter political stability by upsetting the balance of electoral power between the major parties and transforming the coalition of social groups supporting each. What results is a new majority party, a new political elite, and a new array of policy alternatives. The idea of a Reagan realignment gains plausibility as simply one more instance of a periodic phenomenon rather than a unique event.[1]

One can debate, of course, how accurately the idea of party systems punctuated by critical realignments describes American political reality, or quibble about the exact timing, causes, extent, and effects of such realignments.[2] The notion of realignment applies quite well, however, to at least three historical periods, centered around the elections of 1860, 1896, and 1932. In each case political upheaval resulted either from fundamental social strains and conflicts that cut across established political cleavages or from economic depressions: in 1860 slavery and the conflict between North and South; in 1896 the depression of 1893 and the demands of radical farmer and worker groups that government step in to control the power of commercial, financial, and industrial capital; and in 1932 the Great Depression and the debate over what to do about it. In each case the balance of electoral power among the major parties shifted dramatically: 1860 saw the rise of the Republican party as the new majority party; in 1896 the Republican party reestablished uncontested hegemony after two decades of roughly equal party competition; and 1932 witnessed the dramatic resurgence of the Democratic party after decades as little more than a regional presence. Each of the three elections began a period in which one party thoroughly dominated national politics, holding the presidency and both houses of Congress for about fourteen years. In the case of the 1932 election there is clear evidence that the social bases of party support shifted as well, with white ethnics, northern blue-collar workers, and blacks joining white southerners to form the "New Deal Coalition." Finally, in each case electoral shifts were associated with profound changes in government policy or in the range of acceptable policy options: the 1860 election led to the resolution of the slavery issue and to legislation promoting the expansion of industrial capitalism; the 1896 election resulted in the defeat of radical insurgent forces and the political alternatives they offered; and the 1932 election led to the New Deal.[3]

The idea of critical realignment seemed to become relevant to American politics again in the late 1960s. Thirty-six years had elapsed since 1932, about the normal interval between realignments. Major social conflicts wracked American society—over civil rights, the Vietnam War, campus rebellion, and the counterculture. Cleavages on these issues seemed to cross-cut the traditional division between an economically conservative middle class and an economically liberal working class. Traditionally Democratic white southerners, Catholics, and blue-collar workers seemed open to the socially conservative appeals of Nixon, Agnew, and Wallace. Many of the new issues, moreover, seemed to reflect a fundamental transformation of America from an industrial to a postindustrial society, a social world in which increasing affluence and education make personal freedom, democracy and participation, and quality of life central political issues.[4]

Even if realignment did not occur in the late 1960s or early 1970s, both historical precedent and the political upheaval of the time made it inevitable that the election of conservative Ronald Reagan in 1980 and his reelection in 1984 would be viewed through the lens of critical realignment. Reagan's clarion call for the redirection of American politics simply reinforced this perspective. Did the Reagan elections, however, create anything that approximated the kind of political transformation implied by the notion of critical realignment? In essence, this question has three dimensions: Did the Republican party become a new majority party? Did the social bases of support for the two parties shift fundamentally? Did public opinion shift significantly to the right?

To each question the answer is clearly no. Admittedly, the Republicans dominated the presidency from 1968 to 1984, winning four of five elections and a total plurality of 42 million votes. The one Democratic victory, Jimmy Carter's in 1976, was by a very small margin, 50–48 percent, especially given the relatively sluggish economy and the still warm memories of Watergate. In the five elections the Democrats managed to win more than twice in only five states and the District of Columbia, with a total of fifty electoral votes. Yet the GOP failed to make steady progress in Congress or the state legislatures. They were unable to win a majority in the House of Representatives, and they lost control of the Senate in 1986 after holding it for only six years. In the five elections from 1978 through 1986 the GOP netted only thirty-one House seats and seven Senate seats. In contrast, during the New Deal realignment, even after major losses in the 1938 elections, Democrats gained ninety-nine House seats and thirty Senate seats. Similar results for the most part can be seen on the state level as well. Clearly the Republican party did not become the majority party in any electoral sense, and if there was a realignment under Reagan, it was a split-level one.[5]

The 1986 elections dramatized the limits of Republican gains clearly. In an effort to prevent the U.S. Senate from falling back into Democratic hands for the last two years of his presidency, Ronald Reagan campaigned in twenty-two states in the most active presidential midterm effort in many years. He urged voters to make the senatorial races into a national referendum on the Republican policies of a strong national defense and fiscal prudence, calling on the electorate to cast one more vote for him by choosing Republican senatorial candidates. His effort failed: Democrats picked up eight seats and took control of the Senate. Just as striking were the results of exit polls. According to the CBS News/New York Times survey, about three-quarters of those who said they took Reagan's policies into account voted Democratic; two-thirds of those who said they voted as they did because they wanted someone who cared for the middle class voted Democratic. Voters concerned about the economy or about national defense slightly favored the Democrats, and even among self-described Reagan supporters one-third voted Democratic (compared to one-fifth in 1984).[6]

Similarly, much of the wholesale reshuffling of political coalitions predicted since the late 1960s failed to materialize. In particular, class-based and Protestant/Catholic political cleavages, the very stuff of the New Deal realignment, persisted, though sometimes in attenuated form. To be sure, working-class persons and Catholics did vote Republican in often unprecedented proportions, but the relative Democratic advantage among these voters remained. In 1984, according to the CBS News/*New York Times* poll and the *Washington Post*/ABC News poll, Mondale did twenty-two percentage points better among the lowest income group than among the highest, at least ten points better among those with a grade-school education than among college graduates, and at least ten points better among Catholics than among Protestants.[7]

Finally, there is little or no evidence that Americans had become more conservative ideologically on major issues before Reagan's election in 1980, nor that they became so afterward. Throughout the late 1970s and early 1980s a substantial majority of Americans opposed cutting most categories of federal domestic spending or easing most forms of government regulation of the economy. They favored a woman's right to an abortion, at least in some circumstances. As the 1970s progressed, more and more Americans came to believe that military spending needed to be increased; but this trend reversed itself in Reagan's first term, during which a growing majority of Americans favored cuts in military spending rather than in specific domestic programs to balance the federal budget. Nearly all measures of ideology and issue positions used by public-opinion polls showed no substantial move to the right. More important, Republican presidential victories and gains in party identification from 1980 to 1984 came almost totally from that segment of the electorate least attuned to issues and ideology. Among those voters who gave ideological, policy, or interest-group reasons for voting, Democrats actually made up ground. This lack of an ideological move to the right among the electorate was reflected in the uneven effectiveness of conservative political action groups in the elections of the 1980s. After some success in electing conservative senators and congressmen in 1980, these groups fared poorly in subsequent elections.[8]

If a classic critical realignment did not occur in the Reagan years, perhaps what some observers call a second-order realignment did. If the Republican party did not become the new majority party, it still closed the longtime gap in party identification, leaving the two parties at a standoff. For more than three decades America had, in the words of Thomas E. Cavanagh and James L. Sundquist, a "one-and-a-half party relationship":

> From 1950 until the summer of 1984, Gallup polls showed a consistent and substantial Democratic advantage over the Republicans in party identification. . . . In the nation as a whole the Democrats always claimed more than 40 percent of the electorate, and usually 45 to 48 percent, while Republican identification was always below 35 percent and for the last quarter of a century, 29 percent or less.[9]

The Gallup Poll showed consistent 14–22 point Democratic advantages in the early 1980s. In the summer of 1984, however, Republicans suddenly made up ground, and by September they trailed Democrats in the Gallup Poll by only a 35–39 percent margin (with 26 percent of voters declaring themselves independent). Other polls, including the National Election Study, showed similar trends, though of lesser magnitude. A comparison of CBS News/*New York Times* exit polls for the 1980 and 1984 elections shows that this shift, with a few exceptions, occurred across the board, though it was more marked among some groups than others. Only blacks and the unemployed bucked the trend.[10]

A shift in party identification implies significant electoral change only if such identification governs political behavior. Most evidence, however, suggests the opposite—the weakening of party identification and the deterioration of its relationship to political behavior in the 1970s and early 1980s. In other words, the paramount political reality was dealignment, not realignment. The number of Americans considering themselves strong supporters of either party, according to the biennial National Election Study, declined from 38 percent in 1964 to 23 percent in 1978 and inched back up to 29 percent by 1984. The percentage of independents correspondingly rose from about 20 percent to about 38 percent in the mid-1970s. From there it fell somewhat to about 30 percent in the mid-1980s, but Seymour Lipset's assessment of party allegiances at the time still seems sound: "To the 30–33 percent who have described themselves as 'independents' since the early seventies . . . must be added at least another 20 percent who changed their identification as they shift their vote preference. These results are simply another way of documenting that the American electorate has become more volatile."[11] As party identification weakened, the prevalence of split-ticket voting and the power of incumbency in congressional elections increased. In 1956 about one-fifth of all congressional districts voted for presidential and congressional candidates of different parties. That figure rose to one-third in 1964 and hovered between 29 and 44 percent during the next two decades, peaking in 1972 and 1984. Similarly, 14.5 percent of all voters reported splitting tickets in 1956, a figure that rose steadily to 26.7 percent in 1980. As a result of this trend, the impact of the presidential vote on the vote for congressional candidates decreased steadily from the mid-1960s through the 1980 election and the impact of incumbency on that vote increased. The percentage of incumbents in the House of Representatives reelected with at least 60 percent of the major party vote increased from 59 in 1956 to 86 in 1986.[12]

Because of the volatility of the electorate, neither party was able to put together a consistent majority coalition. In the 1980 and 1984 presidential votes Republicans won in every social category except among the poor, the unemployed, blacks, Hispanics, and Jews; but in the midterm elections of 1982 and 1986 they lost in nearly all categories except the highest income group. The implication is that each of the two parties had a relatively small core constituency and that the rest of the electorate was up for grabs.[13]

As Reagan's second term unfolded, the gap between the two parties reopened, from a 37–35 percent standoff in early 1985 to a 42–29 percent Democratic lead in late 1987, according to the Gallup poll.

This did not match the usual Democratic margin of the three decades before 1984, but it did testify to the volatility of the electorate and the uncertainty of even a second-order realignment.[14]

Faced with the lack of evidence of any general electoral realignment, and with the considerable evidence of dealignment, one can easily move to the opposite extreme by arguing in effect that the Reagan elections had little or no ideological implications but simply reflected the changing state of the economy. This image of the Reagan years gains credence from a substantial body of literature that suggests that economic conditions and voters' perceptions thereof are the crucial factor in American elections (and in elections in other Western-style democracies). In this view the key to electoral outcome is such macroeconomic factors as the inflation rate, the unemployment rate, and the rate of growth in personal disposable income as well as individual perceptions of how both personal finances and macroeconomic conditions are faring. Voters tend to support incumbent parties when general economic conditions and personal circumstance are, or are perceived to be, good and to oppose them when these are bad. Thus, according to one analysis, in election years during which personal disposable income rose 3.5 percent or more (1936, 1940, 1948, 1964, and 1984) the presidential candidate of the incumbent party, whether Democratic or Republican, won. In years in which personal disposable income rose 1 percent or less (1932, 1952, 1960, and 1980) the candidate of the incumbent party lost. For election years that fall in between these extremes (1944, 1956, 1968, 1972, and 1976) the results are mixed.[15]

One effort to predict the outcome of presidential elections using the increase in personal disposable income and individual perceptions of changes in personal financial conditions succeeded in predicting the percentage of the popular vote received by the incumbent party's candidate in elections from 1952 to 1984 to within an average of three percentage points. Another analysis of elections between 1979 and 1983 in Western democracies found that when the so-called misery index (unemployment rate plus inflation rate) was above ten, incumbent parties of whatever political stripe lost in seventeen of twenty cases, while in all four instances where the misery index was below ten the incumbent party was reelected.[16]

The economic-voting thesis applies quite well to the Reagan years. In 1980 personal disposable income actually fell slightly, its worst showing since 1932; and a record percentage of Americans (40 percent) told the National Election Survey that their personal financial situation was getting worse. That year incumbent Jimmy Carter lost decisively to challenger Ronald Reagan. In 1984 personal disposable income rose a healthy 5.8 percent, its best showing since 1936, and a near record 45 percent of Americans said their personal financial situation was improving. That year incumbent Ronald Reagan defeated challenger Walter Mondale. According to the *Los Angeles Times* exit poll, 81 percent of those who felt their personal financial circumstances had gotten better voted for Reagan, as opposed to only 27 percent of those who felt they had gotten worse. More to the point, Reagan won 92 percent of the vote among those who felt the economy was beginning a long-term recovery but only 13 percent among those who felt that it was not improving. In a *Washington Post*/ABC News preelection survey those who believed they would prosper financially under Reagan preferred him by large margins even if they disapproved of his handling of the economy (63–35 percent) or foreign policy (66–32 percent) or maintained a more positive view of Mondale than of Reagan. For most of his first term, as well, Reagan's popularity in the polls rose and fell with economic conditions.[17]

Political Mosaic.   It would be misleading, nonetheless, to view the American electorate as simply bending this way or that with the economic winds. Even if a general realignment did not occur in the Reagan years, a mix of important changes of a different order partly reshaped the political terrain in ways that gave advantages to the Republican party for at least the short-term. First, a selective realignment did take place, most markedly among white southerners and evangelical Christians. Second, the economic conditions of the late 1970s and early 1980s may have etched themselves indelibly on the minds of a new cohort of voters, shaping their long-term political allegiances, and may have influenced as well general perceptions of the two parties. Third, dealignment did not work equally against both major parties but favored the Republicans as the smaller, more homogeneous, and, above all, better-organized political party. Thus the key to understanding the Reagan elections is neither a sweeping realignment nor mere economic voting but a series of smaller, but palpable, changes in the political terrain.

I have already discussed (in Chapter 4) the shifting political allegiances of evangelical Christians. Surprisingly, much of that shifting happened after 1980. Whatever the evangelical surge for Reagan in 1980, it was little more than a return to the norm after the 1976 election when evangelicals voted uncharacteristically for Democrat Jimmy Carter. After 1980 the shift to the GOP among evangelicals became undeniable. In 1984 Reagan got about 80 percent of the white evangelical vote, up from about 63 percent in 1980. The white evangelical vote for Republican congressional candidates rose from about 54 percent in 1982 to close to 70 percent in 1986. Party identification among white evangelicals showed a similar trend, moving sharply toward the Republican party, especially among younger and more religiously observant voters.[18]

In contrast, the defection of the once solid South from the Democratic party was certainly nothing new. Ever since the Democrats made their first halting moves toward supporting civil rights for blacks in the 1940s the South has shifted gradually from a Democratic bastion to a region where both parties compete on an almost equal footing. Urban middle-class whites in the so-called outer South were the first to defect, followed by whites in those areas of the Deep South with the highest concentrations of blacks. The net result was that from 1968 to 1984 only Jimmy Carter among Democratic presidential candidates carried a majority of southern states. In a region where Republicans once hardly ever contested elections, let alone won them, after the 1984 elections Republicans held 46 percent of the Senate seats, 36 percent of the House seats, and 21 percent of the seats in the state legislatures. The 1986 midterm elections saw Democrats win back four Senate seats but lose four governorships. In only one of the five southern Senate races where a Democratic candidate won a Republican seat or an open seat did the Democrat win a majority of the white vote. In the other four the victor stitched a majority together from overwhelming black support and about 40 percent of the white vote.[19]

If the South had been slipping from the Democratic grasp for a long time, in its voting behavior, however, it was only after 1980 that its party allegiance shifted dramatically. Between 1960 and 1980 Democratic party allegiance among white southerners eroded rather slowly, from 60 percent to 48 percent, while Republican support inched up only slightly from 21 percent to 25 percent. Between 1980 and 1984 that trend accelerated sharply as the 48–25 percent Democratic lead became a 31–40 percent Republican edge.[20] In white evangelical Christians Republicans gained a new source of solid party allegiance and voting support. In white southerners Democrats lost precisely the same kind of reliable constituency. Both these developments gave new electoral advantages to the Republican party.

Economic voting too may have worked to the advantage of the Republican party. Voters may support or reject an incumbent depending on the state of the economy, but they also make general assessments of the political parties on the same basis. From the 1950s to the 1970s a plurality of Americans fairly consistently identified the Democratic party as doing a "better job of keeping the country prosperous"—in the words of a Gallup Poll question asked regularly since 1951. The Democratic plurality varied from a few percentage points to more than twenty, but only briefly in the early 1970s did it disappear. Through good times and bad the Democratic party was the so-called party of prosperity and only when it led the Republicans by a substantial margin in this respect—by 46–31 percent in 1960, by 53–21 percent in 1964, and by 47–23 percent in 1976—did it manage to win the presidency.

The economic problems of the later Carter years—economic slowdown, rampant inflation, and growing unemployment—undermined the Democrats' image as the party of prosperity. The 47–23 Democratic edge when Carter came into office dwindled to a virtual tie (36–35) when he left and became a 41–28 Republican edge in Reagan's first year in office. That edge disappeared as the recession of 1982 worsened, but it reappeared toward the end of Reagan's first term, with more Americans than ever before (49 percent) identifying the GOP as the party of prosperity, and remained intact through Reagan's second term. The Democrats clearly lost the benefit of the economic doubt. Even if economic voting is a double-edged sword, cutting for or against both parties depending on incumbency and economic conditions, beginning in the early 1980s it cut more deeply against Democrats, just as it once did against Republicans.[21]

Economic voting may also have a long-term impact on the political predispositions of those younger voters whose formative political experiences were bounded by the Carter and Reagan years. Impressed by economic decline under the Democrats and apparent economic rebirth under the Republicans, a cohort of American voters that came of age in the late 1970s and early 1980s gave their loyalty to the Republican party. Ever since the Gallup Poll started examining voting behavior in 1936, Democratic presidential candidates had generally done better among voters under thirty than among older voters. In 1984, however, Reagan actually did slightly better among younger voters than among older ones. Data on party identification reveal the same shift. In 1980, according to the CBS News/*New York Times* poll, Democrats enjoyed an eight-point advantage among whites in all age groups. By 1984 that margin had turned into a Republican advantage among all age groups, with the largest shift occurring in the under-thirty group, which had moved from a 40–32 Democratic tilt to a 30–42 Republican one. Even as the Democratic advantage reemerged in 1987, voters under age thirty remained the most Republican of all age cohorts.[22]

The Republicanization of this cohort of voters probably reflected economic perceptions and concerns. In the summer of 1984 the Gallup Poll asked Americans the question Ronald Reagan had posed in the 1980 campaign: "Would you say you and your family are better off now than you were four years ago or worse off?" The percentage of respondents answering "better" decreased with age—59 percent of those under thirty compared to 34 percent of those over sixty-five. Furthermore, surveys of college freshmen suggested an age cohort increasingly concerned with economic well-being. Seventy percent of the 1986 freshman class considered being well-off financially an important goal, compared to only 40 percent of the 1976 freshman class. A similar percentage of freshmen in 1986 regarded increasing one's earning power as a major reason for attending college, compared to about half of freshmen in the early 1970s. The shift was not an ideological one: entering college students remained fairly liberal on specific issues ranging from national health insurance to legal abortion. They were simply concerned about their economic prospects; they felt less able to take a materially secure future for granted. This shift and its nature were not lost on the Republican party. The College Republicans made a major effort to register and get out the vote on college campuses with an appeal that focused precisely on economics and national self-esteem.[23]

Dealignment also worked to the relative advantage of the Republican party, even though it would seem by definition to work against both parties. It did so for several reasons. First, the GOP as the minority party had less to lose from dealignment and more to gain from the power vacuum it created. Second, the GOP was the more ideologically homogeneous party and thus better able to agree on candidates and make a clear appeal for votes among the uncommitted. Third, the Republican party had more resources and better organization to compete effectively in a dealigned political world.[24] This last reason bears some elaboration.

Dealignment actually occurred in only one of two possible senses. In the late 1960s and 1970s the two major parties appeared not only to be losing the loyalty of the electorate but also to be falling apart organizationally. State and local party organizations declined; candidates for office from the presidency to city councils could, and did, run campaigns independent of any party; parties themselves seemed to be giving way to single-issue groups, political action committees, and social movement organizations. By the early 1980s only the first of these trends still held. Party loyalties continued to be weak and a declining influence on voting behavior, but parties as organizations, especially on the national level, enjoyed a rebirth. This was particularly true of the Republican party.

This odd combination is worth pondering. The decline of subjective party loyalties means a political universe in which a growing percentage of the electorate has no a priori political commitment. The growth of centralized party organization means a party is better able to compete for votes in such a dealigned universe. The Republican party gained political advantage not only from a selective realignment and the residue of economic voting but also from having moved further than the Democrats toward a rationalized, centralized party organization that would be a formidable force under any circumstances but which is especially better able to profit from dealignment.

In a dealigned political universe one of the main findings of voting studies becomes all the more true: in local races "familiarity with and evaluations of the two candidates running in the district" is one of the most important influences on individual voters. One study of the 1982 elections determined that "the better a voter knows and likes a candidate, relative to the opponent, the more likely he or she is to vote for that candidate. This means that the relative quality of candidates and vigor of campaigns is a crucial factor affecting the outcome of congressional contests."[25] The importance of other factors depends on the extent to which they are incorporated in the campaigns and images of the candidates. Where the contest pits an incumbent against a challenger, the quality and resources of the challenger are especially consequential. All other things being equal, the party best able to recruit and support good challengers systematically and to channel adequate funds into close races at the appropriate moment has an advantage.[26]

The Federal Election Campaign Act of 1971, as amended in 1974, sought to democratize the funding of campaigns for federal office by restricting the size of contributions by individuals, interest groups, and parties, by full public funding of general election campaigns for president and partial funding of primary campaigns, and by requiring public disclosure of contributions. Its effect instead was to rationalize and centralize the funding process. By placing higher limits on political action committees and party organizations and by ruling out much of the old-style fat-cat contributions by individuals, the reform law encouraged a more systematic effort to raise a large number of relatively small contributions and to coordinate the distribution of this money.

The Republican party, as the opposition party, had greater incentives to transform itself along these lines and faced fewer obstacles. The 1976 elections threw the GOP out of the White House and left it a small minority in both houses of Congress; it had little left to lose. Its lack of entrenched incumbents and strong local party organizations, moreover, meant relatively little opposition to centralizing party reform. In 1977 William Brock took over as chairman of the Republican National Committee and began systematically to rebuild the party. Most important, he invested a substantial amount of money in direct-mail solicitation to build up a mass base of small contributors. The investment paid off. By 1980 the Republican National Committee was raking in tens of millions of dollars more than its investment and could claim a list of two million active contributors. By 1982 Republican party committees (national, senatorial, and congressional) were outraising their Democratic counterparts by about six to one, with most of the GOP money coming from direct mail. That did not mean Republicans as a whole always raised more money than Democrats, at least in congressional races. But it did mean that the money raised by Republicans was in the hands of the national party, not individual incumbents.[27]

By the early 1980s, as well, Republican organizations were systematically recruiting candidates for legislative and congressional offices and supplying them with advice, funds, and research on issues. They were working closely with sympathetic business and conservative PACs to channel money to Republican candidates.

More and more the Republican party was running itself as a national organization. As a result, it could allocate its resources more rationally than could the Democratic party. Democrats often spent as much as Republicans on House and Senate races in the aggregate because the more numerous entrenched Democratic incumbents could attract substantial contributions even as their national party starved. Republicans, with their centralized control of funds, could direct that money more effectively to close races—to promising challengers or beleaguered incumbents. Political action committees sympathetic to the Republican party followed suit, giving a much higher percentage of their funds to nonincumbents than did Democratic PACs. That allocation was more rational because the relationship between money spent and votes received is stronger for challengers than for incumbents.[28]

Similarly, Republicans were better able to buck the natural tendency of money and good candidates to disappear during unpromising electoral years. The 1982 elections were a good case in point. Given Reagan's modest popularity ratings and the poor state of the economy, the Republicans should have lost at least fifty House seats, according to even the most moderate estimates. They in fact lost less than half that because the Republican party channeled its money into close races, saving a number of otherwise doomed incumbents. In addition, from 1978 to 1984 Republicans won nineteen of twenty-four Senate contests that were decided by less than 4 percent of the vote.[29]

In short, a centralized political party capable of systematically raising and controlling campaign contributions has distinct advantages over a more decentralized system in which funds are controlled by a large number of individual incumbents and fund-raisers. Under the latter system money flows most readily to those who need it least, entrenched incumbents able to translate their congressional power into monetary contributions; under the former system a centralized party, particularly one with effective polling information, can direct money to those candidates who need it most. Under the latter system money dries up when electoral conditions seem bad, in turn reinforcing those conditions; under the former, this tendency, which is partly responsible for the often large midterm election losses suffered by the party in power, can at least be mitigated.

A political party with centralized control of finances is also better positioned to apply the new technologies that became pervasive in American politics in the 1980s. Chief among them was the growing use of computers to enhance the efficiency and effectiveness of various political activities—gathering and analyzing up-to-the-minute polling data, targeting campaign efforts and get-out-the-vote efforts to specific constituencies, collecting and disseminating exhaustive information on opponents' statements and positions, fund-raising, and coordinating other aspects of the campaign. In particular, the Republican party's financial and organizational advantages gave it an edge over the Democrats in tracking polls and opposition research.[30]

Certainly, the advantages of a central party are manifest under any political circumstances, but they seem especially important when traditional political allegiances are weak. In such conditions a larger percentage of voters are uncommitted to either political party and thus make voting decisions based on their evaluations of individual candidates. The capacity to recruit good candidates systematically and to fund them adequately becomes crucial. Thus dealignment coupled with an organizational edge translated into a Republican advantage. This advantage may be short-lived as the Democratic party undertakes its own reorganization, and it may have worked more to limit natural losses than to make political gains. It was, nonetheless, clearly there.[31]

Selective realignment, economic voting, and dealignment all shaped electoral politics in the Reagan era, and they sometimes shifted the balance of party power in unexpected ways. No one grand image or organizing concept therefore can do justice to the period.

Dynamics of a Specific Race: Ideology, Economic Conditions, and Candidates' Images

A similar combination of factors emerges when examining a specific electoral contest, such as the 1984 North Carolina Senate race, in which conservative Republican incumbent Jesse Helms won reelection with just less than 52 percent of the vote, edging his Democratic challenger, two-term governor Jim Hunt. The race was the most expensive nonpresidential contest ever waged in America. Helms raised about $16 million, breaking his own record of $7 million set in 1978; Hunt pulled in about $10 million, making his Senate campaign one of the most expensive ever.[32] The money paid for a year and a half of campaigning, including thousands of television and radio spots, much of it vicious and bitter. Besides the presidential contest, the North Carolina race was perhaps the most important of the 1984 elections. It decided the fate of one of the New Right's founding fathers and its de facto Senate floor leader. In the eyes of most observers it pitted the old South against the new and became one more indicator of where the politically volatile region might go.

The most intriguing fact about the election was that Helms did win reelection. Two years earlier Gary Pearce, codirector of Hunt's campaign, brashly remarked, "If we don't win it, it'll be because we're stupid."[33] There was little basis at the time or in subsequent months on which to dispute his evaluation: Helms had previously won election in the predominantly Democratic state by running against relatively weak and liberal opponents, Congressman Nick Galifianakis in 1972 and state insurance commissioner John Ingram in 1978. Even in the latter race, despite a spending edge of more than ten to one, Helms got less than 55 percent of the vote. But in 1984 Helms's likely opponent was a popular moderate Democrat, twice elected to the governorship by huge majorities more characteristic of an earlier era of Democratic hegemony. Although occasionally identified with liberal issues such as the Equal Rights Amendment, which failed to pass the state legislature several times during his governorship, Hunt was largely a cautious moderate who never got far ahead of, or far behind, public opinion. To be sure, Helms had a powerful political organization centered on the National Congressional Club, the country's largest political action committee, and he could count on the support of an active chapter of the Moral Majority and other groups on the religious Right. The Congressional Club, however, had failed miserably to influence the 1982 state congressional elections, and the more powerful grass-roots efforts seemed to be coming from groups seeking to mobilize blacks, not white evangelicals. Through most of 1983 the polls showed Helms trailing Hunt by as many as twenty points (for example, 31–50 percent in a poll taken in June by the *Charlotte Observer*).[34]

Why, then, did Helms win? There are many easy answers, but

none is wholly satisfactory; together, at first glance, they form a jumble. Yes, Helms outspent Hunt; and being confident of an ample supply of money, he got his campaign into swing earlier and hence was better able to frame the issues of the contest. Hunt's campaign, however, was hardly financially starved, nor was he a political unknown who needed every penny to establish himself as a viable contender. Moreover, he got plenty of free media simply by virtue of his visible public office (as did Helms). Yes, Helms may have ridden Reagan's coattails and the economic recovery, but those coattails, clipped short in much of the nation, somehow proved extra long in North Carolina, where Republicans also won the governorship and gained three seats in the U.S. House of Representatives (for a record total of five) and twenty-four in the state legislature—the party's best showing in the South.[35] And if economic recovery in late 1983 and 1984 led voters to reelect incumbents, one may still ask how exactly recovery impinged on the campaign. Yes, Helms campaigned loudly as a conservative and lost few opportunities for condemning his opponent as a liberal or, even worse, as a Mondale liberal. Hunt, however, often avoided direct ideological confrontation; and at crucial points the campaign devolved into an exchange of apparently nonideological claims and counterclaims about which candidate would best promote North Carolina's economic prosperity.

To restate the question, was Helms's victory that of a man of the Right in conservative times, of an incumbent in economically benign times, or simply of Jesse Helms over Jim Hunt in a political world in which party and ideology held little sway? It was in fact all of these victories (and more), and the trick is to come up with the common thread that links them.

The North Carolina Senate race was first of all a battle of two individuals, or, more correctly, of the personal images that these individuals sought to project in their campaigns. Both Helms and Hunt were well-known figures with clear, well-established political personas, and the central drama was of each seeking to confirm his own image while undermining his opponent's. These images and the battle over them provided the organizing frame of the electoral contest. In this sense, the Helms-Hunt race supported the common argument that candidate evaluation is the primary determinant of a citizen's vote and that all other factors are important to the extent they determine this evaluation.[36] Ideology was also important, however. The personal images of the two candidates assumed very different views of government and its functioning, so that the battle of personal images was implicitly an ideological conflict even though it often appeared nonideological. In addition, specific ideological labeling of Hunt as a Mondale liberal or Helms as a radical right-winger figured explicitly in the construction or destruction of candidate images. The choice between two individuals was thus ideologically charged. At the same time, the state of the economy, or perceptions thereof, also shaped the content and the plausibility of the personal images each candidate presented. Other factors impinged on the race, but they too can be understood in terms of how they affected the battle of personal images.

That the Helms-Hunt race was at all competitive and that Helms was running as a Republican incumbent were the product of several decades of political realignment in North Carolina comparable to what happened throughout the South. Like most of the South, North Carolina was once a consistently Democratic state. Between the end of Reconstruction and 1968 it voted for a Republican presidential candidate only once, preferring Herbert Hoover over Democrat (and Catholic) Al Smith in 1928. To be sure, no Democrat except Franklin Roosevelt rolled up the huge majorities in presidential races that were so common in the Deep South; but North Carolina's support for presidential Democrats survived longer into the postwar period. The state gave Strom Thurmond, running on the States' Rights ticket, only 9 percent of its vote in 1948, his poorest performance in the South; and it gave less support to Goldwater in 1964 than it gave to Nixon in 1960 or Eisenhower in 1952 and 1956. If North Carolina thus stayed longer in the Democratic camp, it ultimately fell away just as far and as quickly as other Southern states. Between 1968 and 1984 North Carolinians voted for four of five Republican presidential candidates and elected two Republican governors, two senators, and numerous congressmen.[37]

Traditionally, the western mountain region of North Carolina, non-slaveholding and anti-Confederate at the time of the Civil War, had been the Republican stronghold.[38] In addition, two long-term trends among white voters that favored the growth of Republicanism throughout the South operated in the state. First, since the 1940s the industrialization and urbanization of the state, especially its central Piedmont region, led to the growth of a white-collar middle class sympathetic to the Republican party. Between 1940 and 1968 Republican voting strength in presidential elections doubled in the Piedmont from 22.5 percent to 44.9 percent while increasing by only one-third elsewhere in the state. Second, civil-rights and law-and-order issues created a mass of disaffected lower-strata white Democrats in the 1960s, especially in the traditionally Democratic and racially conscious coastal region. Clearly, these two trends had different social and political implications. The first involved a growth of Republican support among groups where Republicans always had done well; it thus suggested a certain historical continuity. The second involved new GOP strength where the party had done poorly in the past.

In the 1968 elections Richard Nixon and George Wallace virtually personified these two distinct trends. Nixon became only the second Republican since Reconstruction to win North Carolina, with 39.5 percent of the vote, as Wallace garnered 31.3 percent and fatally split the Democratic vote. The support for the two candidates was quite different and sometimes diametrically opposed. Nixon ran best in the mountain and Piedmont regions, among voters aged 65 and older, and among the college-educated (though not among those with postgraduate schooling), affluent, and professional-managerial strata. Wallace, in contrast, did better in the coastal region, among the young (aged 21–29), and among lower-strata voters. He did especially poorly among the college-educated, professionals and managers, and those in the highest income bracket (more than $15,000 in 1968). In short, the two anti-Democratic trends coalesced into two distinct voting patterns in 1968.

The voting patterns for Republicans in the late 1970s and early 1980s suggest amalgamations of the two trends. Surveys by the *Charlotte Observer* and the University of North Carolina School of Journalism show that Helms in 1978 and Ronald Reagan and Senator John East in 1980 did slightly better among higher-strata whites—the Nixon pattern—but also among whites (especially white Democrats) in the coastal area of the state—the Wallace pattern. In 1984 Helms did best in western North Carolina but ran roughly equally well among all social strata.[39]

Thus, historical conditions made what once would have been a short, lopsided contest into a long, hotly contested race, throughout which Hunt and Helms each put considerable effort into constructing and maintaining images of himself and his opponent. Campaign strategies, issues, and controversies came and went, but the images provided a fairly consistent framework for campaign rhetoric.

Jim Hunt campaigned as a pragmatic, competent, nonideological politician who could use government effectively to get things done for people. As early as October 1983, long before he officially announced his candidacy, Hunt emphasized that his campaign would focus on the "four E's"—the economy, education, the elderly, and the environment, issues on which government can effect positive change in people's lives by actively providing the conditions for economic growth, educating the young, caring for the elderly, and protecting the environment. They are as well noncontroversial issues: the merits of clean air, a secure old age, or a healthy economy are not open to debate as are, say, abortion rights. The four-E's theme appeared again and again in the ensuing months, especially in the fall debates between the two candidates, and Hunt emphasized at various points his advocacy of one or another of them: government support for education, the maintenance of the Social Security system, environmental regulation, and, above all, the development of the infrastructure necessary for economic growth. By February 1984 the theme "He can do more for North Carolina" pervaded Hunt's media ads, and in announcing his candidacy that month Hunt stressed "taking the North Carolina approach, that makes things work, to our nation's capital." The basic theme continued straight into the fall, evident in an October television spot: "Jim Hunt. Progress for North Carolina. More jobs. Better Education. Protecting Social Security and Medicare"; a full-page ad in the *Charlotte Observer* just before the election: "Regardless of who you support for President, think hard about the race for U.S. Senate. What's at Stake for YOU? Jobs . . . Education . . . Social Security . . . Environment. Think about it. And vote for *your* future. Vote for Jim Hunt. For People. For Progress"; and a speech two days before the election: "The question is whether or not North Carolina is going to move forward . . . whether Jesse Helms or Jim Hunt best represents what people really want most, jobs, economic growth, progress, opportunities for themselves and their families, hope for the future. Which one of us will put the people of North Carolina first."[40]

Hunt's political persona built on his established reputation as a two-term incumbent governor who brought industry and jobs to the state and improved public education. This gubernatorial experience received constant reinforcement throughout the campaign in the routine media coverage. Hunt appeared regularly in the state's newspapers in connection with practical, noncontroversial issues of immediate material importance to North Carolinians: traveling to Europe to recruit industrial firms for the state; presiding over the opening of a Dino de Laurentis film studio and an Underwriters Laboratories testing center; launching the Governor's Conference on Women and the Economy; presenting the findings of the Governor's Commission on Education for Economic Growth; speaking across the state about the importance of good schools; shepherding a major education appropriations package through the state legislature.

Moreover, Hunt's political image placed him in the tradition of so-called progressive, modernizing leaders like Terry Sanford, governor in the 1960s and subsequently a senator, who favored government investment in economic infrastructure and an active effort to recruit new industry to the state, coupled with fiscal responsibility and some commitment to civil rights.[41] As he said in his opening statement in the last of four debates with Helms:

> I represent a tradition that has deep roots in the North Carolina soil. A tradition of sound progressive government that has moved the state forward over the years. As your senator, I would continue on the progressive course that has brought jobs and economic growth to North Carolina, a course committed to public education, a course that leads to balanced budgets and fiscal responsibility and a course that is dedicated to equal rights for all of our people.[42]

Jesse Helms struck a different pose. He presented himself as the principled fighter who takes tough stands on controversial issues, often doing battle with the Washington establishment. In the second debate with Hunt he referred to himself as a man "who willingly takes the political heat and stands up and fights." State Republican chairman David T. Flaherty described Helms as "the guy who puts principles above politics. He is the most principled guy even to the point where it sometimes hurts him." Thomas R. Ellis, chairman of the Congressional Club and Helms's political mentor, referred to Helms as a "standup kind of guy, someone who'll take a stand on the issues." Not surprisingly, the range of issues incorporated into Helms's political image was different from those tied to Hunt's political image. Helms for much of the campaign focused on noneconomic issues that evoked controversy and required dramatic stands rather than prosaic programs, including school prayer, abortion, communism, and busing.[43]

As with Hunt's, Helms's political image built on a reputation based on twelve years in the Senate and, before that, more than a decade of experience as a television commentator. It also was reinforced by routine media coverage. In October 1983 the proposal to make Martin Luther King's birthday a national holiday dominated headlines in North Carolina, and Helms's opposition figured prominently. "Senate Rebuffs Helms Effort to Block King Holiday," read one *Charlotte Observer* front-page headline. Although editorial comment was largely critical of Helms, letters to the editor were often supportive of his "outspokenness," and at least one columnist praised the senator for "standing up in front of the Martin Luther King holiday steamroller." Several months later Helms again made headlines for his support for a constitutional amendment to allow organized prayer in public schools. When the amendment went down to defeat, he announced, "Round one is over, but as long as I'm in the U.S. Senate, there are going to be many other rounds."[44]

Helms and Hunt each also presented negative counterimages of his opponent. If Helms pictured himself as principled and outspoken, Hunt pictured him as an ideologue more interested in pushing a partisan New Right agenda than seeing to the needs of North Carolinians and as an extremist whose demagoguery had so alienated him from the political mainstream that he could not effectively guard state interests. He accused Helms of being out of touch with the issues affecting the average North Carolinian (for example, by wanting to phase out Social Security), supporting right-wing Latin American dictators like Roberto D'Aubuisson in El Salvador, and, above all, not doing enough for the state's beleaguered tobacco and textile industries. "We need people who can get things done, not crusaders and lone rangers," said Hunt.[45]

In the last two months of the campaign Hunt focused more explicitly on Helms's ties to the radical Right in both his media spots and the debates. "We're not just running against Jesse Helms," Hunt said in mid-October, "We're running against a whole array of radicals and right-wing groups and interests. We're not going to let these people make North Carolina the home of the radical right wing." Again and again Hunt contrasted his own image as a leader who gets things done, providing jobs, education, and opportunity, to "Senator Helms with his right-wing agenda." The associations with Helms became crisp and clear, as in the following media spot: "Jesse Helms. The Moral Majority. The Congressional Club and all that comes with them. Outlawing abortion. Tax breaks for big oil. Backing military rulers around the world." In Hunt's construction of political reality "principled fighter" became "ideologue" and "extremist," in contrast with a "practical," "constructive" leader.[46]

Helms similarly reconstructed Hunt's political image. If Hunt portrayed himself as competent and pragmatic, Helms transformed these qualities into opportunism, indecision, and lack of principle. He pictured Hunt as a self-interested politician who ducks the tough issues, especially those he would have to deal with as a U.S. Senator. In the fall of 1983 Helms set the tone for the rest of his campaign by beginning a series of "Where Do You Stand, Jim?" ads that challenged Hunt to state his position on such issues as abortion, busing, and school prayer. Helms also sought to undermine Hunt's image of non-ideological pragmatism by portraying the governor as an extreme liberal who served his own list of special interests—"union bosses," "liberal news media," "anti-defense radicals," the "Gay Rights Crowd," the "ultraliberal Democratic Senatorial Committee," and so on. The allegations were less about anything Hunt had done as governor or proposed to do as senator than about the company he would keep as he moved from the state Democratic party to the national party. In this way Helms sought to situate Hunt not in state politics, where Hunt constructed his image, but in national politics, where attention would focus not on Hunt's achievements as governor but on his fellow Democratic senators. If "you vote for Jim Hunt," one Helms supporter wrote to the *Charlotte Observer,* the Democratic party might regain control of the U.S. Senate and "super-liberal Ted Kennedy will become chairman of the Senate Judiciary Committee."[47]

This conflict of personal images implicitly involved a deeper conflict of images of government, especially of the federal government. In presenting himself as a constructive leader who delivers on bread-and-butter issues that affect the lives of average North Carolinians, Hunt necessarily purveyed a distinct image of government as benign, activist, and broadly democratic. In this view government represents—or can represent—the interests of the people as a whole, and it works—or can work—in positive ways to promote those interests. That image was implicit in Hunt's political image and the issues he raised, and it lent an ideological aura to what ostensibly was a non-ideological pitch. Similarly, Hunt's counterimage of Helms was of a politician who either was too busy grinding his own ax to make proper use of government or perverted that proper use by subordinating government to a right-wing agenda.

Helms's political self-image and his counterimage of Hunt also rested on a distinct image of government—at least of the federal government. Helms, after all, presented himself as a principled leader who takes tough stands against a national government dominated by liberal special interests—unions, gays, feminists, secularists, and the like. In this view government is inherently suspect: much of what it does is neither benign nor in the common interest, and political virtue lies not in the ability to use it well but in the courage to stand up against it. Implicit in Helms's appeal was a minimalist, the-less-government-the-better, image that he often honored more in principle than in practice.

Even if Hunt was no flaming liberal, and even if he took pains not to appear ideological, voters in the 1984 North Carolina Senate race were thus confronted not only with a choice between distinctive individual candidates but also with an ideological choice between different images of government. It would have been so even if Helms had not harped on Hunt's liberalism and his own conservatism and Hunt had never breathed a word about right-wing radicals. It would have been so even if most North Carolinians had decided for whom to vote based purely on an evaluation of the competing personal images that Hunt and Helms presented because those personal images embodied broader assumptions about the proper role of government as well.

Ultimately, of course, Helms's images were more successful than Hunt's, as demonstrated not simply in the election results but also in interviews around the state before the election. After traversing the state from mountains to ocean in August and September, Ken Eudy, political reporter for the *Charlotte Observer*, concluded that many North Carolinians, especially white Democrats, were responding to Helms's themes, not Hunt's. They pictured Helms as a man of unswerving principle, not as an ideologue and extremist, and Hunt as an opportunist and liberal, not as a competent, practical leader. Eudy reported that "people are skeptical of the government's ability to solve problems affecting them, and of politicians' honesty," thus rejecting the image of government underlying Hunt's appeal.[48]

A number of quite disparate conditions combined to render Helms's appeal more plausible and attractive than Hunt's during the year preceding the election. Those factors undoubtedly would have been important no matter what images Hunt and Helms chose to purvey, but their distinctive effect was mediated through their impact on the plausibility of the candidates' images.

The two candidates' image construction projects were asymmetrical in an important sense. Helms merely had to defend an established image as a U.S. senator; Hunt had to create a senatorial image, or, more correctly, to transform his established gubernatorial, state-oriented image into a new senatorial, nationally oriented one. He chose to do so largely by stressing continuity—arguing that the issues were the same in Washington, D.C., as in Raleigh and that what worked in one place would work in the other. The emphasis of his campaign on "taking the North Carolina approach" to the nation's capital was thus crucial to the image he hoped to project. To undermine Hunt's effort to build a compelling senatorial image, all Helms had to do was not attack Hunt's solid image as a governor (something he rarely did) but stress discontinuity between state and national politics. His "Where Do You Stand, Jim?" theme succeeded by emphasizing that Hunt vacillated on specifically national issues. His effort to paint Hunt as a dangerous liberal by focusing not on anything Hunt had done as governor but on the company he would keep in the national Democratic party had the same effect: Jim Hunt in Washington would be different from Jim Hunt in Raleigh. Hence Helms could effectively attack Hunt without ever taking on directly his established image as a governor; Hunt, however, necessarily had to confront Helms's established senatorial image.

Given the asymmetry, whatever advantage Hunt had in routine media coverage melts away, and Helms's advantage in campaign spending looms larger than it otherwise would. Most of the media attention Hunt got concerned things he was doing as governor and thus reinforced his gubernatorial image; it did not in itself help build a bridge between that image and a potential senatorial one. Helms's routine media attention, in contrast, consistently reinforced his established senatorial image. Moreover, his campaign started faster, spent more in the early going, and thus allowed him to put Hunt on the defensive by stressing from the beginning state/national discontinuity. By mid-April 1984 Helms had outspent Hunt three to one ($6.7 million to $2.3 million), partly because he had raised more money but also because Hunt held back more of what he had raised for later in the campaign. By that time Hunt's huge early lead had dissipated, and the contest was neck and neck. As late as October 1983 most polls still showed Hunt well ahead. The University of North Carolina School of Journalism poll had Hunt up 56–36 percent (54–41 percent among likely voters) and the Gallup Poll had him ahead 52–43 percent. Polls from the spring of 1984 on, however, typically had the two candidates only about four percentage points apart, with the lead shifting between them.[49]

The tightening of the North Carolina Senate race also corresponded to the growing popularity of Ronald Reagan in the state, especially in comparison to the likely Democratic presidential candidate, Walter Mondale. The October 1983 Gallup Poll gave Mondale the same nine-point advantage over Reagan that it gave Hunt over Helms. The May 1984 Gallup Poll, in contrast, showed Reagan with a twenty-point lead (59–38 percent). Reagan's increasing popularity may have helped in any case, but it was especially important in the context of the Hunt-Helms image battle. It undoubtedly helped spread the negative image of government Reagan purveyed and thus tended to undermine the idea of activist government implicit in Hunt's political image.

The relative strength of Reagan and the national Republican party and the relative weakness of Mondale and the Democrats increased the difficulty of Hunt's attempt to stress continuity between Raleigh and Washington while making it easier for Helms to fend off charges of extremism. Hunt had to build a national political image while simultaneously avoiding being identified with his national party and its unpopular leader. He played hardly any role at his party's national convention, invited no national party leaders except other southerners to campaign for him, and conspicuously avoided Mondale when the latter came to North Carolina. Helms, in contrast, avidly stressed his connections to his national party. He was visible everywhere at the Republican national convention and welcomed virtually all of his party's major figures to the state to campaign for him, including not only Reagan but also Vice President George Bush, Senators Howard

Baker and Robert Dole, and Secretary of Transportation Elizabeth Dole. This activity rendered implausible Hunt's continual claim that Helms was far out of the political mainstream.

A number of specific issues also confirmed Helms's images and undermined Hunt's at various points in the campaign. Proposals for a Martin Luther King national holiday and for legislation permitting organized prayer in public schools made headlines during the campaign, the former in October 1983 and the latter in January 1984 and again in March. Helms forthrightly opposed the King holiday and supported school prayer legislation. Hunt seemed to waffle on both: he was on record supporting the King holiday but avoided public comment on it. His initial response to the school prayer issue was to support voluntary prayer while pleading a lack of familiarity with pending legislation. In March, with debate well under way in the U.S. Senate, Hunt endorsed a constitutional amendment to permit organized prayer in public schools, in effect agreeing with Helms. Both issues thus reinforced Helms's own image as a man of principle and his counterimage of Hunt as waffler and opportunist. Both figured in Helms's "Where Do You Stand, Jim?" ads.

In December 1983 President Reagan, despite obvious contradictions with his own free-market philosophy, signed legislation continuing the tobacco price support program and tightened controls on textile imports, thus buttressing what were respectively North Carolina's largest cash crop and biggest industrial employer. This action undermined Hunt's contention that Helms's outspokenness and political extremism made him an ineffective advocate for the state on bread-and-butter issues. As the *Charlotte Observer*, no friend of Helms, noted in an article at year's end, Helms had actually done fairly well on those issues in the U.S. Senate.[50]

To the extent that Helms's charges that Hunt was either an opportunist or an ultraliberal focused on social issues, his close ties to North Carolina evangelicals and their political mobilization on his behalf certainly gave him a ready audience for his claims. Although Hunt's personal religious credentials as an evangelical matched Helms's, he lacked the direct political ties or appeal that Helms had. Growing ties between Helms and theologically conservative Christians were evident throughout the campaign. Theological conservatives took control of the state Southern Baptist convention in November 1983. The convention elected as its president Norman Wiggins, president of Campbell College (of which Helms was a trustee), a member of the American Family Institute (founded by Helms's aides), and a personal friend of Helms. The Moral Majority and evangelical churches undertook voter registration drives and later get-out-the-vote drives. As a result, the Republican share of the 3.3 million registered voters in the state actually rose during the Hunt-Helms campaign despite active efforts by civil-rights groups to register black voters. In September 1984 a group called Pastors for Helms was formed; there was no Pastors for Hunt. In the voting itself Helms won large enough majorities in the Bible belt between Greensboro and Charlotte to offset Hunt's edge in the eastern part of the state and in the metropolitan areas. All of that suggests both the degree of political mobilization of evangelicals and Helms's close ties to evangelical networks, both of which provided a ready audience for his political message.[51]

Above all, the continuing economic recovery in 1984 made Reagan, the Republicans, and, by extension, Helms appear as the guarantors of economic prosperity and thus put the force of economic voting squarely behind the incumbent senator. That force undermined Hunt's political image in several specific ways. It hurt Hunt's central assertion that North Carolinians would prosper more with his competent, pragmatic presence in the U.S. Senate than with Helms the ideologue there. The equation of economic recovery with Reaganomics and hence with reducing the size and influence of government worked to undermine the legitimacy of the image of activist government implicit in Hunt's persona. Finally, the growing image of the Republican party as the party of prosperity further undercut the popularity of the national Democratic party and thus made it all the more necessary for Hunt to avoid identifying with it even while trying to build a bridge to national politics.

The importance of the economic factor is reflected in two important changes in Helms's campaign appeal by the fall of 1984. The first occurred in the principle connotations that Helms chose to attach to the epithet *liberal* he so often flung at Hunt. In the early part of the campaign he emphasized Hunt's liberalism on a range of social issues, including school prayer, busing, abortion, and the King holiday. *Liberal* thus conjured up images of secularism and permissiveness. As the campaign progressed and economic recovery seemed more and more solid, Helms put more stress on certain economic connotations of liberalism. With greater frequency he accused Hunt not simply of being a liberal but of being a Mondale liberal, as in this memorable passage from his closing statement in the second debate in early September: "Ladies and Gentlemen, Governor Hunt has declared that nowhere in this country do the voters have a clearer choice between candidates than they have in this state. I agree the choice is clear. Mr. Hunt doesn't want you to know it, but he's a Mondale liberal and ashamed of it. I'm a Reagan conservative and I'm proud of it."[52] Clearly, Helms used the phrases *Reagan conservative* and *Mondale liberal* to link himself with a popular presidential candidate and Hunt with an unpopular one, but underlying this choice of words was a clear economic implication: to be a Reagan conservative meant to be for economic recovery and national optimism, whereas Mondale liberalism, as Helms made clear in his closing statement in the third debate, was "liberalism of big spending and high taxes," which would inevitably doom economic recovery. Thus liberalism came to be associated with high taxes and, above all, economic stagnation.[53]

A second change in Helms's campaign rhetoric occurred at a telling moment in mid-October. Helms had held the lead in both the Gallup Poll (49–45 percent) and the *Charlotte Observer* poll (48–45 percent) in September; but an *Observer* poll in early October showed Hunt back ahead, 46–42 percent. With victory possibly slipping from his grasp, Helms toned down the man-of-principle-versus-opportunist rhetoric that had framed most of his campaign and sought instead to steal Hunt's fire by picturing himself, not Hunt, as the competent, pragmatic politician who supported policies—Reagan's policies—responsible for economic recovery and hence increased the well-being of all North Carolinians. In the fourth and final debate in mid-October Helms the fearless fighter and Hunt the furtive opportunist were all but gone. At issue, Helms argued again and again, was economic recovery, pure and simple. His opening statement tied himself to Reagan and economic recovery:

> Ladies and Gentlemen, it's been a long time since we've seen such an upbeat, optimistic attitude in America as we're seeing today. Americans are proud to be Americans again, and they are excited about the most remarkable recovery, economically speaking, in 30 years. Now I'm proud of the record that Ronald Reagan and I have established. We have cut taxes and we have

curbed the growth of federal spending, and more Americans are working today than ever before.

In response to Hunt's charge that he wanted to make North Carolina "the home for radical, right-wing politicians," Helms again invoked the image of economic recovery: "Now, Governor, what is so radical about President Reagan's economic recovery program?" Finally, his closing statement began and ended with an appeal to economic recovery: "The Reagan Economic Recovery Program must be given the strongest possible support by the senator you elect in November. . . . The President and I need your support if the economic recovery is to continue."[54]

The shift in emphasis apparently worked: Polls just before the election showed Helms had regained a three-to-four-point lead. Ultimately, the *Raleigh News and Observer* was probably right to see economic voting as the pivot of the Hunt-Helms race: "After all the biting rhetoric about moral values, foreign dictators, right-wing conspiracies and election fraud, the issue that sent Republican Jesse A. Helms back to the Senate was people's pocketbooks."[55] The pocketbook issue, however, took hold through a set of political images established by each candidate of himself and his opponent, serving largely to undermine Hunt's images of himself and of Helms. Running as a competent, pragmatic politician who delivers a healthy economy can work for an incumbent in good times or a challenger in bad times. Hunt was neither. The pocketbook issue was joined by a host of other factors that affected the plausibility of the candidates' images: issues, ideology, mobilized evangelicals, and presidential prestige.

The Helms-Hunt race was certainly one in which personal images had more direct impact than broader matters of party identification, ideology, issues, or the economy—an exemplary race in an era of dealignment. In another sense, however, it was a race in which ideology mattered, affecting the different views of government just below the surface of the candidates' self-images and motivating the use of terms like *liberal* and *radical right-winger* to maintain or undermine those images. It was also a race in which North Carolinians voted their individual and collective pocketbooks, reelecting an incumbent when times were relatively good; however, the economy had an especially powerful impact because of Hunt's chosen image as the more competent, effective leader. The Helms-Hunt race was many things

at once, because many factors fed into constructing the political im- ~Edelman~
ages upon which voters made their electoral choices.

Conclusion

The analysis of the Helms-Hunt race underlines the point made earlier in this chapter: taken alone, neither realignment nor economic
voting (nor, for that matter, dealignment) captures the essence of
electoral politics in the age of Reagan. There was no essence, no mas-
ter trend that definitively encompassed the shifting political fortunes
of the period. Talk of a durable, across-the-board shift in the balance
of power between the major parties is misleading, as is talk of voters
casting their ballots in accordance with the economic winds. The Republican party gained advantages in the late 1970s and early 1980s,
but the notion of realignment does not accurately depict these advantages, which were at once more diverse, more modest, and probably
more tenuous than that august concept suggests. The party certainly
benefited from a political sea change among a few discrete groups,
such as white evangelicals and white southerners. It also gained from
greater public willingness to see it as the "party of prosperity" and
from its growing ability to use new political technologies and to target resources on close races. Taken together, these changes still are
much less impressive than a realignment, and that is part of the
point. They nonetheless helped to make the Republican party a big-
ger yet faster political vehicle for conservatives to ride to power.

Epilogue

American Conservatism in the Bush Years

Ronald Reagan emerged from eight years in the White House standing tall, his public image untarnished by a second term marked by crisis, corruption, and indirection. The fate of the conservatism that he had led to power was considerably more mixed. The most common assessment was that the Right was *entrenched* but *exhausted*. On the one hand, many of its achievements and assumptions had become part of the framework of American politics. Tax cuts and large budget deficits focused political debate squarely on reducing government spending and made a liberal domestic agenda difficult to contemplate let alone enact. The large military buildup in Reagan's first term greatly raised the baseline of the perennial debates about less or more military spending. Reagan's federal court appointments put a long-term conservative stamp on American jurisprudence, which was most palpably evident in the Supreme Court decisions in 1989 on affirmative action and abortion. Above all, conservative views on most issues had gained legitimacy and acceptability.

On the other hand, the forward momentum of conservatism was largely exhausted, and hence the prospects of the Right making further major gains seemed slight. The Reagan administration in its second term had not pursued, let alone enacted, much of the conservative agenda; the conservative movement was in disarray; and most important, the Reagan years ended with neither a solid Republican nor a conservative popular majority much closer than when they had begun.

Political scientist William Schneider nicely summed up the conventional wisdom about the Right: "The Republicans will learn that Reaganism is a spent political force. . . . The Democrats will learn that Reagan has established a new institutional order."[1] Indeed, George Bush is the very embodiment of this situation: a Republican president lacking deep roots in the conservative movement and committed more to consolidating and modifying the Reagan legacy than to extending it. This assessment of the Right in the Bush years accurately captures the general outlines of the situation, but it misses important details. Not all parts of the political force of conservatism are equally spent, nor has conservatism created a wholly new institutional order. To get a clearer picture of the Right today, let us examine the current condition of the various elements of conservatism discussed in this book and of the ideological climate as a whole.

The New Right

The New Right entered the Reagan years optimistic, aggressive, and, in Richard Viguerie's phrase, "ready to lead." It left them, as one observer put it, in "dismay and disarray." This mood, which became more and more apparent from 1986 on, is reflected in the words of movement leaders themselves. "The conservative movement is directionless," Viguerie sadly concluded; Howard Phillips spoke of "a sense of futility among conservatives"; and R. Emmett Tyrrell, Jr., speculated about a "conservative crack-up." At public conferences and in private interviews in the late 1980s, conservative leaders seemed adrift and apprehensive about the future.[2]

This situation reflected the fact that for the first time in twenty years conservatives faced the future without a leader. Ever since Ronald Reagan had won the California governorship in 1966, he had been the movement's undisputed standard-bearer, around whom conservatives could rally when they chose. With Reagan headed to political retirement, no one of similar stature stood ready to replace him. Conservatives failed to unite around a successor in the Republican primaries in 1988. Partly as a result, the Republican nomination (and ultimately the presidency) went to George Bush, whom neither political history nor political instincts marked as a pure-bred conservative. Conservatives thus faced the Bush years with considerable ambivalence, their emotions ranging from cautious optimism (at best) to bitter alienation.[3]

Dismay among conservatives arose also from their collective sense that however they might assess the Reagan administration's actual achievements, it had bequeathed little momentum to the Right— little, that is, with which to energize conservative activists. Reagan's second term got under way with hardly any program or sense of direction. By 1987 it was mired in scandal and crisis with the Iran-Contra revelations, the continuing investigation of Attorney General Edwin Meese, and the spate of unflattering insider accounts of the Reagan White House. Its main achievement, an arms control agreement with the Soviet Union, contradicted every conservative impulse and hardly inspired the rank and file of the Right. For conservatives as well, the political news from 1986 on was mostly bad: the Republican loss of the Senate, the unsuccessful nomination of Robert Bork to the United States Supreme Court, and the indecisive support for the Nicaraguan Contras.

Loss of leadership and political momentum, however, were only part of the reason for conservative dismay. Important New Right organizations faced considerable financial problems in the late 1980s; though neither pervasive nor necessarily permanent, these problems still absorbed attention and slackened the energy of conservative leaders. The Richard A. Viguerie Company, once the Right's premier direct-mail fundraiser, hit the skids in 1985 for a variety of reasons: too much credit extended to conservative groups, Viguerie's expensive unsuccessful run for the Republican nomination for lieutenant governor of Virginia, competition from other direct mailers, and a bad business investment. Viguerie reestablished solvency, but only after cutting his staff, selling the journal *Conservative Digest* (the New Right's mouthpiece), and focusing on his business direct-mail clients. The Life Amendment Political Action Committee, once a major political force in the antiabortion movement, collapsed under the weight of debt after its unsuccessful effort to unseat Senator Bob Packwood in the Oregon Republican primary in 1986. The National Conservative Political Action Committee, the largest PAC in the early 1980s, saw its fundraising fall precipitously after 1985 and ended the Reagan years in debt and bitterly divided. And the venerable John Birch Society, as far as its extreme secrecy about finances allowed outsiders to estimate, also seemed to be in trouble.[4]

The most important reason for the disarray of the New Right was that its basic political style no longer suited the political tasks it faced. Conservatives had long cultivated the stance of the outsider; as I argued in Chapter 3, their adeptness with antiestablishment rhetoric and their capacity to focus diffuse discontent on concrete political targets had often been a political asset. By the late 1980s, however, these assets had partly become liabilities. What was needed, Republican House Whip Newt Gingrich noted, was "a governing rather than an opposition conservatism."[5] The traits that made for effective opposition did not necessarily lead to effective governing. The title of Richard Viguerie's 1980 prospectus, *The New Right: We're Ready to Lead*, rang ironically in the late 1980s. The New Right was not ready to lead; it never had been. It was ready, as always, to oppose.

Two examples of the New Right's inability to shed its outsider pose were especially striking. The first was the failure of conservatives to unite around the candidacy of Congressman Jack Kemp during the Republican primaries in 1988. For the New Right Kemp came closest to being a natural successor to Reagan; he had a long history in the conservative movement, the correct positions on all but a few issues, and potentially broad popular appeal. Conservatives had so cultivated the outsider style, with its resentment and bitterness, however, that they could not warm to a candidate who did not identify and attack a political enemy. As one observer put it, Kemp's message was too positive; he was not "a hater or polarizer." Or, in the words of conservative leader Richard Viguerie, "[Kemp] could not bring himself to be critical. And failing that his campaign had no chance. Jack never pushed the conservatives' buttons because he could not bring himself to attack."[6]

The second example was the failure of the nomination of conservative Republican John Tower as secretary of defense in early 1989. Although the Senate vote rejecting Tower ultimately fell along party lines (Democrats against, Republicans for), the initial volley against Tower came from New Right activist Paul Weyrich, who surprised the Senate Armed Services Committee by making public the frequent private rumors that Tower was a drunk and a womanizer. Weyrich acted apparently out of deep conviction that political leaders should set moral examples, but that he could so readily translate personal belief into divisive public attack reflects, again, the outsider's mentality of the New Right.[7]

In the Bush years, the New Right seems likely to remain an outsider. Its organizations and activists are unlikely to be central to any conservative advances, which must come through other channels. The New Right's day has passed.

The New Religious Right

The New Religious Right entered the Bush years as a still potent source of Republican votes, conservative activists, and institutional power. It remained, however, not a religious Right, or even a Christian Right, but an evangelical-fundamentalist Right. In the 1988 presidential election, white evangelicals and fundamentalists confirmed their Republican leanings by giving 81 percent of their votes to George Bush. They were thus one of the very few groups from whom Bush got a higher vote percentage than Reagan had in 1984. By 1988 too, the remaining pulses of conservative grass-roots activism were coming primarily from the New Religious Right. In states as diverse as Michigan and Arizona, determined evangelical activists gained control of local Republican party organizations. At the same time, the focal point of the antiabortion movement shifted from conventional political activity to Operation Rescue, an effort to block access to abortion clinics by using civil disobedience tactics. The national leader of Operation Rescue, Randall Terry, and the majority of participants are evangelicals. Thus the antiabortion movement, like the anti-ERA movement before it, has drawn progressively more on the efforts of evangelicals; important elements of the New Religious Right have come to see abortion as the central issue in their political agenda.[8]

Another striking example of the staying power of the New Religious Right has been the fundamentalists' continued dominance over the Southern Baptist Convention. By 1989, fundamentalists had been in power long enough to control nearly every major seminary, publication, and agency. Moderate Baptists vigorously contested national elections and regained control of a number of state conventions, but they began to concede their defeat. In 1987 some moderate Baptists broke away to form the Southern Baptists Alliance; in 1988 moderate faculty members at Southeastern Baptist Theological Seminary, faced with a board of trustees committed to hiring only theological conservatives for future posts, began planning to start another seminary.[9]

The influence of the New Religious Right, however, remained limited in scope: the vision in the early 1980s of an ecumenical religious Right had not materialized as the decade ended. The failure of Pat Robertson's well-financed campaign for the Republican presidential nomination in 1988 to gain more than scant support among nonevangelicals is certainly prime evidence of this limited appeal.[10] That the

New Religious Right will expand its scope in the near future seems unlikely, because the major television preachers who provided visible leadership have been mired in financial trouble. As the audience for televangelism became saturated in the late 1980s and the number of religious programs increased, all the major television preachers saw their revenues fall dramatically, even before the Gospelgate scandals involving Jim Bakker and Jimmy Swaggart. Where once the ministries had expanded confidently, retrenchment became the order of the day. Pat Robertson's Christian Broadcasting Network laid off more than 10 percent of its staff, cut its budget by a similar amount, and abandoned a new nightly news show. After substantially cutting his staff and borrowing millions to maintain the academic accreditation of Liberty University, Jerry Falwell began a phased retreat from active politics, culminating in the disbanding of the Moral Majority in 1989. In the wake of the Gospelgate scandals, revenues fell faster and the popularity of television preachers declined markedly.[11]

To be sure, in the long run some of the television ministries will retain the support of the faithful, reestablish solvency, and generally sort themselves out. In the short run, however, the major television preachers will be preoccupied more with getting their houses in order than with leading a political movement. This will not mean the death knell of the New Religious Right; the epitaphs by some observers are premature. It does mean, however, that opportunities for expansion are limited: the New Religious Right will remain a powerful force within distinct limits. The interesting questions are how long the leadership vacuum will continue and how much it will affect the vitality of the New Religious Right.

Corporate Conservatism

Corporate conservatism remained an important political force as the Reagan years ended, but its aggressiveness, partisanship, and in some ways unity waned. The economic issues of the late 1970s and early 1980s had unified big business, but those of Reagan's second term split it. Disagreements among corporations and industries about trade legislation, budget deficits, and tax reform hobbled the Business Roundtable, divided corporate lobbyists, and pitted policy planning groups against one another.[12]

More important, in the electoral arena, where a high degree of unity still prevailed in contributions to political candidates, big business no longer made a concerted effort to elect conservative Republican challengers to House and Senate seats. Between the early 1970s and 1980, as I discussed in Chapter 5, corporate political action committees (PACs) had moved strikingly from pragmatic support for entrenched incumbents of whatever party to an ideological strategy of electing conservative Republicans. After 1980, however, pragmatism reasserted itself, as corporate PACs gave progressively less money to challengers, conservatives, Republicans, and close races and instead aimed contributions at powerful incumbents of both parties. In 1980, Republican candidates challenging Democratic incumbents or seeking open seats received 29 percent of all corporate PAC money in House races and 58 percent in Senate races; by 1986 the percentages had fallen to 12 and 28 percent respectively. In 1980 in House and Senate races pitting Democratic incumbents against Republican challengers, the Democratic advantage in corporate PAC contributions was virtually nil; in 1986, Democrats in these races enjoyed an eight-to-one advantage. In 1980, too, House and Senate Republican candidates in close races experienced a last-minute surge of corporate money; in 1984, this did not happen.[13]

Big business became more ideological and politically partisan in the late 1970s partly because this strategy appeared to have many benefits and few costs. For a short time, it appeared that Republicans and conservatives could indeed win both houses of Congress as well as the presidency. The deep recession of the early 1980s dimmed those hopes and halted the Republican drive to monopolize corporate PAC money. Democrats, moreover, began to fight more effectively for business money by emphasizing probusiness candidates and stressing the risks of aggressively supporting Republicans as long as Democrats controlled the House. Congressman Tony Coelho, while he chaired the Democratic Congressional Campaign Committee, spearheaded this strategy. His often-quoted admonition to corporate PACs is worth quoting one more time: "You people are determined to get rid of the Democratic Party. The record shows it. I just want you to know we are going to be in the majority of the House for many, many years and I don't think it makes good business sense for you to try to destroy us."[14]

In reverting to a pragmatic strategy, big business hardly became politically neutral. Corporate PAC contributions in the aggregate still favored Republicans over Democrats. A greater percentage of the money contributed to Republican incumbents than to Democratic incumbents, moreover, went to candidates in close races. Above all, the shift in corporate contributions hardly benefited Democrats who challenged Republican incumbents or sought open seats. They received 4 percent of corporate PAC money in House races and 11 percent in Senate races in 1986. Big business was certainly not investing in a new generation of Democrats or liberals.[15]

Just as important, even if corporate conservatism lost its cutting edge in the late 1980s, its most important product remained intact. The network of conservative policy-making and policy-discussion organizations underwritten by business money continued to provide a conduit for conservative ideas and personnel into government. The Heritage Foundation, which remained the vanguard of this network, greeted the incoming Bush administration with *Mandate for Leadership III*, a thick volume of policy recommendations, and 2,500 résumés of conservatives seeking political jobs (the single largest set received by the new president). The American Enterprise Institute, whose financial troubles in the mid-1980s had made it the weak link of the network, was back on its feet again as the 1980s ended. This "conservative counterestablishment" will give legitimacy, plausibility, and visibility to conservative policy alternatives and will sustain a cadre of conservative leaders, activists, and policymakers—the so-called "Third Generation" of conservatives—whatever the overall political climate.[16]

The legacy of the corporate conservative activism of the late 1970s and early 1980s, in short, persists into the 1990s, though that activism itself has proven episodic. Big business remains a conservative force even if in a more sedate way.

The Republican Party

The Republican party left the Reagan years with the gains discussed in Chapter 6 largely intact but far short of the realignment that once seemed possible. The Democratic edge in party identification remained much smaller than before the 1980s; the Republican party held onto its reputation as the party of prosperity and hence continued to enjoy the benefit of the economic doubt; above all, the GOP maintained its financial, organizational, and technological edge. To be sure, Democrats in the late 1980s cut into the Republican advantage in national party fundraising, stemming the flow of business money to their opponents; they made important gains in political technology. The Republicans, nonetheless, have continued to be the more effective national party in channeling resources and services to candidates and in coordinating the activities of sympathetic PACs and other interest-group representatives. Democratic gains in fundraising, especially from business PACs, have also had a considerable cost: they have made the party beholden to business interests, pulled it away from its natural constituencies, and blurred its distinct political identity.[17]

Although Republican gains remained intact, realignment still eluded the GOP as the 1980s ended. The 1988 elections confirmed the mixed electoral success that has been the fate of Republicans since the late 1960s. On the one hand, Republicans won the presidency for the fifth time in the last six elections. George Bush received 54 percent of the popular vote and 426 of 538 electoral votes. His victory was all the more striking because 1988 was widely reputed to be a "Donkey's Year" and because Bush trailed so badly in midyear polls. Democratic candidate Michael Dukakis saw a seventeen-point lead in the polls in July collapse into an eight-point loss in November, a more striking reversal of fortunes than that suffered by Republican Thomas E. Dewey in the fabled 1948 election.

On the other hand, Bush's coattails proved to be as short as any winning presidential candidate's had ever been. Democrats gained five House seats, one Senate seat, and a governorship, while losing only a few dozen state legislature seats across the nation. On all levels, Republicans were worse off (or at most no better off) than after Reagan's initial victory. That 1980 win, which was supposed to be a harbinger of greater Republican gains, has instead turned out to be a last hurrah.[18]

Republican success in winning over and holding new constituencies was also mixed. White southerners as well as white evangelicals again voted heavily Republican, and of all regions Bush did best in the South. Younger voters, however, though maintaining a relatively high level of Republican identification, did not vote disproportionately for Bush. In addition, traditional divisions along class and religious lines remained at least partly intact, with Democrats doing markedly better among the lower strata and among Catholics.[19]

The Broader Ideological Climate

The implications of the 1988 elections for conservatism have been a matter of debate. On the one hand, one can easily minimize the ideological significance of Bush's victory. He was after all the candidate of an incumbent party during prosperity and peace, and so his victory seems no more than another example of economic voting, plebiscitary and retrospective. He bowed at least slightly in a liberal direction by promising to have the federal government do more on education and the environment. The preference of voters for Democrats in other offices, moreover, hardly suggested an electorate intent on sending a conservative message.[20]

On the other hand, one can argue that the 1988 elections sent a clear conservative or at least antiliberal message. From this perspective, Bush overcame his early deficit in the polls primarily by effectively labeling Dukakis a liberal and attaching pejorative connotations to that label (unpatriotic, soft on crime). Democrats, in contrast, were successful in contests for lower offices, because such races are inherently less ideological and issue-oriented than the presidential race and hence allow candidates to stress personal image and constituent services and to use the powers of incumbency. Republicans, according to this argument, win elections that are ideological and issue oriented; Democrats win those that are not.

Both these analyses have an element of truth to them. The message of the 1988 elections and public opinion polls over the last few years is a mixed one. Conservatives have won an important battle, but they are losing the war. They have succeeded in turning *liberal* into a pejorative political label that is a liability for most of those on whom it is pinned. They have failed, however, to push public opinion on most issues to the right.

Bush's attempt to tar Dukakis as a liberal—a strategy developed by his campaign manager, conservative Lee Atwater—apparently bore fruit. As Dukakis collapsed in the polls from July to October, the percentage of Americans identifying him as a liberal increased: in May 1988, 27 percent identified Dukakis as a liberal and 17 percent judged his views too liberal. By October, 43 percent called him a liberal and

31 percent regarded his beliefs as too liberal. This shift was consistent with other survey results as well: in the late summer of 1988, only 13 percent of Americans said they wanted a liberal for president while 40 percent preferred a conservative and 41 percent a moderate. Twenty-nine percent said they would feel less favorable about a public figure described as a liberal (compared to 17 percent in 1985), while only 14 percent would disfavor a conservative. Although the percentage of Americans calling themselves conservatives did not increase during the Reagan years, more Americans consistently identified themselves as conservatives than as liberals. Conservatives, moreover, were more consistent in approving of conservative public figures than liberals were of their fellows.[21]

Conservatives have thus won an important symbolic victory, but it has been a limited one. Liberal may be a less appealing label than conservative, in part because liberals have not consistently given it a positive meaning. When Dukakis did redefine liberalism as economic populism in the last weeks of the 1988 campaign, he revived his sagging fortunes and won handily among voters who made up their minds just before the election.[22]

More important, ideological labels are not the only or even the primary basis upon which Americans organize their political decisions. For many Americans neither label carries much meaning. In practice, how Americans feel about both labels often bears little relation to how they think about specific issues. Indeed in most major policy areas, conservatives have failed to put their imprint on the broad contours of public thinking.[23]

Conservatives have inveighed against the evil Soviet empire and have argued passionately that the United States is involved in an international struggle on which the very fate of humanity rests; yet although their anticommunist rhetoric has sometimes had great appeal, they have failed to get public support for more than the quickest and cheapest assertions of American power in the world. Americans may have applauded bombing Qaddafi or invading Grenada, but they balked at the broader contemporary version of a liberation strategy, the funding of anticommunist insurgents around the world. Despite all the conservatives' efforts to stimulate fear over an alleged Soviet beachhead on the mainland of the Western hemisphere, Americans remained resistant to the idea of aiding the Contras in Nicaragua. Despite the evil empire rhetoric, Americans and even their erstwhile conservative president eagerly grasped at opportunities for peace and rapprochement with the Soviet Union. Indeed, the advance of *glasnost* and *perestroika* in the Soviet Union and their equivalents elsewhere threatens to undermine the very logic of a hardline conservative position. As David Keene, chairman of the American Conservative Union, commented in early 1989: "The glue that held together the movement was the need for a strong anti-communist foreign policy. If Gorbachev survives, reforms the Soviet Union and redirects Soviet foreign policy, that glue will be weakened."[24]

Conservatives have also decried the decline of the traditional family and traditional moral values and the rise of a secular, hedonistic culture. They have called Americans back to a moral consensus about the good and true. Again, this rhetoric has had potent appeal, but it did not lead to public support for the conservative social agenda. Certainly, conservatives have emphasized the abortion issue more than any other, yet by 1989 nearly fifteen years of intense antiabortion activity had failed to budge public opinion more than a few percentage points. Americans seem not to want their morality legislated and seem to seek a more careful balance of personal freedom and social constraint than offered by the Right.[25]

Most important, conservatives have presented an image of society in which government plays a minimal role in producing and distributing goods and services. They have pictured big government as the problem rather than the solution to America's various economic problems. Once again, the general image of less government has appeal, especially when the issue is taxes. Despite eight years of Ronald Reagan and conservative rhetoric, however, a substantial majority of Americans believe government has broad responsibilities for promoting specific areas of social well-being; they oppose cutbacks in government spending in most social welfare areas. In practice, as opposed to rhetoric, most Americans expect an activist government; even Republicans and conservatives have tried to adjust their policies accordingly.[26]

Put simply, Americans are symbolically conservative but substantively liberal.[27] Conservatives have won important symbolic battles but have failed to alter the practical political sentiments of Americans. Those who oppose conservatism—whether they call themselves liberals, progressives, populists, or something else—are often more in tune with these practical sentiments but have failed to artic-ulate an effective political vision. Whatever the strengths and weak-nesses of the various elements of conservatism as the 1990s begin, how this asymmetry plays out may well determine the future of American politics.

Notes

Introduction

1. Daniel Bell, *The End of Ideology: On the Exhaustion of Political Ideas in the Fifties*, rev. ed. (New York: Free Press, 1965), pp. 402–403.

2. *The New American Right*, ed. Daniel Bell (New York: Criterion Books, 1955); *The Radical Right*, ed. Daniel Bell (Garden City, N.Y.: Doubleday, 1963).

3. Bell, *Radical Right*, pp. 84–85.

4. Ibid., pp. 102, 233, 21–22, 16.

5. G. William Domhoff, *The Higher Circles: The Governing Class in America* (New York: Random House, 1970), p. 307.

6. James O'Connor, *The Fiscal Crisis of the State* (New York: St. Martin's Press, 1973).

7. For a different way of making a similar point about sociology and the Right, see Alan Wolfe, "Sociology, Liberalism, and the Radical Right," *New Left Review* 128 (July–August 1981): 3–27.

8. Walter Dean Burnham, "The Eclipse of the Democratic Party," *Society* 21 (July–August 1984): 5–11.

9. George Nash, *The Conservative Intellectual Movement in America since 1945* (New York: Basic Books, 1976).

10. William A. Rusher, *The Rise of the Right* (New York: Morrow, 1984); Alan Crawford, *Thunder on the Right: The "New Right" and the Politics of Resentment* (New York: Pantheon Books, 1980); Kevin P. Phillips, *Post-Conservative America: People, Politics, and Ideology in a Time of Crisis* (New York: Random House, 1982).

11. Everett Carll Ladd, Jr., and Charles D. Hadley, *Transformations of the American Party System: Political Coalitions from the New Deal to the 1970s* (New York: Norton, 1975); Kevin P. Phillips, *The Emerging Re-*

publican Majority (New Rochelle, N.Y.: Arlington House, 1969); idem, *Mediacracy* (Garden City, N.Y.: Doubleday, 1975); idem, *Post-Conservative America*; Ronald Inglehart, *The Silent Revolution* (Princeton, N.J.: Princeton University Press, 1977).

12. Thomas Ferguson and Joel Rogers, *Right Turn: The Decline of the Democrats and the Future of American Politics* (New York: Hill and Wang, 1986); Thomas Byrne Edsall, *The New Politics of Inequality* (New York: Norton, 1984); Sidney Blumenthal, *The Rise of the Counter-Establishment: From Conservative Ideology to Political Power* (New York: Times Books, 1987).

Chapter One

1. *Conservative Digest*, April 1981, pp. 24, 26.

2. Frank S. Meyer, "Conservatism," in *Left, Right and Center: Essays on Liberalism and Conservatism in the United States*, ed. Robert Goldwin (Chicago: Rand McNally, 1965), pp. 1–17, at p. 3 (emphasis added). See also George Nash, *The Conservative Intellectual Movement*, and William Rusher, *The Rise of the Right*.

3. For overviews of the New Deal, see William E. Leuchtenburg, *Franklin D. Roosevelt and the New Deal* (New York: Harper and Row, 1963); Carl N. Degler, *Out of Our Past: The Forces That Shaped Modern America*, 3d ed. (New York: Harper and Row, 1984), pp. 412–450; Michael W. Miles, *The Odyssey of the American Right* (New York: Oxford, 1980), pp. 29–56; and James T. Patterson, *Congressional Conservatism and the New Deal* (Lexington: University Press of Kentucky, 1967).

4. James Holt, "The New Deal and the American Anti-Statist Tradition," in *The New Deal: The National Level*, ed. John Braeman, Robert H. Bremner, and David Brody (Columbus: Ohio State University Press, 1975), pp. 27–49; Theda Skocpol, "The Legacies of New Deal Liberalism," in *Liberalism Reconsidered*, ed. Douglas MacLean and Claudia Mills (Totowa, N.J.: Rowman and Allenheld, 1983), pp. 87–104; Margaret Weir, Ann Shola Orloff, and Theda Skocpol, *The Politics of Social Policy in the United States* (Princeton: Princeton University Press, 1988).

5. Leuchtenberg, *Roosevelt and the New Deal*, pp. 326–336; Degler, *Out of Our Past*, pp. 444–447; Richard Hofstadter, *The Age of Reform* (New York: Random House, 1955), pp. 272–328.

6. Samuel Lubell, *The Future of American Politics*, 3d ed., rev. (New York: Harper and Row, 1965), pp. 43–88; Walter Dean Burnham, *The Current Crisis in American Politics* (New York: Oxford University Press,

1982), pp. 110–113, 146–147, 177–179; James T. Patterson, *Congressional Conservatism*.

7. For the vote on fair labor standards, see Patterson, *Congressional Conservatism*, p. 196. Figures on the outcomes of elections here and elsewhere in this chapter are from *Elections '84* (Washington, D.C.: Congressional Quarterly, 1984) and *Presidential Elections since 1789*, 3d ed. (Washington, D.C.: Congressional Quarterly, 1979).

8. For overviews of American politics in the late 1940s and 1950s, see Godfrey Hodgson, *America in Our Time: From World War II to Nixon, What Happened and Why* (New York: Random House, 1976), pp. 3–98; Eric Goldman, *The Crucial Decade—and After: America, 1945–1960* (New York: Random House, 1960); William H. Chafe, *The Unfinished Journey: America since World War II* (New York: Oxford, 1986), pp. 31–145; Miles, *Odyssey of the American Right*, pp. 80–238; and Alan Wolfe, *America's Impasse: The Rise and Fall of the Politics of Growth* (New York: Pantheon, 1981), pp. 13–48.

9. For voter turnout, see Walter Dean Burnham, "The 1980 Earthquake: Realignment, Reaction, or What?" in *The Hidden Election*, ed. Thomas Ferguson and Joel Rogers (New York: Pantheon, 1981), pp. 98–140, at p. 101. For Truman's campaign appeals, see Goldman, *Crucial Decade*, p. 85. For class polarization of vote, see Robert R. Alford, *Party and Society: The Anglo-American Democracies* (Chicago: Rand McNally, 1963); and Paul R. Abramson, John H. Aldrich, and David W. Rohde, *Change and Continuity in the 1980 Elections*, rev. ed. (Washington, D.C.: Congressional Quarterly, 1983), p. 105.

10. Goldman, *Crucial Decade*, p. 142; Whittaker Chambers, *Witness* (New York: Random House, 1952), pp. 793–794; Frank Meyer, *The Conservative Mainstream* (New Rochelle, N.Y.: Arlington House, 1969), pp. 187–193.

11. Goldman, *Crucial Decade*, pp. 59–60.

12. How much of a role the alleged communist threat at home and abroad played in the 1952 elections is a matter of some debate, but it certainly contributed to Eisenhower's margin of victory. See, for example, Angus Campbell, Philip E. Converse, Warren E. Miller, and Donald E. Stokes, *The American Voter*, abridged ed. (New York: John Wiley, 1964), pp. 15–48; Stephen Hess and Michael Nelson, "Foreign Policy: Dominance and Decisiveness in Presidential Elections," in *The Elections of 1984*, ed. Michael Nelson (Washington, D.C.: Congressional Quarterly, 1985), pp. 129–154.

13. James L. Sundquist, *Dynamics of the Party System: Alignment and Realignment of Political Parties in the United States* (Washington, D.C.: Brookings Institution, 1973), pp. 218–244; George H. Mayer, *The Re-*

publican Party, 1854–1964 (New York: Oxford, 1964), pp. 504–505; Thomas E. Cavanagh and James L. Sundquist, "The New Two-Party System," in *The New Direction in American Politics*, ed. John E. Chubb and Paul E. Peterson (Washington, D.C.: Brookings Institution, 1985), pp. 33–68, esp. p. 43.

14. Wolfe, *America's Impasse*, pp. 9–10, 24–31; Hodgson, *America in Our Time*, pp. 67–98.

15. Barry Goldwater, *The Conscience of a Conservative* (Shepherdsville, Ky.: Victor, 1960), pp. 67–89.

16. The following synopsis of the history of *conservative* and *liberal* as labels in American politics draws on my lengthier account, "The Career of a Concept," an unpublished manuscript. My approach differs from that of others in two ways. First, it focuses on the term *conservative* rather than *liberal*. Second, it argues that both terms came into common use in the Progressive Era rather than with the New Deal. For other accounts, see Samuel H. Beer, "Liberalism and the National Ideal," in *Left, Right, and Center*, ed. Goldwin, pp. 142–169; Ronald Rotunda, "The 'Liberal' Label: Roosevelt's Capture of a Symbol," *Public Policy* 17 (1968): 377–408.

17. Herbert Hoover, "The Consequences of the Proposed New Deal," in *Opposition Politics: The Anti–New Deal Tradition*, ed. Joseph Boskin (Beverly Hills: Glencoe Press, 1968), p. 42; Albert Jay Nock, "A Little Conserva-tive," *The Atlantic Monthly* 158 (October 1936): 481–489.

18. "The Faith of the Freeman," *The Freeman* 1 (1950): 5; William F. Buckley, Jr., *God and Man at Yale: The Superstitions of "Academic Freedom"* (Chicago: Henry Regnery, 1951); Frank Chodorov, "What Individualism Is Not," *National Review* 2 (1956): 15–17; Nash, *Conservative Intellectual Movement*, pp. 16–18, 30–31.

19. Editorial, *National Review* 1 (1955): 5–6; William F. Buckley, Jr., *Up from Liberalism* (New York: McDowell, Obolensky, 1959); Goldwater, *Conscience of a Conservative; What Is Conservatism?* ed. Frank Meyer (New York: Holt, Rinehart and Winston, 1964); Willmoore Kendall, *The Conservative Affirmation* (Chicago: Henry Regnery, 1963); Rusher, *Rise of the Right*, p. 90; William F. Buckley, Jr., "Notes toward an Empirical Definition of Conservatism," in *What Is Conservatism*, ed. Meyer, pp. 211–226. A good example of conservatives defending their absolute right to their new name is their response to M. Morton Auerbach's *The Conservative Illusion* (New York: Columbia, 1959); see M. Stanton Evans, "Exorcising Conservatism," *National Review* 8 (1960): 81–82; Richard M. Weaver, "Illusions of Illusion," *Modern Age*

4 (1960): 316–320; and an exchange between Auerbach and various *National Review* editors in *National Review* 12 (1962): 57–59, 74.

Chapter Two

1. Nash, *The Conservative Intellectual Movement*, is the indispensable starting point for any examination of the making of contemporary conservative ideology. Its major shortcoming is that it looks at the process of ideological construction largely from the vantage point of the finished product and thus pays little attention to what got left out in the transformation and synthesis, or to the influence of social context on the formation of ideology. Other works of interest in understanding the construction of conservative ideology include Rusher, *The Rise of the Right*, pp. 11–53; Garry Wills, *Confessions of a Conservative* (New York: Penguin, 1980), pp. 3–70; John Chamberlain, *A Life with the Printed Word* (Chicago: Regnery Gateway, 1982), pp. 134–167; Charles Lam Markmann, *The Buckleys: A Family Examined* (New York: Morrow, 1973); William F. Buckley, Jr., Introduction to *Did You Ever See a Dream Walking?* (Indianapolis: Bobbs-Merrill, 1970), pp. xv–xl; M. Stanton Evans, "Varieties of Conservative Experience," *Modern Age* 15 (1971): 130–137; Donald Atwell Zoll, "Philosophical Foundations of the American Right," *Modern Age* 15 (1971): 114–129; "A Generation of the Intellectual Right," *Modern Age* 26 (1982): 226–460; and Jeffrey Hart, *The American Dissent: A Decade of American Conservatism* (Garden City, N.Y.: Doubleday, 1966).

2. Meyer, "Conservatism," pp. 1–17, at 3–4.

3. Murray N. Rothbard, "The Transformation of the American Right," *Continuum* 2 (1964): 220–231, at p. 220; Nash, *Conservative Intellectual Movement*, pp. 123–130.

4. My account of isolationism in the following paragraphs draws especially on Manfred Jonas, *Isolationism in America* (Ithaca, N.Y.: Cornell University Press, 1966); Wayne S. Cole, *America First: The Battle against Intervention*, 2d ed. (1953; New York: Octagon, 1971); idem, *Roosevelt and The Isolationists, 1932–1945* (Lincoln: University of Nebraska Press, 1983); Justus D. Doenecke, *Not to the Swift: The Old Isolationists in the Cold War Era* (Lewisburg, Pa.: Bucknell University Press, 1979); and Michael Rogin, *The Intellectuals and McCarthy: The Radical Specter* (Cambridge: MIT Press, 1967), pp. 75–84. For a good annotated bibliography of isolationist scholarship to the early 1970s, see Justus D. Doenecke, *The Literature of Isolationism: A Guide to Non-Interventionist Scholarship, 1930–1972* (Colorado Springs: Ralph Myles, 1972).

5. Miles, *Odyssey of the American Right*, pp. 49–79, falsely sees isolationism by the 1930s as monopolized by the Right and supported only by conservative arguments. Lubell, *Future of American Politics*, pp. 131–155, combines this political image of isolationism with an ethnic one by picturing German-Americans as its major constituency. (See n. 4 for sources that adequately refute both these notions.) In reaction to this image of a purely right-wing isolationism, Ronald Radosh, *Prophets on the Right: Profiles of Conservative Critics of American Globalism* (New York: Simon and Schuster, 1975), bends over backward to portray some isolationist critics of American foreign policy in the late 1940s and 1950s as precursors of the New Left of the 1960s: "These conservatives raised issues and defined problems that . . . opened the way for liberal and leftist critics of a future epoch" (p. 15). This statement is true enough, but it omits a range of less radical arguments made by these same critics. Although 1950s isolationists like Robert Taft sometimes sounded like 1960s New Left critics of the Vietnam War, they also often sounded like Barry Goldwater. For a more balanced view of the fate of onetime isolationist themes in the 1960s and 1970s, see Jonas, *Isolationism in America*, pp. 273–287 and Doenecke, *Not to the Swift*, pp. 231–247.

6. *Congressional Record*, 82d Cong., 1st sess., 1951, 97, pt. 1: 55–69. For a fuller account of Taft's position, see Robert A. Taft, *A Foreign Policy for Americans* (Garden City, N.Y.: Doubleday, 1951). For a dissection of Taft's contradictions, see Alonzo L. Hamby, *Liberalism and Its Challengers* (New York: Oxford, 1985), pp. 106–115.

7. *Congressional Record*, 81st Cong., 2d sess., 1950, 96, pt. 12: 17018–17019.

8. Felix Morley, "The Early Days of *Human Events*," *Human Events* 34 (April 27, 1974): 26, 28, 31; Frank Chodorov, *One Is a Crowd* (New York: Devin-Adair, 1952), p. 116; Aubrey Herbert [Murray Rothbard], "The Real Aggressor," *Faith and Freedom*, April 1954, pp. 22–27.

9. James Burnham, *The Struggle for the World* (New York: John Day, 1947); idem, *The Coming Defeat of Communism* (New York: John Day, 1950); idem, *Containment or Liberation?* (New York: John Day, 1953). As an example of the still unsettled political implications of interventionism and noninterventionism even in the late 1940s, Burnham's first foreign policy work received a favorable review from liberal and interventionist Arthur M. Schlesinger, Jr., in *The Nation*, but a critical one from socialist and noninterventionist Norman Thomas in, of all places, the noninterventionist and soon-to-be conservative *Human Events* (Doenecke, *Not to the Swift*, pp. 37–40, 80).

10. Burnham, *Containment or Liberation?* p. 41.

11. Ibid., p. 43.

12. Burnham, *Coming Defeat of Communism*, p. 142; idem, *Containment or Liberation?*

13. For a detailed and insightful account of four who moved from the Left to the far Right, including Burnham, see John P. Diggins, *Up from Communism: Conservative Odysseys in American Intellectual History* (New York: Harper and Row, 1975).

14. Frank Chodorov, "The Return of 1940?" *The Freeman* 5 (1954): 81–82; William S. Schlamm, "But It Is Not 1940," *The Freeman* 5 (1954): 169–170; Frank Chodorov, "A War to Communize America," *The Freeman* 5 (1954): 171–174.

15. Eric F. Goldman, *The Crucial Decade—and After: America, 1945–1960* (New York: Random House, 1960), p. 114.

16. William F. Buckley, Jr., "Making a Man Out of a Soldier," *The Freeman* 5 (1954): 20–21.

17. William F. Buckley, Jr., "A Dilemma of Conservatives," *The Freeman* 5 (1954): 51–52.

18. Letter to the editor, *The Freeman* 5 (1955): 244.

19. Meyer, *Conservative Mainstream*, pp. 38–43. The ease with which conservatives accepted their ultimate position is reflected in the nonchalance of William Rusher's retrospective remark: "The fact that combatting communism sometimes requires a scope and level of government activity that made conservatives uncomfortable was simply one of those paradoxes in which politics abounds." William Rusher, "The New Right: Past and Prospects," in *The New Right Papers*, ed. Robert W. Whitaker (New York: St. Martin's Press, 1982), p. 7.

20. Two examples of the debate are especially apt: Ronald Hamowy and William F. Buckley, Jr., " 'National Review': Criticism and Reply," *New Individualist Review* 1 (November 1961): 3–11; and Murray N. Rothbard, "The New Libertarian Creed," *New York Times*, February 9, 1971, p. 39, and William F. Buckley, Jr., "The Conservative Reply," *New York Times*, February 16, 1971, p. 33. The debate between self-labeled conservatives and self-labeled libertarians ought not to be confused with the debate within conservatism between traditionalist and libertarian tendencies, though the arguments in each case sometimes overlap. The former involves disagreements over substantive policy issues; the latter involves disagreement over what general philosophical principles to use to justify a set of shared political positions.

21. Barry Goldwater, *Conscience of a Conservative;* Richard A. Viguerie, *The New Right: We're Ready to Lead* (Falls Church, Va.: The Viguerie Company, 1980).

22. T. V. Smith and Robert A. Taft, *Foundations of Democracy* (New York: Knopf, 1939); George Wolfskill, *The Revolt of the Conservatives: A History of the American Liberty League, 1934–1940* (Boston: Houghton Mifflin, 1962); Herbert Hoover, *American Ideals versus the New Deal* (New York: Scribner, 1936).

23. Friedrich A. Hayek, *The Road to Serfdom* (Chicago: University of Chicago Press, 1944), pp. 14, 17.

24. Ibid., pp. 21, 56.

25. Ibid., pp. 57–60, 112.

26. See, for example, Leo Strauss, *Natural Right and History* (Chicago: University of Chicago Press, 1953); Eric Voegelin, *The New Science of Politics: An Introduction* (Chicago: University of Chicago Press, 1952); Robert Nisbet, *The Quest for Community* (New York: Oxford, 1953); Russell Kirk, *A Program for Conservatives* (Chicago: Henry Regnery, 1954); Richard M. Weaver, *Ideas Have Consequences* (Chicago: University of Chicago Press, 1948).

27. Weaver, *Ideas Have Consequences*, p. 3.

28. Ibid., p. 38.

29. Ibid., p. 171; Richard M. Weaver, "Up from Liberalism," *Modern Age* 3 (1958): 21–32.

30. Weaver, *Ideas Have Consequences*, pp. 73–74.

31. Ibid., pp. 91, 113–114.

32. Ibid., pp. 130–133.

33. Ibid., pp. 133–134.

34. Friedrich A. Hayek, "Why I Am Not a Conservative," in *What is Conservatism?* ed. Meyer, pp. 88–103; Frank S. Meyer, "Richard M. Weaver: An Appreciation," *Modern Age* 14 (1970): 243–248.

35. All self-respecting libertarians argue that they assume a set of absolute values; none makes a case for moral relativism. What they do contend, however, is that the formulation and pursuit of values belong properly to individuals in voluntary association with one another, not to the state and hence not to political philosophy. They argue that libertarianism as a political philosophy, not a moral or aesthetic one, is concerned only with "the important subset of moral theory that deals with the proper role of violence in social life," especially the organized, legitimate violence of the state. Since libertarians believe that the only legitimate use of violence is "to defend person and property against violence"—that is, to insure liberty—it has nothing to say about other values or goals not within its limited pur-

view; hence my use of the term *moral agnosticism*. See Murray N. Rothbard, "Myth and Truth about Libertarianism," *Modern Age* 24 (1980): 9–15. See also Frank Chodorov, "What Individualism Is Not," *National Review* 2 (June 20, 1956): 15–17; Murray Rothbard, "Conservatism and Freedom: A Libertarian Comment," *Modern Age* 5 (1961): 217–220; James M. O'Connell, "The New Conservatism," *New Individualist Review* 2 (Spring 1962): 17–21; Ralph Raico, "The Fusionists on Liberalism and Tradition," *New Individualist Review* 3 (August 1964): 29–36; Tibor Machan, "Libertarians and Conservatives," *Modern Age* 24 (1980): 21–33; idem, "Libertarians and Conservatives: Further Considerations," *Modern Age* 26 (1982): 39–48; and idem, *The Libertarian Reader* (Totowa, N.J.: Rowman and Littlefield, 1982).

36. Robert Nisbet, "Conservatives and Libertarians: Uneasy Cousins," *Modern Age* 24 (1980): 2–8; John East, "The American Conservative Movement of the 1980's: Are Traditional and Libertarian Dimensions Compatible?," *Modern Age* 24 (1980): 34–38; George W. Carey, "Conservatives and Libertarians View Fusionism: Its Origins, Possibilities, and Problems," *Modern Age* 26 (1982): 8–18; Dante Germino, "Traditionalism and Libertarianism: Two Views," *Modern Age* 26 (1982): 49–56. See also James C. Roberts, *The Conservative Decade* (Westport, Conn.: Arlington House, 1980), pp. 319–326.

37. John H. Hallowell, review of *The Conservative Affirmation*, by Willmoore Kendall, and *In Defense of Freedom*, by Frank S. Meyer, *American Political Science Review* 58 (1964): 687–688; Evans, "Varieties of Conservative Experience," p. 130; Nash, *Conservative Intellectual Movement*, p. 340; Walter Berns, "The Need for Public Authority," *Modern Age* 24 (1980): 16–20; *ISI Campus Report*, Spring 1981, p. 7.

38. Meyer, "Conservatism," pp. 7–12.

39. Meyer, *Conservative Mainstream*, pp. 43–51. Other efforts by Meyer to reconcile libertarian and traditionalist themes include *Conservative Mainstream*, pp. 35–38; *What Is Conservatism?* pp. 7–20, 229–232; and "In Defense of John Stuart Mill," *National Review* 1 (March 28, 1956): 23–24.

40. Meyer, *Conservative Mainstream*, pp. 184–187.

41. William F. Buckley, Jr., *Up from Liberalism* (New York: McDowell, Obolensky, 1959), pp. 161, 180–181; M. Stanton Evans, "A Conservative Case for Freedom," in *What Is Conservatism?* ed. Meyer, pp. 67–77.

42. Meyer, *Conservative Mainstream*, pp. 74–77.

43. Whittaker Chambers, "Big Sister Is Watching You," *National Review* 4 (1957): 594–596; M. Stanton Evans, "The Gospel according to Ayn Rand," *National Review* 19 (1967): 1059–1063. See also John

Chamberlain, "An Open Letter to Ayn Rand," *National Review* 5 (1958): 118; E. Merrill Root, "What about Ayn Rand?" *National Review* 8 (1960): 76–77; and Garry Wills, "But Is Ayn Rand Conservative?" *National Review* 8 (1960): 139. Only Root made a case for Rand, which Wills eviscerated in the next issue.

44. M. Stanton Evans, "Raico on Liberalism and Religion," *New Individualist Review* 4 (Winter 1966): 19–25. This is a reply to Raico, "Fusionists on Liberalism and Tradition"; Raico rejoins in "Reply to Mr. Evans," *New Individualist Review* 4 (Winter 1966): 25–31.

45. Frank S. Meyer, *In Defense of Freedom: A Conservative Credo* (Chicago: Henry Regnery, 1962), p. 128; idem, "Richard M. Weaver." For critical comments on Meyer's synthesis by important traditionalists, see Russell Kirk, "An Ideologue of Liberty," *Sewanee Review* 72 (1964): 349–350; Richard M. Weaver, "Anatomy of Freedom," *National Review* 13 (1962): 443–444; and L. Brent Bozell, "Freedom or Virtue?" *National Review* 13 (1962): 181–187, 206.

46. Theodore Draper, "Neoconservative History," *The New York Review of Books*, January 16, 1986, pp. 5–15.

Chapter Three

1. See, for example, William A. Gamson, *The Strategy of Social Protest* (Chicago: Dorsey, 1975), and Charles Tilly, *From Mobilization to Revolution* (Reading, Mass.: Addison-Wesley, 1978).

2. The most important works used here for reconstructing the history of the conservative movement from the mid-1950s to the early 1980s include the following: Rusher, *Rise of the Right*; Nash, *Conservative Intellectual Movement*; Miles, *Odyssey of the American Right*; David W. Reinhard, *The Republican Right since 1945* (Lexington: University Press of Kentucky, 1983); Arnold Forster and Benjamin R. Epstein, *Danger on the Right* (New York: Random House, 1964); F. Clifton White and William J. Gill, *Why Reagan Won: The Conservative Movement, 1964–1981* (Chicago: Regnery Gateway, 1981); M. Stanton Evans, *Revolt on the Campus* (Chicago: Henry Regnery, 1961); James C. Roberts, *The Conservative Decade—Emerging Leaders of the 1980s* (Westport, Conn.: Arlington House, 1980); Erling Jorstad, *The Politics of Doomsday* (Nashville: Abingdon, 1970); Seymour Martin Lipset and Earl Raab, *The Politics of Unreason: Right-Wing Extremism in America, 1790–1977*, 2d ed. (Chicago: University of Chicago Press, 1978); K. Phillips, *Post-Conservative America*; Viguerie, *New Right*; and John T. Saloma III, *Ominous Politics: The New Conservative Labyrinth* (New York: Hill and Wang, 1984).

3. Reinhard, *Republican Right*, p. 153.

4. Forster and Epstein, *Danger on the Right,* p. 212.

5. Reinhard, *Republican Right,* p. 140.

6. Jorstad, *Politics of Doomsday,* p. 80.

7. Forster and Epstein, *Danger on the Right,* pp. 11–46; Bell, *Radical Right,* p. 422.

8. Reinhard, *Republican Right,* p. 155.

9. Evans, *Revolt on the Campus,* p. 110.

10. Nash, *Conservative Intellectual Movement,* p. 293.

11. Evans, *Revolt on the Campus,* p. 38.

12. Rusher, *Rise of the Right,* p. 161.

13. Rusher, *Rise of the Right,* pp. 119–121, 189–190; Nash, *Conservative Intellectual Movement,* pp. 292–293; Forster and Epstein, *Danger on the Right,* pp. 217, 197–202, 108, 230; *Group Research Reports* 24 (1985): 25, 33. Rusher and Nash both play down the role of the Birch Society.

14. Nash, *Conservative Intellectual Movement,* pp. 293–294.

15. Viguerie, *New Right,* pp. 26–27.

16. Rusher, *Rise of the Right,* pp. 154–155.

17. William F. Buckley, Jr., *Inveighing We Will Go* (New York: Berkley Publishing, 1973), p. 63.

18. Nash, *Conservative Intellectual Movement,* pp. 293–294, 334–335.

19. K. Phillips, *Emerging Republican Majority;* Richard M. Scammon and Ben J. Wattenberg, *The Real Majority* (New York: Coward, McCann, and Geoghegan, 1970).

20. The classic statements of a status politics theory of the postwar American Right are found in Bell, *Radical Right.* Lipset and Raab, *Politics of Unreason,* extend the basic argument from the 1950s and 1960s backward and forward in history. Critics of the status politics thesis as applied to McCarthyism include Rogin, *Intellectuals and McCarthy;* Nelson W. Polsby, "Toward an Explanation of McCarthyism," *Political Studies* 8 (1960): 250–271; Thomas C. Reeves, "McCarthyism: Interpretations since Hofstadter," *Wisconsin Magazine of History* 60 (Autumn 1976): 42–54. For a good summary of the literature on status politics, see Clarence Y. H. Lo, "Countermovements and Conservative Movements in the Contemporary U.S.," *Annual Review of Sociology* 8 (1982): 107–134.

21. Bell, *Radical Right;* Lipset and Raab, *Politics of Unreason.*

22. Lipset and Raab, *Politics of Unreason,* p. 497. After an exhaustive examination of survey data on right-wing movements since the 1930s, Lipset and Raab concluded that right-wing leaders and organizations appeal to varying combinations of three groups: economic conservatives, whose high socioeconomic status gives them an interest in opposing the growth of government; status preservatists,

whose changing or inconsistent social status gives them a desire to return to an idealized past; and the less educated, whose values give them what Lipset and Raab call "low democratic restraint." See *Politics of Unreason*, especially pp. 474, 496.

23. I am not denying the real diversity of support for right-wing movements. I merely want to direct attention as well to a foundation of common support that is often ignored in the preoccupation with diversity. According to a 1954 Gallup Poll, those favorable to McCarthy were more likely than those unfavorable to have voted for Eisenhower in 1952 (76 to 49 percent), to intend to vote Republican in the 1954 Congressional elections (53 to 29 percent), and to consider themselves Republicans (46 to 24 percent). Polsby, "Explanation of McCarthyism," p. 262. See also Lipset and Raab, *Politics of Unreason*, p. 225. Seventy-two percent of Birch Society supporters in a 1962 California Poll (compared to 41 percent of the entire sample) were Republicans, as were 43 percent of supporters in a 1962 national Gallup Poll (compared to 28 percent of the entire sample). Seymour Martin Lipset, "Three Decades of the Radical Right," in Bell, *Radical Right*, pp. 425, 429. Two-thirds of those attending a 1962 anticommunism school in Oakland, California, sponsored by the Christian Anti-Communism Crusade, called themselves Republicans, and 92 percent of those who voted in the 1960 presidential election supported Nixon. Raymond E. Wolfinger, Barbara Kaye Wolfinger, Kenneth Prewitt, and Sheilah Rosenhack, "America's Radical Right: Politics and Ideology," in *Ideology and Discontent*, ed. David E. Apter (New York: Free Press, 1964). A 1960 survey of ISI members found that about 63 percent reported that their parents were Republicans and 70 percent called themselves Republicans. Evans, *Revolt on the Campus*, pp. 46–50. A 1967 study of campus political activists found that YAF members were disproportionately Republican in comparison to a control group of inactive students (though not in comparison to a sample of Young Republicans). Richard G. Braungart, "Family Status, Socialization, and Student Politics: A Multivariate Analysis," *American Journal of Sociology* 77 (1971): 108–130. A study of the 1964 California delegation to the Republican National Convention found that Goldwater delegates were significantly more likely than Rockefeller delegates to have served on county (86 to 24 percent) and state (82 to 34 percent) committees, to have contributed more than one thousand dollars to the party in 1962 (51 to 17 percent), to have been a delegate to a previous national convention (41 to 21 percent), and to have been involved in the Republican party for twenty or more years (41 to 28 percent). Edmond Constantini and Kenneth H. Craik, "Competing

Elites within a Political Party: A Study of Republican Leadership," *Western Political Quarterly* 22 (1969): 879–903. See also James McEvoy III, *Radicals or Conservatives: The Contemporary American Right* (Chicago: Rand McNally, 1971).

24. McCarthy's support among Texas businessmen, especially oilmen H. L. Hunt, Clint Murchison, and Roy Cullen, was legendary. He visited the state so often and received so much financial support from it that he was sometimes known as Texas's third senator. Charles J. V. Murphy, "McCarthy and the Businessman," *Fortune,* April 1954, pp. 156–158, 180–194; idem, "Texas Business and McCarthy," *Fortune,* May 1954, pp. 100–101, 208–216. See also Lipset and Raab, *Politics of Unreason,* pp. 227–228, 310–312; Alan F. Westin, "The John Birch Society," in Bell, *Radical Right,* pp. 249–250; and Forster and Epstein, *Danger on the Right,* pp. 8–9, 272–280.

25. Studies of Birch Society and Christian Anti-Communism Crusade activists in the mid-1960s found that from 17 to 40 percent (depending on the sample) earned more than fifteen thousand dollars a year (compared to 4 percent of all Americans), 30 to 52 percent were college graduates (compared to 10 percent of a national sample), and 31 to 58 percent had professional or managerial jobs (compared to 23 percent of a national sample). A 1962 California Poll found that Birch Society supporters tended to be of higher than average socioeconomic status: 36 percent had three or more years of college, in comparison to 27 percent of Birch opponents and 20 percent of the entire sample; 35 percent were classified as of a high economic level, in comparison to 23 percent of opponents and 26 percent of the entire sample. Lipset and Raab, *Politics of Unreason,* pp. 288–326, especially pp. 298–299; Lipset, "Three Decades," pp. 425, 429. See also Barbara S. Stone, "A Profile of the John Birch Society," *Journal of Politics* 36 (1974): 184–197. In a 1965 ad pitched to potential advertisers, the *National Review* claimed on the basis of a marketing survey that its subscribers had an average annual income of $19,500 and an average net worth of $151,000, that two-thirds were college graduates and one-third had postgraduate degrees, and that more than half owned two cars. *National Review* 17 (October 19, 1965): 903; Evans, *Revolt on the Campus,* p. 61.

On the Conservative party, see Robert A. Schoenberger, "Conservatism, Personality, and Political Extremism," *American Political Science Review* 62 (1968): 868–877. On McCarthy, see Lipset and Raab, *Politics of Unreason,* pp. 226–229. A 1960 study of ISI members found that about half came from families with annual incomes greater than five thousand dollars, half from families with incomes below that level.

Evans, *Revolt on the Campus,* pp. 46–50. A 1967 study at one major university classified 28 percent of YAF members as from upper middle-class families (defined by occupational status and education), about the same as for a control group (25 percent), but much less than for any other group of campus activists (Young Republicans, 59 percent; Young Democrats, 41 percent; Students for a Democratic Society, 55 percent). Braungart, "Student Politics," p. 119. See also David L. Westby and Richard G. Braungart, "Class and Politics in the Family Backgrounds of Student Political Activists," *American Sociological Review* 31 (1966): 690–692. Studies of national YAF samples gave similar results, but studies of YAF members at Harvard and other eastern universities showed them to be a more affluent lot. See summary in *Student Politics,* ed. Seymour Martin Lipset (New York: Basic Books, 1967), pp. 213–224. For one way of reconciling these findings with theories of status politics and older theories of authoritarian personality, see Schoenberger, "Conservatism," who distinguishes "political" conservatism (conservative political affiliation) from "psychological" conservatism (conservative political belief).

For data on Wallace, see Lipset and Raab, *Politics of Unreason,* pp. 358–390, esp. pp. 380–382. In the 1964 Democratic primaries in Wisconsin, Indiana, and Maryland, Wallace carried working-class districts in which Goldwater failed miserably a few months later in the general election. In his 1968 presidential bid Wallace did best among the lower strata. He got 17 percent of the vote of manual workers but only 9 percent of the vote of nonmanual workers; 19 percent of the vote of those with a grade-school education but only 9 percent of the vote of those with at least some college education; and about 18 percent of the vote of those with incomes of less than seven thousand dollars but only 6 percent of the vote of those with incomes of more than fifteen thousand dollars. All in all, this pattern of support is different from that of the conservative movement in the 1950s and 1960s.

Three qualifications need to be noted to this analysis of the class basis of the Wallace vote. First, in one instance, the Wisconsin Democratic primary in 1964, Wallace did run better in middle-class neighborhoods than in working-class ones, but that appears to have been an idiosyncratic result. In the Indiana and Maryland primaries that year the bases of his support were similar to those in the 1968 general election. Second, in 1968, outside the South, Wallace did a better job of winning the vote of middle-class sympathizers than of working-class sympathizers. Third, middle-class Wallace supporters tended to be more conservative in racial and economic views than his working-class supporters. Michael Rogin, "Wallace and the Middle Class: The White Backlash in Wisconsin," *Public Opinion Quarterly* 30 (1966): 98–108; Michael Rogin, "Politics, Emotion, and the Wallace Vote," *The British Journal of Sociology* 20 (1969): 27–49; M. Margaret Conway, "The White Backlash Re-examined: Wallace and the 1964 Primaries," *Social Science Quarterly* 49 (1968): 710–719; Seymour Martin Lipset and Earl Raab, "The Wallace Whitelash" *Trans-action* 7 (December 1969): 23–35; Richard F. Hamilton, *Class and Politics in the United States* (New York: Wiley, 1972).

26. Kirkpatrick Sale, *Power Shift: The Rise of the Southern Rim and Its Challenge to the Eastern Establishment* (New York: Random House, 1975).

27. Murphy, "Texas Business and McCarthy"; Forster and Epstein, *Danger on the Right*, p. 39; Lipset and Raab, *Politics of Unreason*, p. 305.

28. Sundquist, *Dynamics of the Party System*, pp. 245–274.

29. Among white voters in presidential elections from 1944 to 1964 Democratic candidates on the average did 22 percentage points better among union members than nonmembers, 20 points better among voters from blue-collar families than among those from white-collar families, and 24 points better among Catholics than Protestants. (In each case, however, one exceptional year inflates the average—1948 for union membership and class, 1960 for religious affiliation.) In 1968 those differences were 13, 10, and 30; in 1972 they fell to 1, 2, and 13. In 1976 and 1980, however, they recovered much of the lost ground. See Abramson, Aldrich, and Rohde, *Change and Continuity*, p. 105.

30. Seymour Martin Lipset and William Schneider, *The Confidence Gap: Business, Labor, and Government in the Public Mind* (New York: Free Press, 1983).

31. Lipset and Raab, *Politics of Unreason*, p. 348; William F. Buckley, Jr., *The Governor Listeth* (New York: Putnam, 1970), pp. 57–71. See also Meyer, *The Conservative Mainstream*, pp. 285–288. As reported by Buckley, the *Human Events* poll had only 8 percent of conservatives supporting Wallace against Nixon and 23 percent supporting him against Rockefeller. About three-quarters of respondents said Wallace's candidacy would hurt the conservative movement in America.

32. Rusher, *Rise of the Right*, pp. 239–252. For the opinions of two later leaders of the New Right, see Howard Phillips, "A New Right Perspective," in *The New Right at Harvard*, ed. Howard Phillips (Vienna, Va.: Conservative Caucus, 1983), pp. 3–13, and Viguerie, *New Right*, pp. 31–32.

33. Everett Carll Ladd, Jr., *Where Have All the Voters Gone?: The*

Fracturing of America's Political Parties (New York: Norton, 1982), p. 13; Jonathan Rieder, *Canarsie: The Jews and Italians of Brooklyn against Liberalism* (Cambridge: Harvard University Press, 1985), p. 5, 240–241.

34. Viguerie, *New Right*, p. 51.

35. Ibid., p. 52.

36. Ibid., pp. 32, 52, 53, 49.

37. The cover of the October 1980 issue of *Conservative Digest*, published until 1986 by Viguerie, pictured eight persons marching under a banner proclaiming "The New Right: We're Ready to Lead"—Viguerie, Phillips, Dolan, Weyrich, Helms, Blackwell, Schlafly, and Falwell. In his insider's view of American conservatism, Burton Pines identified the "small circle of the movement's founding fathers" as including Viguerie, Phillips, Dolan, Weyrich, Feulner, and Blackwell, as well as Schlafly, Helms, McAteer, and Billings. Burton Yale Pines, *Back to Basics: The Traditionalist Movement That Is Sweeping Grass-Roots America* (New York: Morrow, 1982), p. 293. The September 1983 *Conservative Digest* reported that Crane, Helms, and McDonald topped a preference poll of its readers as leaders most suited to succeed Reagan. Falwell, Buchanan, Crane, Helms, McDonald (posthumously), Kemp, and Schlafly all ranked high in *Conservative Digest*'s tenth anniversary list of "most admired conservatives of the decade" in its May 1985 issue. (Ronald and Nancy Reagan, Buckley, James Watt, Jeremiah Denton, Beverly LaHaye, Jeanne Kirkpatrick, and Sandra Day O'Connor also made it into the top five in one of the three categories: conservatives in Congress, conservative men not in Congress, conservative women not in Congress.) Crane and Helms have perennially won among the highest ratings from conservative organizations for their congressional voting records. See, for example, *Washington Times*, November 14, 1986, p. 3A. Well into 1986 Kemp topped presidential preference polls of *Conservative Digest* readers. See, for example, *Conservative Digest*, April 1986, pp. 23–26.

38. "Conservative Cry: Our Time Has Come," *U.S. News and World Report*, February 26, 1979, pp. 52–54; E. J. Dionne, Jr., "Fund-Raising Data Worry Democrats," *New York Times*, September 25, 1980, p. 8; Adam Clymer, "Conservative Political Action Committee Evokes Both Fear and Adoration," *New York Times*, May 31, 1981, p. 1; Lee Edwards, "Paul Weyrich: Conscience of the New Right," *Conservative Digest*, July 1981, pp. 2–8.

39. Viguerie, *New Right*, pp. 32–33; Rusher, *Rise of the Right*, pp. 263–290.

40. *Conservative Digest*, October 1980, p. 17. For a more detailed discussion of the New Right and the social issues, see Jerome L. Him-

melstein, "The New Right," in *The New Christian Right: Mobilization and Legitimation*, ed. Robert Liebman and Robert Wuthnow (Hawthorne, N.Y.: Aldine, 1983), pp. 13–30. By the late 1980s the emphasis on social issues was being recycled as "cultural conservatism." See Paul Weyrich, "Reshaping the Political Debate: Cultural Conservatism and American Politics," *Election Politics* 4 (Fall 1987): 15–16.

41. Dudley Clendinen, "TV Evangelists and Small Group Lead 'Christian New Right's' Rush to Power," *New York Times*, August 18, 1980, p. 14; "Roundtable's President Ed McAteer Is Music Man of Religious Right," *Conservative Digest*, January 1981, pp. 2–7; James L. Guth, "The New Christian Right," in *New Christian Right*, ed. Liebman and Wuthnow, pp. 31–45.

42. *Conservative Digest*, November 1980, pp. 4, 5, 7, 40; Roberts, *Conservative Decade*; Rusher, *Rise of the Right*, p. 310.

43. K. Phillips, *Post-Conservative America*, p. 14. "During the 1960s and 1970s," wrote Phillips in the same work, "the nature of 'conservatism' underwent a transformation—not complete by any means, but substantial. . . . Conservatism . . . increasingly took on the coloration of popular, even populist, animosity" (pp. 31–32). "The 'New' Right," he added, "did then and still does represent a major cultural and tactical departure for a 'conservative' politics" (p. 47) See *Post-Conservative America*, pp. 31–52. Others who made the neo-populist argument include Crawford, *Thunder on the Right*; Gillian Peele, *Revival and Reaction: The Right in Contemporary America* (Oxford: Oxford University Press, 1984); John L. Kater, Jr., *Christians on the Right* (New York: Seabury Press, 1982); Pines, *Back to Basics*; and Nicholas Lemann, "The Evolution of the Conservative Mind," *The Washington Monthly*, May 1981, pp. 34–41. Blumenthal, *Rise of the Counter-Establishment*, also flirts with the populist analogy, though he confesses that if the New Right is populist, it is "populism turned on its head" (pp. 321–323). The irony of using a populist analogy to distinguish a new Right from an older one is that a prior generation of social commentators had used the same analogy to characterize the Old Right of the 1950s. See especially Hofstadter, *Age of Reform*, pp. 3–22, and Peter Viereck, "The Revolt against the Elite," in *Radical Right*, ed. Bell, pp. 161–183. The analogies are about equally misleading, drawing heavily on superficial similarities in rhetoric rather than real historical continuities or commonalities in policies. Certainly Rogin, *Intellectuals and McCarthy*, convincingly showed the flaws in that earlier use of the populist analogy. Others have criticized the neo-populist analogy as applied to the New Right, especially Saloma, *Ominous Politics*, pp. 38–49.

44. Richard Viguerie, "Money, Message, and Marketing," in *New Right at Harvard*, ed. H. Phillips, p. 116.

45. Roberts, *Conservative Decade*, p. 7.

46. The brief political biographies in the following paragraphs are drawn from a number of sources. On Viguerie: Viguerie, *New Right*, pp. 19–37. On Phillips: H. Phillips, *New Right at Harvard*, pp. vii–viii, 3–10. On Dolan: Milton Ellerin and Alisa H. Kesten, "The New Right: What Is It?," *Social Policy* 11 (March-April 1982): 54–62. On Weyrich: Ellerin and Kesten, "The New Right"; Edwards, "Paul Weyrich." On Schlafly: Carol Felsenthal, *The Sweetheart of the Silent Majority* (Garden City, N.Y.: Doubleday, 1981); Sasha Gregory-Lewis, "Stop-ERA: A Choice or an Echo?," *The Advocate*, November 2, 1977, pp. 12–15, and November 16, 1977, pp. 6–8. On Crane: White and Gill, *Why Reagan Won*, p. 76; Viguerie, *New Right*, p. 74. On Buchanan: Rusher, *Rise of the Right*, pp. 197–198; White and Gill, *Why Reagan Won*, p. 77; Crawford, *Thunder on the Right*, p. 190. On McDonald: *Newsweek*, September 12, 1983, p. 27. On Blackwell: H. Phillips, *New Right at Harvard*, p. 133. On Feulner: *ISI Campus Report*, Spring 1981; Saloma, *Ominous Politics*, p. 42. On Kemp: Rowland Evans and Robert Novak, "Is He the GOP's Future?" *Reader's Digest*, June 1982, pp. 108–112; *Washington Post*, August 12, 1984, p. B8. On Helms: Elizabeth Drew, "Jesse Helms," *The New Yorker*, July 20, 1981, pp. 78–95; Bill Arthur, "Helms, Outspoken Symbol of the Right," *Charlotte Observer*, February 12, 1984, p. 1A. On Falwell: Dinesh D'Souza, *Falwell: Before the Millennium* (Chicago: Regnery Gateway, 1984); Frances Fitzgerald, "A Disciplined, Charging Army," *The New Yorker*, May 18, 1981, pp. 53–141. On McAteer: "Roundtable's President McAteer."

47. Roberts, *Conservative Decade*, pp. 19–35; *ISI Campus Report*, Spring 1981.

48. Viguerie, *New Right*, pp. 21, 39, 11, 41.

49. *Conservative Digest*, March 1981, pp. 2–7.

50. Ibid., p. 26.

51. Ibid., pp. 28–29.

52. Rebecca Klatch, "Perceptions of Gender among Women of the New Right," paper presented at the annual meetings of the American Anthropological Association, 1983. See also idem, *Women of the New Right* (Philadelphia: Temple University Press, 1987). In the latter work Klatch divides New Right women into "social conservatives" and "laissez-faire conservatives" and rightfully argues that most research has focused on the former. She exaggerates the division, however, by ignoring the ample number of hybrids and by lumping members of the Libertarian party among the laissez-faire group. Some observers

have seen in the traditionalist themes invoked by antifeminist women a nascent critique of both capitalism and patriarchy. See, for example, Andrea Dworkin, *Right-Wing Women* (New York: Putnam, 1983). There is, however, nothing inherently anticapitalist or antipatriarchal in traditionalist themes; their broader implications depend on the overall political position into which they are integrated. In Chapter 2 I have shown how conservatives have long since expunged the critical elements of traditionalism.

53. For a discussion of supply-side economics as part of conservative ideology, see Jerome L. Himmelstein, "God, Gilder, and Capitalism," *Society* 18 (September-October, 1981): 68–72. For detailed accounts of how it developed, see John Brooks, "Annals of Finance: The Supply Side," *The New Yorker,* April 19, 1982, pp. 97–150; and Blumenthal, *Rise of the Counter-Establishment,* pp. 166–209.

54. For the selling of supply-side economics to Republicans, see David A. Stockman, *The Triumph of Politics: Why the Reagan Revolution Failed* (New York: Harper and Row, 1986), pp. 47–76. For the conversion of Ronald Reagan in particular from a traditional Republican emphasis on austerity, balanced budgets, and painful solutions to the more optimistic approach of tax cuts and instant economic growth, see Robert W. Merry, "Growth Agent: Reagan Transformed," *Wall Street Journal,* September 13, 1985.

55. Cavanagh and Sundquist, "New Two-Party System," p. 37.

56. George Gilder, *Wealth and Poverty* (New York: Basic Books, 1980).

57. Viguerie, *New Right,* p. 59; *National Review* 1 (November 19, 1955), p. 5; John Dillin, "U.S. Conservatives on the March: Economic Philosophy and Outlook," *Christian Science Monitor,* March 18, 1986, p. 22.

58. John Judis, "Pop-Con Politics," *The New Republic* 191 (September 3, 1984): 20; Richard A. Viguerie, *The Establishment vs. the People: Is a New Populist Revolt on the Way?* (Chicago: Regnery Gateway, 1983). For a summary of conservative use of populist rhetoric, see Nash, *Conservative Intellectual Movement,* pp. 250–251, 338. For another instance of the New Right playing up its populism, see Whitaker, *New Right Papers.*

59. See almost any issue of *Conservative Digest* between 1981 and 1988 for criticism of the Reagan administration, but especially February 1981, August 1981, February 1982, April 1982, July 1982, and September 1983. *Human Events,* March 7, 1981; *National Review* 35 (March 8, 1983): 294; *Conservative Digest,* May 1985; *Group Research Report* 24 (October 1985): 35.

Chapter Four

1. Jerry Falwell, *Listen, America!* (New York: Bantam, 1981), pp. 6, 60, 101.

2. J. Craig Jenkins, "Resource Mobilization Theory and the Study of Social Movements," *Annual Review of Sociology* 9 (1983): 527–553.

3. Ladd and Hadley, *Transformations of the American Party System*, pp. xx, xxi.

4. See, for example, Louis Harris, *The Anguish of Change* (New York: Norton, 1973); Inglehart, *Silent Revolution;* Everett Carll Ladd, Jr. "The New Lines Are Drawn: Class and Ideology in America," *Public Opinion* 1 (July 1978): 48–53, and 1 (September 1978): 4–20; Ladd and Hadley, *Transformation of the American Party System;* K. Phillips, *Mediacracy;* and Scammon and Wattenberg, *Real Majority.*

5. Harris, *Anguish of Change*, p. 52.

6. Jane J. Mansbridge, *Why We Lost the ERA* (Chicago: University of Chicago Press, 1986), pp. 98–117; Kathleen Gerson, *Hard Choices: How Women Decide about Work, Career, and Motherhood* (Berkeley and Los Angeles: University of California Press, 1985), pp. 186–190; idem, "Emerging Social Divisions among Women: Implications for Welfare State Policies," *Politics and Society* 15 (1986–1987): 213–221; Rosalind Pollack Petchesky, "The Antiabortion Movement and the Rise of the New Right," in *Abortion and Women's Choice: The State, Sexuality, and Reproductive Freedom* (Boston: Northeastern University Press, 1984), pp. 241–285; Zillah R. Eisenstein, "Antifeminism in the Politics and Presidential Election of 1980," in *Feminism and Sexual Equality: Crisis in Liberal America* (New York: Monthly Review Press, 1984), pp. 19–39; Kristin Luker, *Abortion and the Politics of Motherhood* (Berkeley and Los Angeles: University of California Press, 1984).

7. For a detailed discussion of these points, see Jerome L. Himmelstein, "The Social Basis of Antifeminism: Religious Networks and Culture," *Journal for the Scientific Study of Religion* 25 (1986): 1–15; Jerome L. Himmelstein and James A. McRae, Jr., "Social Issues and Socioeconomic Status," *Public Opinion Quarterly* 52 (1988): 492–512; Steven Brint, "'New Class' and Cumulative Trend Explanations of Liberal Political Attitudes of Professionals," *American Journal of Sociology* 90 (1984): 30–71; and idem, "The Political Attitudes of Professionals," *Annual Review of Sociology* 11 (1985): 389–414.

8. Donald Granberg, "The Abortion Activists," *Family Planning Perspectives* 13 (1981): 157–163; Donald Granberg and Donald Denney, "The Coathanger and the Rose," *Society* 19 (1982): 39–51; Luker, *Abortion and the Politics of Motherhood*, pp. 196–197.

9. For a review of the literature on the determinants of beliefs on abortion and the ERA and for a more detailed discussion and documentation of the argument presented here, see Himmelstein, "Social Basis of Antifeminism." As Klatch points out in *Women of the New Right*, none of the factors discussed here distinguishes feminists from laissez-faire conservatives, both of whom tend to be secular and professional. She does not explain, however, what leads to the different political outcomes.

10. For a detailed account of the changing religious landscape, see Wade Clark Roof and William McKinney, *American Mainline Religion: Its Changing Shape and Future* (New Brunswick, N.J.: Rutgers University Press, 1987). The picture they paint belies the notion that secularization, at least in the form of a decline in personal religious belief and participation, is an inevitable part of modern industrial societies. Their conclusions simply confirm, however, that the United States is a striking exception to an otherwise valid rule. Aside from the United States, the level of economic development in a given society is inversely related to the percentage of its members declaring that their religious beliefs are important. The percentage of Americans declaring strong religious beliefs, however, is much greater than for other advanced industrial societies. Moreover, American church attendance has not declined markedly over the last half century. See Burnham, "The 1980 Earthquake"; and Michael Hout and Andrew M. Greeley, "Church Attendance in the United States," *American Sociological Review* 52 (1987): 325–345. Roof and McKinney's image of religious polarization also cuts the other way, however: if secularization is an inadequate notion, so is the idea of a major religious revival in America. The 1970s and early 1980s witnessed no surge in church attendance or in the importance given religion. Despite the rapid growth of conservative churches, their reach into the secular world was limited: their growing membership came primarily from more effective retention of old members and high birth rates. New members were overwhelmingly reaffiliates and the relatives and friends of old members. See John M. Benson, "The Polls: A Rebirth of Religion?" *Public Opinion Quarterly* 45 (1981): 576–585; Reginald W. Bibby, "Circulation of the Saints Revisited: A Longitudinal Look at Conservative Church Growth," *Journal for the Scientific Study of Religion* 22 (1983): 253–262; and *Public Opinion*, September-October 1988, pp. 24–25.

11. "The 70's; Decade of Second Thoughts," *Public Opinion* 2 (January 1980): 19–42; Carol Mueller, "In Search of a Constituency for the 'New Religious Right,'" *Public Opinion Quarterly* 47 (1983): 213–229; Warren E. Miller and J. Merrill Shanks, "Policy Directions and Presi-

dential Leadership: Alternative Interpretations of the 1980 Presidential Election," *British Journal of Political Science* 12 (1982): 299–356; *Baron Report*, March 1, 1982. Pamela Johnston Conover and Virginia Gray, *Feminism and the New Right* (New York: Praeger, 1983), present a more mixed picture of the changing importance of issues like ERA and abortion than does Mueller. They agree that there was no heightened polarization on these issues in the 1970s, but they argue that position on abortion and ERA had a growing association with ideological label and party. The poll referred to in the *Baron Report* was a 1982 Harris Poll.

12. Michael J. Malbin, "The Conventions, Platforms, and Issue Activists," in *The American Elections of 1980*, ed. Austin Ranney (Washington, D.C.: American Enterprise Institute, 1981), pp. 99–141; Albert R. Hunt, "The Campaign and the Issues," in *American Elections of 1980*, ed. Ranney, pp. 142–176; Adam Clymer, "Displeasure with Carter Turned Many to Reagan," *New York Times*, November 9, 1980, p. 18. For a more detailed analysis of the 1980 elections, see Jerome L. Himmelstein and James A. McRae, Jr., "Social Conservatism, New Republicans, and the 1980 Elections," *Public Opinion Quarterly* 48 (1984): 592–605. Even in the South, with its disproportionately high percentage of churchgoers and fundamentalists, the social issues have had uneven political impact. Hastings J. Wyman, Jr., "Yes, But Then Again, No: Social Issues and Southern Politics," *Election Politics* 4 (Summer 1987): 15–18.

13. Himmelstein, "Social Basis of Antifeminism." Similar results are found among pro-life and pro-choice activists. See Granberg, "Abortion Activists"; and Granberg and Denney, "Coathanger and Rose."

14. Carol Mueller and Thomas Dimieri, "The Structure of Belief Systems among Contending ERA Activists," *Social Forces* 60 (1982): 657–675; Donald Mathews and Jane DeHart Mathews, "The Threat of Equality: The Equal Rights Amendment and the Myth of Female Solidarity," unpublished manuscript. Luker, *Abortion and the Politics of Motherhood*, found similar differences in worldview among abortion activists. Gerson, *Hard Choices*, pp. 186–190, also found such differences between women who chose motherhood and women who chose careers. For other accounts of the worldview of antifeminists, see Dworkin, *Right-Wing Women;* Deirdre English, "The War against Choice: Inside the Anti-Abortion Movement," *Mother Jones* 6 (1981): 16–32; Susan Harding, "Family Reform Movements: Recent Feminism and Its Opposition," *Feminist Studies* 7 (1981): 57–75; and Klatch, *Women of the New Right*, pp. 119–147.

15. Theodore S. Arrington and Patricia A. Kyle, "Equal Rights Amendment Activists in North Carolina," *Signs* 3 (1978); 666–680; Iva E. Deutchman and Sandra Prince-Embury, "Political Ideology of Pro- and Anti-ERA Women," *Women and Politics* 2 (1982): 39–55; Mueller and Dimieri, "Structure of Belief Systems"; David Brady and Kent L. Tedin, "Ladies in Pink: Religion and Political Ideology in the Anti-ERA Movement," *Social Science Quarterly* 56 (1976): 564–575; Luker, *Abortion and the Politics of Motherhood*, pp. 138–139; Faye Ginsburg, *Contested Lives: The Abortion Debate in an American Community* (Berkeley and Los Angeles: University of California Press, 1988).

16. James L. Guth, "Political Converts: Partisan Realignment among Southern Baptist Ministers," *Election Politics* 3 (Winter 1985–1986): 2–6.

17. James L. Guth and John C. Green, "Politics in a New Key: Religiosity and Activism Among Political Contributors," paper presented at the meetings of the Society for the Scientific Study of Religion, Knoxville, Tenn., November 4–6, 1983; idem, "Party, PAC, and Denomination: Religiosity among Political Contributors," paper presented at the meetings of the American Political Science Association, Chicago, September 1–4, 1983; idem, "Faith and Politics: Religion and Ideology among Political Contributors," *American Politics Quarterly* 14 (1986): 186–200; idem, "The Christian Right in the Republican Party: The Case of Pat Robertson's Supporters," *Journal of Politics* 50 (1988): 150–165; idem, "God and the GOP: Varieties of Religiosity among Political Contributors," paper presented at the meetings of the American Political Science Association, Chicago, September 3–6, 1987.

18. "Roundtable's President Ed McAteer Is Music Man of Religious Right," *Conservative Digest*, January 1981, pp. 2–7; D'Souza, *Falwell*; Fitzgerald, "A Disciplined, Charging Army"; Arthur H. Miller and Martin P. Wattenberg, "Politics from the Pulpit: Religiosity and the 1980 Elections," *Public Opinion Quarterly* 48 (1984): 301–317; Stuart Rothenberg and Frank Newport, *The Evangelical Voter: Religion and Politics in America* (Washington, D.C.: Free Congress Research and Education Foundation, 1984).

19. George M. Marsden, *Fundamentalism and American Culture: The Shaping of Twentieth-Century Evangelicalism, 1870–1925* (New York: Oxford University Press, 1980), p. 3; "America's Evangelicals: Genesis or Evolution?," *Public Opinion*, April-May 1981, pp. 22–27; James Davison Hunter, *American Evangelicalism: Conservative Religion and the Quandary of Modernity* (New Brunswick, N.J.: Rutgers University Press, 1983), pp. 49–60. For perceptive discussion of the analytic problems in defining *evangelical*, see Corwin Smidt, "Evangelicals in

Presidential Elections: A Look at the 1980s," *Election Politics* 5 (Spring 1988): 2–11; idem, "Evangelicals and the 1984 Election: Continuity or Change?" *American Politics Quarterly* 15 (1987): 419–444; Corwin Smidt and Lyman Kellstedt, "Evangelicalism and Survey Research: Interpretive Problems and Substantive Findings," in *The Bible, Politics, and Democracy,* ed. Richard J. Neuhaus (Grand Rapids, Mich.: Eerdmans, 1987). Charismatics, who emphasize the spiritual experience of the indwelling of the Holy Spirit, overlap partly with evangelicals. See Smidt, " 'Praise the Lord' Politics: A Comparative Analysis of the Social Characteristics and Political Views of American Evangelical and Charismatic Christians," *Sociological Analysis,* forthcoming.

20. "America's Evangelicals"; Hunter, *American Evangelicalism,* pp. 49–60; Lyman A. Kellstedt, "Evangelicals and Political Realignment," paper presented at the conference, "Evangelical Political Involvement in the 1980s," Calvin College, Grand Rapids, Mich., October 17–18, 1986; Miller and Wattenberg, "Politics from the Pulpit."

21. Hunter, *American Evangelicalism,* pp. 7–8; George Marsden, "The Evangelical Denomination," in *Piety and Politics: Evangelicals and Fundamentalists Confront the World,* ed. Richard John Neuhaus and Michael Cromartie (Washington, D.C.: Ethics and Public Policy Center, 1987), pp. 55–68; A. James Reichley, "The Evangelical and Fundamentalist Revolt," in *Piety and Politics,* ed. Neuhaus and Cromartie, pp. 69–95.

22. John H. Simpson, "Moral Issues and Status Politics," in *The New Christian Right: Mobilization and Legitimation,* ed. Robert Liebman and Robert Wuthnow (New York: Aldine, 1983), pp. 188–207; J. Milton Yinger and Stephan J. Cutler, "The Moral Majority Viewed Sociologically," in *New Christian Politics,* ed. David G. Bromley and Anson Shupe (Macon, Ga.: Mercer University Press, 1984), pp. 69–90; Gary D. Gaddy, "Some Potential Causes and Consequences of the Use of Religious Broadcasts," in *New Christian Politics,* ed. Bromley and Shupe, pp. 117–128; James L. Guth, "Sex and the Single Issue Activist: Female Campaign Contributors in the 1982 Elections," paper presented at the meetings of Southern Political Science Association, Savannah, Ga., November 1–3, 1984; David Knoke, "Stratification and the Dimensions of American Political Orientations," *American Journal of Political Science* 23 (1979): 772–791; Himmelstein, "The Social Basis of Antifeminism"; Jeffrey K. Hadden and Charles E. Swann, *Prime Time Preachers: The Rising Power of Televangelism* (Reading, Mass.: Addison-Wesley, 1981). There has been considerable discussion over whether socioeconomic or cultural characteristics are most telling in

shaping social conservatism. See, for example, Charles L. Harper and Kevin Leicht, "Explaining the New Religious Right: Status Politics and Beyond," in *New Christian Politics*, ed. Bromley and Shupe, pp. 101–110; and Michael Wood and Michael Hughes, "The Moral Basis of Moral Reform: Status Discontent vs. Culture and Socialization as Explanations of Anti-Pornography Social Movement Adherence," *American Sociological Review* 49 (1984): 86–99.

23. William G. McLoughlin, *Revivals, Awakenings, and Reform: An Essay on Religion and Social Change in America, 1607–1977* (Chicago: University of Chicago Press, 1978); Ann Douglas, *The Feminization of American Culture* (New York: Knopf, 1977); A. James Reichley, *Religion in American Public Life* (Washington, D.C.: Brookings Institution, 1985).

24. Marsden, *Fundamentalism and American Culture*, p. 11.

25. Reichley, *Religion in American Public Life*.

26. The discussion of the transformation of evangelicalism in the following paragraphs draws on Marsden, *Fundamentalism and American Culture*; Hunter, *American Evangelicalism*; James A. Speer, "The New Christian Right and Its Parent Company: A Study in Political Contrasts," in *New Christian Politics*, ed. Bromley and Shupe, pp. 19–40; Gary Clabaugh, *Thunder on the Right: The Protestant Fundamentalists* (Chicago: Nelson-Hall, 1974).

27. The account of fundamentalism and evangelicalism since the 1920s draws on Jorstad, *Politics of Doomsday;* Leo P. Ribuffo, *The Old Christian Right* (Philadelphia: Temple University Press, 1983); Hunter, *American Evangelicalism;* Clabaugh, *Thunder on the Right;* and Speer, "New Christian Right."

28. Reichley, *Religion in American Public Life;* James L. Guth, "The New Christian Right," in *New Christian Right,* ed. Liebman and Wuthnow, pp. 31–45.

29. Carol Flake, *Redemptorama: Culture, Politics, and the New Evangelicalism* (New York: Penguin Books, 1984), p. 52, citing William Martin, *Texas Monthly,* September 1979.

30. "Northside Baptist Church and Dr. W. Jack Hudson Celebrating 30 Years of Service to the Carolinas," *Charlotte Observer,* September 6, 1984, special advertising supplement.

31. Hadden and Swann, *Prime Time Preachers*.

32. "Power, Glory, and Politics: Right-Wing Preachers Dominate the Dial," *Time,* February 17, 1986, pp. 62–69; Gaddy, "Causes and Consequences"; Razelle Frankl, *Televangelism: The Marketing of Popular Religion* (Carbondale, Ill.: Southern Illinois University Press, 1987); Jeffrey K. Hadden, "Religious Broadcasting and the Mobilization of

the New Christian Right," *Journal for the Scientific Study of Religion* 26 (1987): 1–24.

33. Robert C. Liebman, "Mobilizing the Moral Majority," in *New Christian Right*, ed. Liebman and Wuthnow, pp. 50–74; Guth, "New Christian Right."

34. Although evangelicals tended to vote Republican in presidential elections, survey data suggest that until the early 1980s their party loyalties were Democratic. Albert J. Menendez, *Religion at the Polls* (Philadelphia: Westminster Press, 1977); Kellstedt, "Evangelicals and Political Realignment."

35. Robert Wuthnow, "The Political Rebirth of American Evangelicals," in *New Christian Right*, ed. Liebman and Wuthnow, pp. 168–187; James L. Guth, "The Politics of Preachers: Southern Baptist Ministers and Christian Right Activism," in *New Christian Politics*, ed. Bromley and Shupe, pp. 235–250.

36. Speer, "New Christian Right."

37. D'Souza, *Falwell*, pp. 80–81.

38. D'Souza, *Falwell*; Fitzgerald, "A Disciplined, Charging Army."

39. The discussion in this and the following two paragraphs draws especially on Guth, "New Christian Right"; and Liebman, "Mobilizing the Moral Majority."

40. "A Tide of Born-Again Politics," *Newsweek*, September 15, 1980, pp. 28–36.

41. Anson Shupe and William A. Stacey, "Public and Clergy Sentiments toward the Moral Majority: Evidence from the Dallas–Fort Worth Metroplex," in *New Christian Politics*, ed. Bromley and Shupe, pp. 91–100. See also Anson Shupe and William A. Stacey, *Born-Again Politics and the Moral Majority: What Social Surveys Really Show* (New York: Edwin Mellen Press, 1982); and Hadden and Swann, *Prime Time Preachers*.

42. "A Tide of Born-Again Politics"; "America's Evangelicals"; Frank M. Newport and V. Lance Tarrance, Jr., "Evangelicals, Fundamentalists, and Political Issues in the 1984 Elections," *Election Politics* 1 (Winter 1983–1984): 2–6; Rothenberg and Newport, *Evangelical Voter*; D'Souza, *Falwell*, pp. 172–173; Reichley, "Evangelical and Fundamentalist Revolt." When *evangelical* or *fundamentalist* is defined more stringently, differences on social issues are more marked. A 1981 Roper Poll done for the National Broadcasting Company found that the 5 percent of respondents who scored "very high" on a fundamentalism scale opposed the ERA 60–28 percent (compared to 71–20 percent support among the quarter of respondents who scored

zero on the scale). Sixty-one percent of the fundamentalist group supported a law against all abortions in comparison to 9 percent of those who scored zero. National Broadcasting Company, "Sex, Profanity, and Violence: An Opinion Survey about Seventeen Television Programs," June 30, 1981.

43. James L. Guth, "Southern Baptist Clergy: Vanguard of the New Right," in *New Christian Right,* ed. Liebman and Wuthnow, pp. 118–132.

44. Thomas E. Mann and Norman J. Ornstein, "The Republican Surge in Congress," in *American Elections of 1980,* ed. Ranney, pp. 263–302; Stephen Johnson and Joseph B. Tamney, "The Christian Right and the 1980 Presidential Election," *Journal for the Scientific Study of Religion* 21 (1982): 123–131; Robert Zwier, "The New Christian Right and the 1980 Election," in *New Christian Politics,* ed. Bromley and Shupe, pp. 173–194; Richard V. Pierard and James L. Wright, "No Hoosier Hospitality for Humanism: The Moral Majority in Indiana," in *New Christian Politics,* ed. Bromley and Shupe, pp. 195–212; Seymour Martin Lipset and Earl Raab, "The Elections and the Evangelicals," *Commentary* 71 (March 1981): 25–31; Himmelstein and McRae, "Social Conservatism"; Seymour Martin Lipset, "The Revolt against Modernity," in *Mobilization, Center-Periphery Structures, and Nation-Building,* ed. Per Torsvik (Bergen: Universitetsforlaget, 1981); Smidt, "Evangelicals in Presidential Elections"; Miller and Wattenberg, "Politics from the Pulpit." My own analysis of 1980 National Election Study data suggests that neither religiosity nor born-again experience had much influence on whether or not Carter voters in 1976 defected to Reagan in 1980. Among 1976 Carter voters 61.9 percent of those claiming a born-again experience voted for Carter in 1980 and 21.6 percent went over to Reagan; among those not claiming a born-again experience the comparable figures were 61.1 percent and 24.1 percent. Of those 1976 Carter voters who said religion gave them a great deal of guidance, 65.7 percent voted for Carter in 1980 and 22.9 percent voted for Reagan. Among those who said religion was not important to them only 42.7 percent voted for Carter again, with 22.7 percent voting for Reagan and 16.4 percent for independent John Anderson.

45. *The Elections of 1984,* ed. Michael Nelson (Washington, D.C.: Congressional Quarterly, 1985), p. 290; Chubb and Peterson, *New Direction in American Politics,* p. 46; *New York Times,* November 6, 1986, p. A29; Smidt, "Evangelicals in Presidential Elections"; Kellstedt, "Evangelicals and Political Realignment." The political shift among

evangelicals as a religious group ought not to be confounded with that within the South as a region, though evangelicals represent a disproportionate percentage of the electorate in the South. If anything, the shift is more marked among evangelicals outside the South. The biggest shift to Reagan in 1984 came among nonsouthern evangelicals; moreover, turnout among this group rose in 1984 whereas it fell among southern evangelicals. By 1986 evangelicals may have been drifting back to the Democratic party in terms of party identification; but they were still more likely than nonevangelicals to support Republican presidential candidates, a difference that stayed significant even when region and party identification were controlled. Again, see Smidt, "Evangelicals in Presidential Elections."

46. "Power, Glory, and Politics"; *Freedom Writer,* October 1986; *Washington Times,* November 14, 1986, p. 2A.

47. John Herbers, "Reagan Beginning to Get Top Billing in Christian Bookstores for Policies," *New York Times,* September 28, 1984, p. A23.

48. *Charlotte Observer,* June 13, 1984, p. 1E; *Raleigh News and Observer,* June 17, 1984, p. 25A; *New York Times,* June 15, 1986, section 4, p. 6; *Boston Globe,* June 15, 1986, p. 11; Guth, "Political Converts."

49. Liebman, "Mobilizing of the Moral Majority," p. 57. See also Charles Tilly, *From Mobilization to Revolution;* and John D. McCarthy and Mayer N. Zald, "Resource Mobilization and Social Movements: A Partial Theory," *American Journal of Sociology* 82 (1977): 1212–1239.

50. Wuthnow, "Political Rebirth of American Evangelicals."

51. Liebman, "Mobilizing of the Moral Majority"; idem, "The Making of the New Christian Right," in *New Christian Right,* ed. Liebman and Wuthnow, pp. 227–238.

52. Corwin Smidt, "Partisanship of American Evangelicals: Changing Patterns over the Past Decade," paper presented at the meetings of the Society for the Scientific Study of Religion, Washington, D.C., November 14–16, 1986; *New York Times,* March 10, 1988, p. A26. Among religious contributors to conservative political action committees in the early 1980s, strong support for the Moral Majority was limited to a few fundamentalist groups. See James L. Guth and John C. Green, "The Moralizing Minority: Christian Right Support Among Political Contributors," *Social Science Quarterly* 68 (1987): 598–610.

53. Mansbridge, *Why We Lost the ERA,* pp. 74–77. See Ginsburg, *Contested Lives,* for a somewhat similar shift in antiabortion ranks in North Dakota.

54. Smidt, "Partisanship of American Evangelicals."

Chapter Five

1. Frances Fox Piven and Richard A. Cloward, *The New Class War: Reagan's Attack on the Welfare State and Its Consequences* (New York: Pantheon Books, 1982), pp. xi, 9, 13; Ferguson and Rogers, *Right Turn,* pp. 46, 109; Jospeh G. Peschek, *Policy-Planning Organizations: Elite Agendas and America's Rightward Turn* (Philadelphia: Temple University Press, 1987). See also Dan Clawson and Mary Ann Clawson, "Reagan or Business? Foundations of the New Conservatism," in *The Structure of Power in America: The Corporate Elite as Ruling Class,* ed. Michael Schwartz (New York: Holmes and Meier, 1987), pp. 201–217.

2. Edsall, *New Politics of Inequality,* pp. 13–14.

3. Alan Wolfe, "Toward a Political Sociology of Reaganism," *Contemporary Sociology* 16 (1987): 31.

4. For a summary of these and related indicators, see Ferguson and Rogers, *Right Turn,* pp. 79–82; and Samuel Bowles, David M. Gordon, and Thomas E. Weisskopf, *Beyond the Waste Land: A Democratic Alternative to Economic Decline* (Garden City, N.Y.: Doubleday, 1983), pp. 19–61.

5. The argument in the following paragraphs draws especially on Bowles, Gordon, and Weisskopf, *Beyond the Waste Land.*

6. Ferguson and Rogers, *Right Turn,* p. 81.

7. Samuel Bowles, "The Post-Keynesian Capital-Labor Stalemate," *Socialist Review* 12 (September-October 1982): 45–72.

8. Piven and Cloward, *New Class War,* pp. 14–15.

9. Ferguson and Rogers, *Right Turn,* pp. 51–57.

10. Bowles, Gordon, and Weisskopf, *Beyond the Waste Land,* pp. 84–91; Piven and Cloward, *New Class War,* pp. 13–39.

11. Dan Clawson, Karen Johnson, and John Schall, "Fighting Union Busting in the 1980s," *Radical America* 16 (1982): 45–64; Dan Georgine, "From Brass Knuckles to Briefcases: The Modern Art of Union Busting," in *The Big Business Reader,* ed. Mark Green and Robert Massie, Jr. (New York: Pilgrim Press, 1980), pp. 91–110; Thomas Ferguson and Joel Rogers, "The Knights of the Roundtable," *The Nation* 229 (1979): 620–628. For a general discussion of the strategies corporations used to cut labor costs, see Bennett Harrison and Barry Bluestone, *The Great U-Turn: Corporate Restructuring and the Polarizing of America* (New York: Basic Books, 1988).

12. Silk and Vogel, *Ethics and Profits.*

13. Silk and Vogel, *Ethics and Profits,* p. 52; Michael Useem, "Company vs. Classwide Rationality in Corporate Decision-Making," *Administrative Science Quarterly* 27 (1982): 199–226; idem, "Business and

Politics in the United States and the United Kingdom," *Theory and Society* 12 (1983): 281–308; idem, *The Inner Circle: Large Corporations and the Rise of Business Political Activity in the U.S. and the U.K.* (New York: Oxford, 1984); Murray Weidenbaum, "The High Cost of Government Regulation," *Challenge*, November-December 1981, pp. 32–39.

14. Silk and Vogel, *Ethics and Profits*, pp. 57–58.

15. Ibid., p. 75.

16. Ibid., pp. 104, 126.

17. "The Reindustrialization of America," *Business Week*, June 30, 1980, pp. 56–114; Silk and Vogel, *Ethics and Profits*, pp. 75–101.

18. Edsall, *New Politics of Inequality*, p. 128. Good overviews of the political mobilization of business in the 1970s and 1980s include Ferguson and Rogers, *Right Turn*, pp. 78–219; Edsall, *New Politics of Inequality*, pp. 107–140; Blumenthal, *The Rise of the Counter-Establishment*, pp. 32–86; Saloma, *Ominous Politics*, pp. 7–37, 63–80; Pines, *Back to Basics*, pp. 31–98.

19. Grant McConnell, *Private Power and American Democracy* (New York: Random House, 1966), pp. 336–368; G. William Domhoff, *The Powers That Be: Processes of Ruling-Class Domination in America* (New York: Random House, 1979), pp. 53–60. Interestingly, corporate officials sometimes agree about the minimal role of the Chambers of Commerce and the National Association of Manufacturers in coordinating business political activity. These organizations may be good for exchanging information, they say, but not for organized political action. Conversations with Don Hendriksen, former vice president for government relations at Arco, and John Burton, a public-affairs officer first at Fluor Corporation and later at CooperVision, Sloan Workshop on Political Technology, Claremont, California, January 6, 1988.

20. Ferguson and Rogers, "Knights of the Roundtable," p. 621.

21. Ibid.; Peter Slavin, "The Business Roundtable: New Lobbying Arm of Big Business," *Business and Society Review*, Winter 1975–1976, pp. 28–32; Edsall, *New Politics of Inequality*, pp. 120–123; G. William Domhoff, *Who Rules America Now?* (Englewood Cliffs, N.J.: Prentice-Hall, 1983), pp. 135–136; Blumenthal, *Rise of the Counter-Establishment*, pp. 69–80; Kim McQuaid, *Big Business and Presidential Power from FDR to Reagan* (New York: Morrow, 1982), pp. 284–305.

22. See Chapter 6 for a more detailed discussion of the impact of campaign reform laws and of electoral politics in general. In fact, the business elite played a major role in framing the Federal Election Campaign Act of 1971. See Tom Koenig, "Business Support for Dis-

closure of Corporate Campaign Contributions: An Instructive Paradox," in Schwartz, *Structure of Power in America,* pp. 82–96.

23. Gary C. Jacobson, "The Republican Advantage in Campaign Finance," in *New Direction in American Politics,* ed. Chubb and Peterson, p. 147; Edsall, *New Politics of Inequality,* p. 131; Useem, "Business and Politics," p. 299.

24. Dan Clawson, Alan Neustadtl, and James Bearden, "The Logic of Business Unity: Corporate Contributions to the 1980 Congressional Elections," *American Sociological Review* 51 (1986): 810.

25. Common Cause, *1972 Federal Campaign Finances* (Washington, D.C.: Common Cause, 1973); idem, *1976 Federal Campaign Finances* (Washington, D.C.: Common Cause, 1977); Federal Elections Commission, computer tape of PAC contributions to candidates for federal office, 1981; Gary C. Jacobson, "The Effects of Campaign Spending in Congressional Elections," *American Political Science Review* 72 (1978): 469–471. Dan Clawson provided me with the data on the changing patterns of corporate PAC contributions to congressional candidates. Of course, a preference for incumbents could reflect an ideological strategy rather than a pragmatic one if indeed most corporate money so targeted went to incumbents in close races and hence reflected an intent to keep politically suitable persons in office. In fact, however, such money went disproportionately to incumbents who carried 60 percent of the vote or more in the previous election. This suggests the goal was not to save embattled incumbents with ideologies favorable to business but to win access to entrenched incumbents with considerable clout. See Dan Clawson and Alan Neustadtl, "Corporate Political Strategies: Classwide Rationality and Conservatism in PAC Contributions to the 1980 Congressional Elections," unpublished paper.

26. Clawson, Neustadtl, and Bearden, "Logic of Business Unity," p. 801. See also Stuart Rothenberg and Richard R. Roldan, *Business PACs and Ideology: A Study of Contributions in the 1982 Elections* (Washington, D.C.: Free Congress Research and Education Foundation, 1983).

27. For a lucid summary of different arguments about the bases of political divisions among corporations, see Val Burris, "The Political Partisanship of American Business: A Study of Corporate Political Action Committees," *American Sociological Review* 52 (1987): 732–744.

28. Dan Clawson, Allen Kaufman, and Alan Neustadtl, "Corporate PACs for a New Pax Americana," *Insurgent Sociologist* 13, no. 1–2 (1985): 63–77; Clawson and Neustadtl, "Corporate Political Strategies"; Burris, "Partisanship of American Business." In the first two

works the measures of centrality included total sales, foreign sales, capital intensity, and director interlocks. Only the last of these was significantly related to contribution strategy, with the more inter-locked corporations more likely to support incumbents. In Burris's work the measures of centrality comprised these as well as profit rate, an oligopoly index, Business Roundtable membership, and several others. Only capital intensity was significantly related to contribution strategy, and then weakly. In both sets of studies the factor that best distinguished contribution strategies was relationship to govern-ment: corporations in traditional regulated industries with long-standing ties to specific government agencies and congressional com-mittees and those with substantial government contracts were most likely to support incumbents. The finding of Clawson and his co-authors that the more interlocked corporations were most likely to pursue a contribution strategy rooted in a narrow company rational-ity runs counter to the idea that inner-circle corporations are apt to take a broad class view of politics.

29. Clawson, Neustadtl, and Bearden, "Logic of Business Unity," p. 803.

30. Elizabeth Drew, *Power and Money* (New York: Macmillan, 1983); Edsall, *New Politics of Inequality*, pp. 136–138; Alan Neustadtl and Dan Clawson, "Corporate Political Groupings: PAC Contributions to the 1980 Congressional Elections," *American Sociological Review* 53 (1988): 172–190. There are of course less formal modes of coordination. The chief contributions officers of individual corporations do not make decisions about political contributions in a vacuum. They share data bases and sometimes meet to listen to and discuss candidates. Con-versations with Don Hendriksen.

31. David Vogel, "Business's 'New Class' Struggle," *The Nation* 229 (1979): 609, 625–628; Ann Crittenden, "The Economic Wind's Blow-ing toward the Right—for Now," *New York Times*, July 16, 1978, sec-tion 3, pp. 1, 9; Richard Goldstein, "The War for America's Mind," *The Village Voice*, June 8, 1982, pp. 1, 11–20; Useem, *Inner Circle*, pp. 129–132.

32. I noticed the ad in question in *Commentary*, June 1980. The re-sults of the survey itself are from "The Vital Consensus: American Attitudes on Economic Growth," provided by Union Carbide on my request.

33. See, for example, Domhoff, *Powers That Be*, pp. 61–127. For a more thorough analysis, see Peschek, *Policy-Planning Organizations*.

34. William E. Simon, *A Time for Truth* (New York: Berkley, 1978), pp. 208–257; quotations at pp. 245, 248, 249. The growing power of

the New Class, its ideological unity, and its hostility to business were articles of faith among neoconservative intellectuals, who contributed to developing an image of America as a postindustrial society in which businessmen play a declining role. See the essays in *The Third Century,* ed. Seymour Martin Lipset (Stanford: Hoover Institution Press, 1979) and *The New Class?* ed. B. Bruce-Briggs (New York: McGraw-Hill, 1979). See also Peter Steinfels, *The Neoconservatives: The Men Who Are Changing America's Politics* (New York: Simon and Schuster, 1979), pp. 188–213. For the best analysis of the actual political beliefs of the New Class, see Steven Brint, "The Political Attitudes of Professionals," *Annual Review of Sociology* 11 (1985): 389–414; and idem, " 'New Class' and Cumulative Trend Explanations of the Liberal Political Attitudes of Professionals," *American Journal of Sociology* 90 (1984): 30–71.

35. Crittenden, "Economic Wind's Blowing toward the Right"; Malcolm Scully, "More than GOP's 'Government in Exile,' " *Chronicle of Higher Education* 21 (December 15, 1980): 3; Peter Stone, "Conservative Brain Trust," *New York Times Magazine,* May 10, 1981, p. 18; "A Think Tank at the Brink," *Newsweek,* July 7, 1986, p. 87; "The Tale of Two Right-Wing 'Think Tanks,' " *Group Research Reports* 25 (1986): 22. Unpublished sources of expenditure figures cited here and in the following paragraphs include annual reports for the Heritage Foundation and the Brookings Institution; and conversations with public-affairs officers for AEI and the Hoover Institution. My thanks again to Dan Clawson for supplying many of these statistics. By 1988 at least one major corporation, Arco, which runs the largest corporate foundation, had decided it had given too much to right-wing think tanks and was moving back to the center. Arco, however, has a relatively liberal reputation among major corporations. Conversation with George Dunn, director of public affairs at Arco, Sloan Workshop on Political Technology, Claremont, California, January 6, 1988.

36. Crittenden, "Economic Wind's Blowing toward the Right"; Janet Hook, "Georgetown's 'Intellectual Brokerage House,' " *Chronicle of Higher Education* 21 (December 8, 1980): 3–4; Stewart McBride, "Leaning to the Right," *Christian Science Monitor,* April 2, 1980; Jack McCurdy, "A Reagan 'Brain Trust': Hoover Institution Finds It's in the Public Eye," *Chronicle of Higher Education* 21 (December 1, 1980): 3.

37. Morton Kondracke, "The Heritage Model," *The New Republic* 183 (December 20, 1980): 10; Dom Bonafede, "Issue-Oriented Heritage Foundation Hitches Its Wagon to Reagan's Star," *National Journal,* March 20, 1982, pp. 502–507; "Heritage Foundation Booms on the Right," *Group Research Report* 25 (1986): 22.

38. The list included the Institute for Contemporary Studies, Center for Law and Economics, Center for Public Choice, Center for the Study of the Economy and the State, International Institute for Economic Research, Center for Free Enterprise, Center for Research in Government Policy and Business, Ethics and Public Policy Center, Center for the Study of American Business, Institute for Foreign Policy Analysis, National Strategy Information Center, the Manhattan Institute, the Lehrman Institute, and many others. Dan Morgan, "Conservatives: A Well-Financed Network," *Washington Post*, January 4, 1981, pp. A1, A14.

39. Karen Rothmyer, "Citizen Scaife," *Columbia Journalism Review*, July-August 1981, pp. 41–50; David Warner, "Scaife: Financier of the Right," *Pittsburgh Post-Gazette*, April 20, 1981; Bernard Weinraub, "Foundations Support Conservatism by Financing Scholars and Groups," *New York Times*, January 20, 1981, p. 17.

40. Peter Stone, "The Counter-Intelligentsia," *Village Voice*, October 27, 1979, pp. 14–19; Blumenthal, *Rise of the Counter-Establishment*, pp. 66–68.

41. Chris Welles, "The Supply-Side Cabal," *This World*, September 20, 1981, pp. 8–12; Geoffrey Norman, "Neo-Conservatism: An Idea Whose Time Is Now," *Esquire*, February 13, 1979, pp. 23–42; Walter Goodman, "Irving Kristol: Patron Saint of the New Right," *New York Times Magazine*, December 6, 1981, p. 90; Stone, "Counter-Intelligentsia." For detailed accounts of the development of supply-side economics, see Blumenthal, *Rise of the Counter-Establishment*, pp. 166–209; Stockman, *Triumph of Politics*, pp. 30–76; and Brooks, "Annals of Finance," pp. 97–150.

42. Peter Stone, "The I.E.A.—Teaching the Right Stuff," *The Nation* 233 (1981): 231–235; Goldstein, "War for America's Mind"; Blumenthal, *Rise of the Counter-Establishment*, pp. 66–68. After noting that as many as sixty conservative campus papers began publication in the early 1980s, one sympathetic observer candidly admitted, "Without IEA there would not be a conservative student newspaper movement to speak of." Stephen Weeks, "Notes from the Underground," *National Review* 38 (September 26, 1986): 36–40.

43. Bonafede, "Issue-Oriented Heritage Foundation"; *Mandate for Leadership: Policy Management in a Conservative Administration*, ed. Charles Heatherly (Washington, D.C.: Heritage Foundation, 1981); Blumenthal, *Rise of the Counter-Establishment*, pp. 292–296.

44. Blumenthal, *Rise of the Counter-Establishment*, pp. 35–37, 328.

45. Alexander Haig, Reagan's first secretary of state, was president of United Technologies, a director of several other corporations,

and a member of the Council on Foreign Relations. George Schultz, his successor, was president of the Bechtel Corporation and a director of the Council on Foreign Relations. Caspar Weinberger, Reagan's first defense secretary, was a vice president of Bechtel and a member of the Trilateral Commission. Finally, Donald Regan, first Reagan's treasury secretary and later his chief of staff, was head of Merrill Lynch, a trustee of the Committee for Economic Development, and a member of the Council on Foreign Relations. The first three all had prior governmental experience. See Domhoff, *Who Rules America Now?* pp. 139–140.

46. As I noted in Chapter 3, conservatives never lacked business support. What changed from the 1950s to the 1970s was the breadth of support. Where once one could identify an idiosyncratic business Right of rich individuals, family-owned companies, and a few corporations distinct from a corporate mainstream, by the late 1970s that mainstream too had moved right. See Forster and Epstein, *Danger on the Right,* for data on business contributions to right-wing groups in the 1950s and early 1960s.

47. Blumenthal, *Rise of the Counter-Establishment,* p. 33.

48. William Spinrad, "Power in Local Communities," in *Class, Status, and Power,* ed. Reinhard Bendix and Seymour Martin Lipset, 2d ed. rev. (New York: Free Press, 1966), p. 229.

49. Daniel Bell, *End of Ideology,* p. 45. See also idem, *Radical Right,* pp. 21–22.

50. Robert A. Dahl, "A Critique of the Ruling Elite Model," in *C. Wright Mills and the Power Elite,* ed. G. William Domhoff and Hoyt B. Ballard (Boston: Beacon Press, 1968), pp. 25–36; Ivar Berg and Mayer Zald, "Business and Society," *Annual Review of Sociology* 4 (1978): 137; Bell, *End of Ideology,* pp. 39–45, 66; Arnold M. Rose, *The Power Structure: Political Process in American Society* (New York: Oxford University Press, 1967), pp. 101–102. For a recent revival of pluralism, see David Vogel, "The New Political Science of Corporate Power," *The Public Interest* 87 (Spring 1987): 63–79.

51. Edsall, *New Politics of Inequality;* Piven and Cloward, *New Class War;* Blumenthal, *Rise of the Counter-Establishment.* The titles themselves imply a pluralist approach. Of the major works on the politics of big business in the 1970s and 1980s, only Ferguson and Rogers, *Right Turn,* avoids assuming that big business sat on its hands politically for years before the 1970s.

52. Useem, "Classwide Rationality," p. 221; idem, *Inner Circle.*

53. Useem, *Inner Circle,* pp. 34–48.

54. The instrumentalist/structuralist distinction was articulated in

the mid-1970s in two articles by Erik Olin Wright and his colleagues. See David Gold, Clarence Y. H. Lo, and Erik Olin Wright, "Some Recent Developments in Marxist Theories of the Capitalist State," *Monthly Review* 27 (October 1975): 29–43, and 27 (November 1975): 36–51; and Gosta Esping-Andersen, Rodger Friedland, and Erik Olin Wright, "Modes of Class Struggle and the Capitalist State," *Kapitalistate* 4–5 (1976): 186–220. They certainly did not mean these categories to be static or final; indeed, in articulating them, these writers also sought to transcend them. In general, Marxist theories of the state and the broader discussion of which they are a part have for some time gone beyond the simple instrumentalist/structuralist dichotomy by stressing the independent impact of state structures and the range of possible capitalist states, the contradictory nature of the relationship between the state and capitalist relations of production, and the role of class struggle. For a general discussion, see Martin Carnoy, *The State and Political Theory* (Princeton: Princeton University Press, 1984), and Bob Jessop, "Recent Theories of the Capitalist State," *Cambridge Journal of Economics* 1 (1977): 353–373. See also Fred Block, "Beyond Corporate Liberalism," *Social Problems* 24 (1977): 352–361; idem, "The Ruling Class Does Not Rule: Notes on the Marxist Theory of the State," *Socialist Revolution* 7 (1977): 6–28; and Theda Skocpol, "Political Response to Capitalist Crisis: Neo-Marxist Theories of the State and the Case of the New Deal," *Politics and Society* 10 (1980): 155–201. The instrumentalist/structuralist dichotomy is also problematic because virtually no one has embraced the instrumentalist label. Domhoff in particular has rejected it vehemently. See G. William Domhoff, "I Am Not an 'Instrumentalist': A Reply to *Kapitalistate* Critics," *Kapitalistate* 4–5 (1976): 221–224. Although the terms thus have limited utility in describing contemporary ruling-class theories of the state, they still denote with some accuracy two ideal-typical images of the political role of the capitalist class, two poles toward which a diversity of theories of the state inevitably gravitate.

55. Nicos Poulantzas, "The Problem of the Capitalist State," in *Ideology in Social Science*, ed. Robin Blackburn (New York: Random House, 1973), pp. 238–253; quotations at pp. 245–247.

56. Domhoff, *Higher Circles*; idem, *Powers That Be*; idem, *Who Rules America Now?*; James Weinstein, *The Corporate Ideal in the Liberal State* (Boston: Beacon Press, 1968); Gabriel Kolko, *The Triumph of Conservatism* (Chicago: Quadrangle, 1967); Lawrence Shoup and William Minter, *Imperial Brain Trust: The Council on Foreign Relations and United States Foreign Policy* (New York: Monthly Review Press, 1977).

57. For other works on policy-planning organizations, see Pes-

chek, *Policy-Planning Organizations;* Thomas R. Dye, *Who's Running America? The Conservative Years,* 4th ed. (Englewood Cliffs, N.J.: Prentice-Hall, 1986); Shoup and Minter, *Imperial Brain Trust;* Robert Collins, *The Business Response to Keynes, 1929–1964* (New York: Columbia University Press, 1981); McQuaid, *Big Business and Presidential Power.*

58. Domhoff, *Higher Circles,* pp. 217–218.

59. Gold, Lo, and Wright, "Some Recent Developments," p. 48.

60. See, for example, Erik Olin Wright, *Class, Crisis and the State* (New York: Schocken Books, 1979), pp. 111–179; Claus Offe, *Contradictions of the Welfare State* (Cambridge: MIT Press, 1984).

61. David Vogel, "Why Businessmen Distrust their State," *British Journal of Political Science* 8 (1978): 45–78. The combination of early democracy and late bureaucracy also helps to explain the late and uneven development of the U.S. welfare state. See Weir, Orloff, and Skocpol, *Politics of Social Policy.*

62. I mean this point to dovetail with major criticisms of the notion of corporate liberalism. See, for example, Block, "Beyond Corporate Liberalism," and Skocpol, "Political Response to Capitalist Crisis." See also Collins, *Business Response to Keynes.*

63. McQuaid, *Big Business and Presidential Power,* perhaps comes closest to capturing the image I have in mind.

Chapter Six

1. Walter Dean Burnham, *Critical Elections and the Mainsprings of American Politics* (New York: Norton, 1970); idem, *The Current Crisis in American Politics* (New York: Oxford University Press, 1982); Sundquist, *Dynamics of the Party System;* Bruce A. Campbell and Richard J. Trilling, eds. *Realignment in American Politics: Toward a Theory* (Austin: University of Texas Press, 1980; *The Evolution of American Electoral Systems,* ed. Paul Kleppner (Westport, Conn.: Greenwood Press, 1981); Jerome M. Clubb, William H. Flanigan, and Nancy H. Zingale, *Partisan Realignment: Voters, Parties, and Government in American History* (Beverly Hills, Ca.: Sage Publications, 1980).

2. For critical perspectives on the notion of realignment, see Clubb, Flanigan, and Zingale, *Partisan Realignment;* David H. Nixon, "Methodological Issues in the Study of Realignment," in *Realignment in American Politics,* ed. Campbell and Trilling, pp. 52–65; Ferguson and Rogers, *Right Turn,* pp. 41–46.

3. Sundquist, *Dynamics of the Party System.*

4. K. Phillips, *Emerging Republican Majority,* was one of the first to voice this idea. See Chapter 4 of the present volume for a discussion

of theories that stress the emergence of new alignments in the 1960s and 1970s.

5. See *Statistical Abstracts of the United States, 1986* (Washington, D.C.: Government Printing Office, 1987), pp. 250–252, for data on governorships and state legislatures. Even after Reagan's 1984 landslide victory Republicans had only slightly narrowed the gap in state legislative seats. The Democratic edge in governorships varied erratically through much of the 1980s.

6. R. W. Apple, "Voters' Rebuff to Reagan's Vision," *New York Times,* November 6, 1986, p. 1.

7. For data on changes in the social bases of support for the major parties, see Abramson, Aldrich, and Rohde, *Change and Continuity,* p. 105; Everett Carll Ladd, Jr., "Is Election '84 Really a Class Struggle?" *Public Opinion,* April-May 1984, pp. 41–47, 51; and Nelson, *Elections of 1984,* pp. 106, 290. In 1984, according to the CBS News/*New York Times* poll, Mondale got the votes of 44 percent of Catholics versus 26 percent of white Protestants, 53 percent of those earning under $12,500 versus 31 percent of those earning over $50,000, 49 percent of those with less than a high-school education versus 40 percent of college graduates. The *Washington Post*/ABC News exit poll gave Mondale the vote of 44 percent of Catholics and 33 percent of Protestants, 51 percent of those without a high-school diploma and 37 percent of college graduates. In the 1986 midterm House elections only 36 percent of northerners from households with at least one union member voted Republican; 55 percent of that group had voted for Reagan in 1984. Nonunion Catholics, however, gave Republicans a 53 percent majority in both years. See Frederick T. Steeper and John R. Petrocik, "Ratification of the Reagan Realignment: The 1986 Election," *Election Politics* 4 (Winter 1986–1987): 10–13, and John R. Petrocik, "Realignment: New Party Coalitions and the Nationalization of the South," *Journal of Politics* 49 (1987): 347–375.

8. For summaries of public-opinion data, see Seymour Martin Lipset, "The Economy, Elections, and Public Opinion," *Tocqueville Review* 5 (1983): 431–470; Everett Carll Ladd, Jr., Marilyn Potter, Linda Basilick, Sally Daniels, and Dana Suszkiw, "The Polls: Taxing and Spending," *Public Opinion Quarterly* 43 (1979): 126–135; Donald Granberg and Beth Wellman Granberg, "Abortion Attitudes, 1965–1980: Trends and Determinants," *Family Planning Perspectives* 12 (1980): 250–261; "The 70's: Decade of Second Thoughts," *Public Opinion,* December-January 1980, pp. 19–42; Miller and Shanks, "Policy Directions and Presidential Leadership," pp. 299–356; John Magney, "Mountains, Molehills, and Media Hypes: The Curious Case of the New Conserv-

atism," *Working Papers*, May-June 1979, pp. 28–34; Warren E. Miller, "A New Context for Presidential Politics: The Reagan Legacy," *Political Behavior* 9 (1987): 91–113; and *Public Opinion*, March-April 1987, pp. 21–29, and November-December 1987, pp. 30–40. For analysis of the source of Republican gains, see Miller, "New Context for Presidential Politics." For discussions of the political effectiveness of conservative groups, see Loch Johnson and Charles S. Bullock III, "The New Religious Right and the 1980 Congressional Elections," paper presented at the annual meeting of the Southwestern Political Science Association, San Antonio, Tex., March 17–21, 1982; Seymour Martin Lipset and Earl Raab, "The Elections and the Evangelicals," *Commentary* 71 (March 1981): 25–31; Michael J. Robinson, "The Media in 1980: Was the Message the Message?" in *American Elections of 1980*, ed. Ranney, pp. 177–211; Marjorie Randon Hershey, "Single-Issue Groups and Political Campaigns: Six Senatorial Races and the Pro-Life Challenge in 1980," paper presented at the annual meeting of the Midwest Political Science Association, 1981; "Organized Right Took a Beating in the Elections," *Group Research Report* 25 (1986): 33.

9. Cavanagh and Sundquist, "New Two-Party System," p. 43.

10. Ibid., p. 46; Steeper and Petrocik, "Ratification of the Reagan Realignment." See also "Special Issue: The State of Public Opinion in the States," *Election Politics* 5 (Winter 1977–1978).

11. Norman E. Nie, Sidney Verba, and John R. Petrocik, "The Decline of Partisanship," in *Controversies in Voting Behavior*, ed. Richard G. Niemi and Herbert F. Weisberg, 2d ed. (Washington, D.C.: Congressional Quarterly, 1984), pp. 496–518; Seymour Martin Lipset, "The Elections, the Economy, and Public Opinion," *PS* (Winter 1985): 35; Arthur Sanders, "Political Parties and the Mass Media," *Election Politics* 3 (Fall 1986): 21–25.

12. John A. Ferejohn and Morris P. Fiorina, "Incumbency and Realignment in Congressional Elections," in *New Direction in American Politics*, ed. Chubb and Peterson, pp. 91–116; *Public Opinion*, January-February, 1989, p. 11.

13. Nelson, *Elections of 1984*, pp. 106, 290; *New York Times*, November 6, 1986, p. A29.

14. George Gallup, Jr., *The Gallup Poll: Public Opinion 1987* (Wilmington, Del.: Scholarly Resources, 1988), pp. 6–9, 123–135, 235–237.

15. Ferguson and Rogers, *Right Turn*, p. 34.

16. Gregory B. Markus, "The Impact of Personal and National Economic Conditions on the Presidential Vote: A Pooled Cross-Sectional Analysis," unpublished paper; Lipset, "The Economy, Elec-

tions, and Public Opinion." See also D. Roderick Kiewiet, *Macro-Economics and Micro-Politics: The Electoral Effects of Economic Issues* (Chicago: University of Chicago Press, 1983); Morris P. Fiorina, *Retrospective Voting in American National Elections* (New Haven: Yale University Press, 1981); and Donald R. Kinder and D. Roderick Kiewiet, "Economic Discontent and Political Behavior: The Role of Personal Grievances and Collective Economic Judgments in Congressional Voting," *American Journal of Political Science* 23 (1979): 495–517.

17. Ferguson and Rogers, *Right Turn*, pp. 27, 34; Markus, "Impact of Economic Conditions"; William Schneider, "An Uncertain Consensus," *National Journal*, November 10, 1984, pp. 2130–2132. See also Paul J. Quirk, "The Economy: Economists, Electoral Politics, and Reagan Economics," in *Elections of 1984*, ed. Nelson, pp. 155–187; D. Roderick Kiewiet and Douglas Rivers, "The Economic Basis of Reagan's Appeal," in *New Direction in American Politics*, ed. Chubb and Peterson, pp. 69–90.

18. Nelson, *Elections of 1984*, pp. 106, 290; Kellstedt, "Evangelicals and Political Realignment"; Smidt, "Partisanship of American Evangelicals"; *New York Times*, November 6, 1986, p. A29.

19. Sundquist, *Dynamics of the Party System*, pp. 245–274; "Right-Wing Drive to Control State Houses," *Southern Exposure*, January-February 1985, pp. 6–7; Steeper and Petrocik, "Ratification of the Reagan Realignment."

20. Cavanagh and Sundquist, "New Two-Party System," p. 46. Given the general shift of white southerners into the GOP and the disproportionate number of evangelicals in the South, it is tempting to see the religious shift as an artifact of the regional one. However, this is not the case. Evangelicals outside the South moved toward the Republican party as much as, or more than, their Southern counterparts. See Smidt, "Evangelicals in Presidential Elections."

21. George Gallup, Jr., *The Gallup Poll: Public Opinion 1986* (Wilmington, Del.: Scholarly Resources, 1987), p. 100; idem, *Public Opinion 1987*, p. 322.

22. Cavanagh and Sundquist, "New Two-Party System" pp. 46, 48–49; Gallup, *Public Opinion 1987*, pp. 7, 124, 236.

23. Gallup Poll, reported in *Raleigh News and Observer*, August 26, 1984, p. 15A; results of American Council on Education survey of college freshmen reported in *New York Times*, October 31, 1986. See also "The Conservative Student," *Newsweek on Campus*, March 1985, pp. 6–14. For a discussion of the College Republicans, see Crocker Coulson, "Lost Generation: The Politics of Youth," *The New Republic* 195 (December 1, 1986): 21–25.

24. Charles O. Jones, "The Republican Challenge," *Society* 21 (July-August, 1984): 21–24. The following argument is similar to that in Robert Kuttner, *The Life of the Party: Democratic Prospects in 1988 and Beyond* (New York: Viking, 1987), pp. 72–108.

25. Gary Jacobson and Samuel Kernell, "Strategy and Choice in the 1982 Elections," in *Controversies in Voting Behavior*, ed. Niemi and Weisberg, p. 240. See also Gregory B. Markus and Philip E. Converse, "A Dynamic Simultaneous Equation Model of Electoral Choice," in *Controversies in Voting Behavior*, ed. Niemi and Weisberg, pp. 132–153.

26. Gary C. Jacobson, "The Republican Advantage in Campaign Finance," in *New Direction in American Politics*, ed. Chubb and Peterson, pp. 143–174.

27. A. James Reichley, "The Rise of National Parties," in *New Direction in American Politics*, pp. 175–200; Jacobson, "Republican Advantage"; Edsall, *New Politics of Inequality*, pp. 67–106; idem, "Republican America," *New York Review of Books*, April 24, 1986, pp. 3–6; Larry J. Sabato, *The Rise of the Political Consultants* (New York: Basic Books, 1981), pp. 220–263; David C. Adamany, "Political Parties in the 1980s," in *Money and Politics in the United States: Financing Elections in the 1980s*, ed. Michael J. Malbin (Washington, D.C.: American Enterprise Institute, 1984), pp. 70–121; for data on party fund-raising, see Malbin, *Money and Politics*, pp. 277–311.

28. Drew, *Power and Money*; Jacobson, "Republican Advantage."

29. Jacobson, "Republican Advantage"; idem, "Congress: Politics after a Landslide without Coattails," in *Elections of 1984*, ed. Nelson, pp. 215–238; idem, "Money in the 1980 and 1982 Congressional Elections," in Malbin, *Money and Politics*, pp. 38–69. Robert Kuttner, "Fat and Sassy," *The New Republic* 196 (February 23, 1987): 21–23.

30. Kuttner, "Fat and Sassy"; Alan Ehrenhalt, "Technology, Strategy Bring New Campaign Era," *Congressional Quarterly* 43 (1985): 2559–2565; Bob Davis, "Grand Old Party Tunes Up New Technology to Battle Democrats in Next Year's Election," *Wall Street Journal*, August 19, 1987, p. 38; Michael J. Bayer and Joseph Rodota, "Computerized Opposition Research: The Instant Parry," *Campaigns and Elections* 6 (Spring 1985): 25–29. At least one former member of the House Republican leadership staff told me in 1988, however, that the GOP's edge in technology is deceptive because information is used so poorly.

31. More precisely, politics in the 1980s has pitted a Democratic party whose strength (outside of the presidency, obviously) lies in the power of incumbency against a Republican party whose strength lies

in the capacity occasionally to counteract the effects of incumbency by systematically recruiting and funding good challengers and injecting national issues into local races.

32. Bob Hall, "Jesse Helms: The Meaning of His Money," *Southern Exposure*, January-February 1985, pp. 14–25.

33. *Charlotte Observer*, November 8, 1984, p. 13A. My data on the Helms-Hunt race come largely from reading two major North Carolina newspapers, the *Charlotte Observer* (hereafter *CO*) and the *Raleigh News and Observer* (hereafter *RNO*) from October 1983 through November 1984. For two especially insightful overviews of the race— one prospective, the other retrospective—see Rob Christensen, "Helms, Hunt Prepare for All-Out Battle," *RNO*, November 6, 1983, p. 1D, and Ken Eudy, "Sharply Drawn Images Define Senate Race," *CO*, November 4, 1984, p. 1A.

34. *RNO*, February 20, 1984, p. 11A. Data on previous North Carolina elections here and in the remainder of the chapter are from Richard Scammon and Alice V. McGillivray, *America Votes 15* (Washington, D.C.: Congressional Quarterly, 1982), pp. 262–264.

35. The summary of the 1984 election results is from *CO*, November 7 and 8, 1984, and *RNO*, November 8, 1984.

36. Some of the best material on Helms and Hunt as political figures came from the daily reporting in *RNO* and *CO*. See, for example, Bill Arthur, "Helms: Outspoken Symbol of the Right," *CO*, February 12, 1984, p. 1A; idem, "Jesse Helms's Unwavering Conservatism," *CO*, September 29, 1984, p. 1A; Rob Christensen, "Helms' Career in Senate Series of Ideological Stands," *RNO*, October 21, 1984, p. 1A; Ken Eudy, "For Jim Hunt, Public Career Is a Calling," *CO*, February 5, 1984, p. 1A; Ken Eudy and Katherine White, "Hunt's Years: Practical Man Makes Mark," *CO*, October 6, 1984, p. 1A; Ginny Carroll, "Politics Taught Hunt 'What Government Can Do for People,'" *RNO*, October 7, 1984, p. 1A; and Elizabeth Leland, "Hunt Progressive Governor with a Cautious Approach," *RNO*, October 21, 1984, p. 1A. Outside of North Carolina, of course, Helms has also received intense scrutiny. See Drew, "Jesse Helms," pp. 78–95; Peter Ross Range, "Inside the New Right War Machine," *Playboy*, August 1981, pp. 99–102, 116, 216–221; and "The Helms Network," *Congressional Quarterly Special Report*, March 6, 1982, pp. 499–505.

37. *Presidential Elections since 1789*, 2d ed. (Washington, D.C.: Congressional Quarterly, 1979).

38. Thad L. Beyle and Peter B. Harkins, "North Carolina," in *Explaining the Vote: Presidential Choices in the Nation and the States, 1968,*

ed. David M. Kovenock and James W. Prothro (Chapel Hill: Institute for Research in Social Science, 1973), pp. 376–424.

39. I wish to thank the School of Journalism of the University of North Carolina, Dr. Robert Stevenson, Dr. Jane Brown, and research assistant Stan Wearden for providing data from the School of Journalism poll. I also want to thank the *Charlotte Observer*, its marketing research director John Koslick, and research analyst Rob Daves for providing the data from the *Observer* poll. For a fuller discussion of this data, see Jerome L. Himmelstein, "Conservative Republicans in North Carolina," unpublished manuscript.

40. *RNO*, October 18, 1983, p. 1A; *CO*, December 18, 1983, p. 1A; *RNO*, February 5, 1984, p. 1A; *CO*, February 7, 1984, p. 1B; *RNO*, October 19, 1984, p. 1A; *CO*, November 4, 1984; *CO*, November 5, 1984, p. 1C.

41. Paul Luebke, Stephen Peters, and John Wilson, "The Political Economy of Microelectronics," in *High Hopes for High Tech: The Microelectronics Industry in North Carolina*, ed. Dale Whittington (Chapel Hill: University of North Carolina Press, 1985); Paul Luebke, "North Carolina—Still in the Progressive Mold?," *RNO*, July 1985 (special North Carolina quartercentury edition).

42. *RNO*, October 15, 1984, p. 4C.

43. *RNO*, September 11, 1984, p. 3C; *RNO*, November 6, 1983, p. 7D; *CO*, December 18, 1983, p. 1A.

44. *CO*, October 19, 1983, p. 1A; John York, "Helms Showed Courage in Questioning King Holiday," *CO*, October 27, 1983, p. 1B; *RNO*, March 21, 1984, p. 9A.

45. *RNO*, February 26, 1984, p. 25A.

46. *RNO*, October 8, 1984, p. 9A; October 16, 1984, p. 1A; October 28, 1984, p. 1A; October 19, 1984, p. 1A.

47. *CO*, January 18, 1984, p. 2E; *RNO*, January 22, 1984, p. 1A; *CO*, July 7, 1984.

48. Ken Eudy, "N.C. Politics: Hunt, Mondale Are in Trouble," *CO*, September 16, 1984, p. 3B; idem, " 'Registered' Democrat May Mean 'But I'll Vote for Helms,' " *CO*, September 12, 1984, p. 1E.

49. On Hunt's and Helms's fund-raising, see *CO*, April 27, 1984, p. 1C. For polls, see *RNO*, November 6, 1983, p. 1D; *RNO*, January 18, 1984, p. 1A; *RNO*, May 28, 1984, p. 1A; *RNO*, May 29, 1984, p. 1A; *CO*, July 1, 1984, p. 1A; *CO*, September 16, 1984, p. 1A; *RNO*, September 16, 1984, p. 1A; *RNO*, September 17, 1984, p. 1A; *CO*, October 7, 1984, p. 1A; and *CO*, October 30, 1984, p. 1A. The May Gallup Poll had Helms up 50–46 percent, but the June *Observer* Poll

gave Hunt a 47–42 percent lead. By September Helms had a slight lead in both polls (48.5–44.5 in the Gallup Poll, 48–45 in the *Observer* poll). An early October *Observer* poll had Hunt back in front, 46–42, but two polls in late October gave Helms the edge again, 49–46 and 47–43.

50. *CO*, December 30, 1983, p. 1A. A multivariate analysis of a February poll by the University of North Carolina School of Journalism showed that among whites, attitude toward the King holiday was second only to party loyalty in explaining preference for Helms or Hunt. *RNO*, June 24, 1984, p. 1D.

51. Paul Luebke, "Grass-Roots Organizing: The Hidden Side of the 1984 Helms Campaign," *Election Politics* 3 (Winter 1985–1986): 30–33; *RNO*, November 16, 1983, p. 1A; *RNO*, September 2, 1984, p. 1A; *RNO*, September 6, 1984, p. 19A.

52. *RNO*, September 11, 1984, p. 4C.

53. *RNO*, September 25, 1984, p. 16C.

54. *RNO*, October 15, 1984, pp. 4C–5C.

55. See Elizabeth Leland, "Pocketbook Issues Decided the Campaign That Had Everything," *RNO*, November 8, 1984, p. 15A.

Epilogue

1. William Schneider, "The Political Legacy of the Reagan Years," in *The Reagan Legacy*, ed. Sidney Blumenthal and Thomas Byrne Edsall (New York: Pantheon, 1988), pp. 51–98. See also John Judis, "Conservatism and the Price of Success," in *The Reagan Legacy*, pp. 135–171.

2. Viguerie, *New Right*; E. J. Dionne, Jr., "Leaderless Conservatives Approach '88 in Splinters," *New York Times*, December 13, 1987, p. E4; Richard A. Viguerie, "What Reagan Revolution?" *Washington Post*, August 21, 1988, p. C2; Peter Osterlund, "New Right Gropes for Old Momentum," *Christian Science Monitor*, November 27, 1987, p. 1; R. Emmett Tyrrell, Jr., "The Coming Conservative Crack-up," *The American Spectator* 20 (September 1987): 17–19, 51. For other comments on the state of the conservative movement in the late 1980s by outside observers and by conservatives themselves, see Tim W. Ferguson, "What Next for the Conservative Movement?" *The American Spectator* 20 (January 1987): 14–18; Charlotte Low, "The Pro-Life Movement in Disarray," *The American Spectator* 20 (October 1987): 23–26; Amy Moritz, "The New Right: It's Time We Led," *Policy Review* 44 (Spring 1988): 22–25; George Nash, "Completing the Revolution: Challenges for Conservatism after Reagan," *Policy Review* (Spring

1986): 35–39; "Ten Years That Shook the World," *Policy Review* 41 (Summer 1987): 2–5, 72–79; E. J. Dionne, Jr., "High Tide for Conservatives, but Some Fear What Follows," *New York Times*, October 13, 1987, p. 1; Charlotte Saikowski, "Will 'Reagan Revolution' Leave Mark?" *Christian Science Monitor*, April 30, 1987, p. 1; David Shribman, "With Reagan Gone, Conservatives Weigh Strategy to Bring New Energy, Direction to Movement," *Wall Street Journal*, March 2, 1989, p. A18.

3. For the Right's response to Bush, see Fred Mann, "And They're Off," *National Review* 40 (February 5, 1988): 36–40; Richard Brookhiser, "The Establishment Man," *National Review* 40 (November 7, 1988): 34–38; Edwin Feulner, "A Conservative Manifesto: Bush Can Do for Right What Reagan Couldn't," *Washington Post*, December 4, 1988, p. L1; Charlotte Saikowski, "Bush Nominees Leave GOP Right Feeling Uneasy," *Christian Science Monitor*, December 16, 1988, p. 3; Howard Fineman, "Goodbye to the 'Old Sheriff': Will Reagan's Conservative Posse Follow Bush?" *Newsweek*, December 26, 1988, p. 26; Marcia Schwartz, "Conservatives Survey Post-Reagan Landscape," *Washington Post*, February 24, 1989, p. A5; E. J. Dionne, Jr., "Conservatives Like Bush, but They're Watching Him," *New York Times*, February 26, 1989, p. E4.

4. Larry Martz, "Trouble on the Far Right," *Newsweek*, April 14, 1986, pp. 24–25; David Brooks, "Please, Mr. Postman: The Travails of Richard Viguerie," *National Review* 38 (June 20, 1986): 28–32; Thomas B. Edsall, "Head of Conservative PAC Quits in Dispute with Board," *Washington Post*, March 1, 1987, p. A2; Wallace Turner, "Hard Times Descend upon an Anti-abortion PAC," *New York Times*, August 9, 1987, p. 25; "Money Problems at Birch Society," *New York Times*, August 9, 1987, p. 42; Judis, "Conservatism and the Price of Success"; "The John Birch Society Is Broke and Fighting Internally," *Group Research Report* 25 (1986): 25–26.

5. Shribman, "With Reagan Gone, Conservatives Weigh Strategy."

6. Fred Barnes, "Kemp and the Cons," *The New Republic* 198 (December 28, 1987): 10, 12–13; Viguerie quoted in *New York Times*, March 11, 1988, p. D16. See also William Schneider, "The Harumph of the Will," *The New Republic* 198 (December 21, 1987): 39–41.

7. E. J. Dionne, Jr., "It's Straight and Narrow for Architect of Right," *New York Times*, March 16, 1989, p. B12; Andrew Rosenthal, "Tower's Personal Life Is Scrutinized," *New York Times*, February 1, 1989, p. A14.; Robin Toner and Michael Oreskes, "Tower Vote: Heavy Blows, Deftly Dealt," *New York Times*, March 12, 1989, p. 1; Tom Morganthau, "Tower's Troubles," *Newsweek*, March 6, 1989, pp. 16–22.

8. *New York Times*, November 10, 1988, p. B6; Harrison Donnelly,

"Getting Religion into Politics," *Editorial Research Reports*, September 12, 1986, pp. 667–684; Richard W. Bruner, "GOP Mainstream Fights Right Wing," *Christian Science Monitor*, March 29, 1989, p. 8; Garry Wills, " 'Save the Babies': Operation Rescue—A Case Study in Galvanizing the Antiabortion Movement," *Time*, May 1, 1989, pp. 26–27.

9. Ronald Smothers, "Baptists War over Hearts and Minds," *New York Times*, October 19, 1987, p. A18; Marshall Ingiverson, "Baptists Factions Struggle over Church Direction," *Christian Science Monitor*, November 23, 1987, p. 3; Marjorie Hoyer, "Moderate Baptists Rallying," *Washington Post*, November 16, 1987, p. A1; Peter Waldman, "Fundamentalists Fight to Capture the Soul of Southern Baptists," *Wall Street Journal*, March 7, 1988, p. 1; "Southern Baptist Election Is Won by Fundamentalist," *Wall Street Journal*, June 20, 1988, p. 18; Katherine S. Mangan, "Moderate Baptists Vote to Concede Control of Seminary to Fundamentalists and to Found Own Institution," *The Chronicle of Higher Education*, December 7, 1988, p. A15.

10. See Chapter 4.

11. Samuel G. Freedman, "Evangelicals Fight over Both Body and Soul," *New York Times*, May 31, 1987, p. 1; Laura Sessions Stepp, "TV Preachers Have a Devil of a Year," *Washington Post*, November 29, 1987, p. A14; "TV Preaching's 'Free Fall,' " *Washington Post*, July 19, 1987, p. A15; Marshall Ingiverson, "Troubles of Prominent TV Evangelists Ripple through Industry," *Christian Science Monitor*, June 1, 1988, p. 3; Larry Martz, "TV Preachers on the Rocks," *Newsweek*, July 11, 1988, pp. 26–28; Laura Sessions Stepp, "IRS Probes Evangelists' Operations," *Washington Post*, December 10, 1988, p. A1.

12. Alan Murray, "Lobbyists for Business Are Deeply Divided," *Wall Street Journal*, March 25, 1987, p. 1; Curtis M. Grimm and John M. Holcomb, "Choices among Encompassing Organizations: Business and the Budget Deficit," in *Business Strategy and Public Policy*, ed. Alfred A. Marcus, Allen M. Kaufman, and David R. Beam (New York: Quorum Books, 1987), pp. 105–118.

13. Theodore J. Eismeier and Philip H. Pollock III, *Business, Money, and the Rise of Corporate PACs in American Elections* (New York: Quorum Books, 1988), pp. 79–96; Dan Clawson, personal communication to author, June 1, 1989; Theodore J. Eismeier and Philip H. Pollock III, "The Retreat from Partisanship: Why the Dog Didn't Bark in the 1984 Election," in *Business Strategy and Public Policy*, ed. Marcus, Kaufman, and Beam, pp. 137–147. See also Ann B. Matasar, *Corporate PACs and Federal Campaign Financing Laws* (New York: Quorum Books, 1986), pp. 51–70; Tie-ting Su and Dan Clawson, "Corporate PACs and Conservative Realignment: A Comparison of 1980 and 1984," working

draft, May 1989; Tie-ting Su, Dan Clawson, and Alan Neustadtl, "A Dynamic Analysis of Corporate PAC Groupings, 1978–1986," paper presented at the annual meetings of the American Sociological Association, Atlanta, August 1988; Theodore J. Eismeier and Philip H. Pollock III, "Politics and Markets: Corporate Money in American National Elections," *British Journal of Political Science* 16 (1986): 287–306.

14. Eismeier and Pollock, *Business, Money, and Corporate PACs*, p. 92; idem, "Politics and Markets."

15. Eismeier and Pollock, *Business, Money and Corporate PACs*, pp. 83–88.

16. Barbara Vobejda, "A Conservative Agenda for the Bush Administration," *Washington Post*, December 9, 1988, p. A8; Judith Havemann, "Bush to Get 2,500 Conservative Resumes," *Washington Post*, November 15, 1988, p. A17; Edward Sussman, "Conservative Think Tank Comes Back from Brink of Financial Disaster, Leaning More to Right," *Wall Street Journal*, September 3, 1987, p. 42; Blumenthal, *The Rise of the Counter-Establishment*; Benjamin Hart, ed., *The Third Generation: Young Conservatives Look to the Future* (Washington, D.C.: Regnery Gateway, 1987); Judis, "Conservatism and the Price of Success."

17. Brooks Jackson, *Honest Graft: Big Money and the American Political Process* (New York: Knopf, 1988); Paul S. Herrnson, *Party Campaigning in the 1980s* (Cambridge, Mass.: Harvard University Press, 1988); Kuttner, *The Life of the Party*.

18. For the results of the 1988 elections generally, see "Opinion Roundup," *Public Opinion* 11 (January–February 1989): 21–40; *Washington Post*, November 10, 1988, p. 1; *New York Times*, November 10, 1988, p. B6; E. J. Dionne, Jr., "Voters Delay Republican Hopes of Dominance in Post-Reagan Era," *New York Times*, November 10, 1988, p. A1; Thomas B. Edsall and Richard Morin, "Reagan's 1984 Voter Coalition Is Weakened in Bush Victory," *Washington Post*, November 9, 1988, p. A29, A34; R. W. Apple, "The G.O.P. Advantage," *New York Times*, November 9, 1988, p. A1; E. J. Dionne, Jr., "Bush Is Elected by a 6–5 Margin," *New York Times*, November 9, 1988, p. A1; Fred Barnes, "Dream On: The Republican Realignment Quest," *The New Republic* 200 (January 23, 1989): 9–10. The phrase "Donkey's Year" comes from Fred Barnes, "A Donkey's Year," *The New Republic* 199 (February 29, 1988): 16–18.

19. "Opinion Roundup," *Public Opinion* 11 (January–February 1989): 21–40.

20. For an example of the debate over the ideological significance of the 1988 elections, see the articles on the Op-Ed page of the *New York Times*, November 13, 1988, p. C7, including George F. Will,

"There They Go Again . . . "; James A. Baker III, "It's Not a Triumph of Slick Campaigning"; Michael Barone, "Beware the Populist Trap"; Mark Green, "Liberalism Didn't Lose the Election."

21. "Conservatism and Liberalism: A National Review," *Public Opinion* 11 (November–December 1988): 30–35; Celinda Lake and Stanley Greenberg, "What's Left for Liberalism," *Public Opinion* 12 (March–April 1989): 4–7; John P. Robinson and John A. Fleishman, "Ideological Identification: Trends and Interpretations of the Liberal-Conservative Balance," *Public Opinion Quarterly* 52 (1988): 134–145.

22. *Public Opinion* 11 (January–February 1989): 27.

23. See "Opinion Roundup" in the following issues of *Public Opinion*: March–April 1987, 21–29; September–October 1987, 26–35; November–December, 1987, 30–40.

24. Keene quoted in Shribman, "With Reagan Gone, Conservatives Weigh Strategy."

25. Tamar Lewin, "Views on Abortion Are Sharply Split 16 Years after Supreme Court Ruling," *New York Times*, January 22, 1989, p. 21.

26. See n. 24.

27. Lake and Greenberg, "What's Left for Liberalism." This is hardly new; it has simply become more significant politically. The point was first emphasized over twenty years ago by Lloyd A. Free and Hadley Cantril, *The Political Beliefs of Americans* (New Brunswick: Rutgers University Press, 1967).

Bibliography

Abramson, Paul R., John Aldrich, and David W. Rohde. *Change and Continuity in the 1980 Elections*. Rev. ed. Washington, D.C.: Congressional Quarterly, 1983.

Alford, Robert R. *Party and Society: The Anglo-American Democracies*. Chicago: Rand McNally, 1963.

"America's Evangelicals: Genesis or Evolution?" *Public Opinion*, April-May 1981, pp. 22–27.

Apple, R. W. "Voters' Rebuff to Reagan's Vision." *New York Times*, November 6, 1986, p. 1.

Arrington, Theodore S. and Patricia A. Kyle. "Equal Rights Amendment Activists in North Carolina." *Signs* 3 (1978): 666–680.

Arthur, Bill. "Helms, Outspoken Symbol of the Right." *Charlotte Observer*, February 12, 1984, p. 1A.

Bayer, Michael J., and Joseph Rodota. "Computerized Opposition Research: The Instant Parry." *Campaigns and Elections* 6 (Spring 1985): 25–29.

Bell, Daniel, *The End of Ideology: On the Exhaustion of Political Ideas in the Fifties*. Rev. ed. New York: Free Press, 1965.

————, ed. *The Radical Right*. Garden City, N.Y.: Doubleday, 1963.

Benson, John M. "The Polls: A Rebirth of Religion?" *Public Opinion Quarterly* 45 (1981): 576–585.

Berg, Ivar, and Mayer Zald. "Business and Society." *Annual Review of Sociology* 4 (1978): 115–143.

Berns, Walter. "The Need for Public Authority." *Modern Age* 24 (1980): 16–20.

Beyle, Thad L., and Peter B. Harkins. "North Carolina." In *Explaining the Vote: Presidential Choices in the Nation and the States, 1968*, edited by David M. Kovenock and James W. Prothro, pp. 376–424. Chapel Hill: Institute for Research in Social Science, 1973.

Bibby, Reginald W. "Circulation of the Saints Revisited: A Longitudinal Look at Conservative Church Growth." *Journal for the Scientific Study of Religion* 22 (1983): 253–262.

Block, Fred. "Beyond Corporate Liberalism." *Social Problems* 24 (1977): 352–361.

———. "The Ruling Class Does Not Rule: Notes on the Marxist Theory of the State." *Socialist Revolution* 7 (1977): 6–28.

Blumenthal, Sidney. *The Rise of the Counter-Establishment: From Conservative Ideology to Political Power.* New York: Times Books, 1987.

Bonafede, Dom. "Issue-Oriented Heritage Foundation Hitches Its Wagon to Reagan's Star." *National Journal,* March 20, 1982, pp. 502–507.

Boskin, Joseph, ed. *Opposition Politics: The Anti–New Deal Tradition.* Beverly Hills, Calif.: Glencoe Press, 1968.

Bowles, Samuel. "The Post-Keynesian Capital-Labor Stalemate." *Socialist Review* 12 (September-October 1982): 45–72.

Bowles, Samuel, David M. Gordon, and Thomas E. Weisskopf. *Beyond the Waste Land: A Democratic Alternative to Economic Decline.* Garden City, N.Y.: Doubleday, 1983.

Brady, David, and Kent L. Tedin. "Ladies in Pink: Religion and Political Ideology in the Anti-ERA Movement." *Social Science Quarterly* 56 (1976): 564–575.

Braungart, Richard G. "Family Status, Socialization, and Student Politics: A Multivariate Analysis." *American Journal of Sociology* 77 (1971): 108–130.

Brint, Steven. "'New Class' and Cumulative Trend Explanations of Liberal Political Attitudes of Professionals." *American Journal of Sociology* 90 (1984): 30–71.

———. "The Political Attitudes of Professionals." *Annual Review of Sociology* 11 (1985): 389–414.

Bromley, David G., and Anson Shupe. *New Christian Politics.* Macon, Ga.: Mercer University Press, 1984.

Brooks, John. "Annals of Finance: The Supply Side." *The New Yorker,* April 19, 1982, pp. 97–150.

Buckley, William F., Jr. "The Conservative Reply." *New York Times,* February 16, 1971, p. 33.

———. Introduction to *Did You Ever See A Dream Walking?* Indianapolis: Bobbs-Merrill, 1970.

———. "A Dilemma of Conservatives." *The Freeman* 5 (1954): 51–52.

————. *God and Man at Yale: The Superstitions of "Academic Freedom."* Chicago: Henry Regnery, 1951.

————. *The Governor Listeth.* New York: Putnam, 1970.

————. *Inveighing We Will Go.* New York: Berkley, 1973.

————. Letter to the Editor. *The Freeman* 5 (1955): 244.

————. *Up from Liberalism.* New York: McDowell, Obolensky, 1959.

Burnham, James. *The Coming Defeat of Communism.* New York: John Day, 1950.

————. *Containment or Liberation?* New York: John Day, 1953.

————. *The Struggle for the World.* New York: John Day, 1947.

Burnham, Walter Dean. *Critical Elections and the Mainsprings of American Politics.* New York: Norton, 1970.

————. *The Current Crisis in American Politics.* New York: Oxford University Press, 1982.

————. "The Eclipse of the Democratic Party." *Society* 21 (July-August 1984): 5–11.

————. "The 1980 Earthquake: Realignment, Reaction, or What?" In *The Hidden Election,* edited by Thomas Ferguson and Joel Rogers, pp. 98–140. New York: Pantheon, 1981.

Burris, Val. "The Political Partisanship of American Business: A Study of Corporate Political Action Committees." *American Sociological Review* 52 (1987): 732–744.

Campbell, Angus, Philip E. Converse, Warren E. Miller, and Donald E. Stokes. *The American Voter.* Abridged ed. New York: John Wiley, 1964.

Campbell, Bruce A., and Richard J. Trilling, eds. *Realignment in American Politics: Towards a Theory.* Austin: University of Texas Press, 1980.

Carey, George W. "Conservatives and Libertarians View Fusionism: Its Origins, Possibilities, and Problems." *Modern Age* 26 (1982): 8–18.

Carnoy, Martin. *The State and Political Theory.* Princeton: Princeton University Press, 1984.

Cavanagh, Thomas E., and James L. Sundquist. "The New Two-Party System." In *The New Direction in American Politics,* edited by John E. Chubb and Paul E. Peterson, pp. 33–68. Washington, D.C.: Brookings Institution, 1985.

Chafe, William H. *The Unfinished Journey: America since World War II.* New York: Oxford University Press, 1986.

Chamberlain, John. *A Life with The Printed Word.* Chicago: Regnery Gateway, 1982.

Chambers, Whittaker. "Big Sister Is Watching You." *National Review* 4 (1957): 594–596.

———. *Witness*. New York: Random House, 1952.

Chodorov, Frank. *One Is a Crowd*. New York: Devin-Adair, 1952.

———. "The Return of 1940?" *The Freeman* 5 (1954): 81–82.

———. "A War to Communize America." *The Freeman* 5 (1954): 171–174.

———. "What Individualism Is Not." *National Review* 2 (1956): 15–17.

Christensen, Rob. "Helms, Hunt Prepare for All-Out Battle." *Raleigh News and Observer*, November 6, 1983, p. 1D.

Chubb, John E., and Paul E. Peterson, eds. *The New Direction in American Politics*. Washington, D.C.: Brookings Institution, 1985.

Clabaugh, Gary. *Thunder on the Right: The Protestant Fundamentalists*. Chicago: Nelson-Hall, 1974.

Clawson, Dan, and Mary Ann Clawson. "Reagan or Business? Foundations of the New Conservatism." In *The Structure of Power in America: The Corporate Elite as Ruling Class*, edited by Michael Schwartz, pp. 201–217. New York: Holmes and Meier, 1987.

Clawson, Dan, Karen Johnson, and John Schall. "Fighting Union Busting in the 1980s." *Radical America* 16 (1982): 45–64.

Clawson, Dan, Allen Kaufman, and Alan Neustadtl. "Corporate PACs for a New Pax Americana." *Insurgent Sociologist* 13, No. 1–2 (1985): 63–77.

Clawson, Dan, and Alan Neustadtl. "Corporate Political Strategies: Classwide Rationality and Conservatism in PAC Contributions to the 1980 Congressional Elections." Unpublished paper.

Clawson, Dan, Alan Neustadtl, and James Bearden. "The Logic of Business Unity: Corporate Contributions to the 1980 Congressional Elections." *American Sociological Review* 51 (1986): 797–811.

Clendinen, Dudley. "TV Evangelists and Small Group Lead 'Christian New Right's' Rush to Power." *New York Times*, August 18, 1980, p. 14.

Clubb, Jerome M., William H. Flanigan, and Nancy H. Zingale. *Partisan Realignment: Voters, Parties, and Government in American History*. Beverly Hills, Calif.: Sage, 1980.

Clymer, Adam. "Conservative Political Action Committee Evokes Both Fear and Adoration." *New York Times*, May 31, 1981, p. 1.

———. "Displeasure with Carter Turned Many to Reagan." *New York Times*, November 9, 1980, p. 18.

Cole, Wayne S. *America First: The Battle against Intervention*. 2d ed. New York: Octagon, 1971.

————. *Roosevelt and the Isolationists, 1932–1945.* Lincoln: University of Nebraska Press, 1983.

Collins, Robert. *The Business Response to Keynes, 1929–1964.* New York: Columbia University Press, 1981.

Common Cause, *1972 Federal Campaign Finances.* Washington, D.C.: Common Cause, 1973.

————. *1976 Federal Campaign Finances.* Washington, D.C.: Common Cause, 1977.

Conover, Pamela Johnston, and Virginia Gray. *Feminism and the New Right.* New York: Praeger, 1983.

"Conservative Cry: Our Time Has Come." *U.S. News and World Report,* February 26, 1979, pp. 52–54.

Conway, M. Margaret. "The White Backlash Re-examined: Wallace and the 1964 Primaries." *Social Science Quarterly* 49 (1968): 710–719.

Constantini, Edmond, and Kenneth H. Craik. "Competing Elites within a Political Party: A Study of Republican Leadership." *Western Political Quarterly* 22 (1969): 879–903.

Coulson, Crocker. "Lost Generation: The Politics of Youth." *The New Republic* 197 (December 1, 1986): 21–25.

Crawford, Alan. *Thunder on the Right: The "New Right" and the Politics of Resentment.* New York: Pantheon Books, 1980.

Crittenden, Ann. "The Economic Wind's Blowing toward the Right—for Now." *New York Times,* July 16, 1978, section 3, pp. 1, 9.

Dahl, Robert A. "A Critique of the Ruling Elite Model." In *C. Wright Mills and the Power Elite,* edited by G. William Domhoff and Hoyt B. Ballard, pp. 25–36. Boston: Beacon Press, 1968.

Davis, Bob. "Grand Old Party Tunes Up New Technology to Battle Democrats in Next Year's Election." *The Wall Street Journal,* August 19, 1987, p. 38.

Degler, Carl N. *Out of Our Past: The Forces That Shaped Modern America.* 3d ed. New York: Harper and Row, 1984.

Deutchman, Iva E., and Sandra Prince-Embury. "Political Ideology of Pro- and Anti-ERA Women." *Women and Politics* 2 (1982): 39–55.

Diggins, John P. *Up from Communism: Conservative Odysseys in American Intellectual History.* New York: Harper and Row, 1975.

Dillin, John. "U.S. Conservatives on the March: Economic Philosophy and Outlook." *Christian Science Monitor,* March 18, 1986, p. 22.

Dionne, E. J., Jr. "Fund-Raising Data Worry Democrats." *New York Times,* September 25, 1980, p. 8.

Doenecke, Justus D. *The Literature of Isolationism: A Guide to Non-Interventionist Scholarship, 1930–1972.* Colorado Springs: Ralph Myles, 1972.

————. *Not to the Swift: The Old Isolationists in the Cold War Era.* Lewisburg, Pa.: Bucknell University Press, 1979.

Domhoff, G. William. *The Higher Circles: The Governing Class in America.* New York: Random House, 1970.

————. "I am Not an 'Instrumentalist': A Reply to *Kapitalistate* Critics." *Kapitalistate* 4–5 (1976): 221–224.

————. *The Powers That Be: Processes of Ruling-Class Domination in America.* New York: Random House, 1979.

————. *Who Rules America Now?* Englewood Cliffs, N.J.: Prentice-Hall, 1983.

Douglas, Ann. *The Feminization of American Culture.* New York: Knopf, 1977.

Drew, Elizabeth. "Jesse Helms." *The New Yorker,* July 20, 1981, pp. 78–95.

————. *Power and Money.* New York: Macmillan, 1983.

D'Souza, Dinesh. *Falwell: Before the Millennium: A Critical Biography.* Chicago: Regnery Gateway, 1984.

Dworkin, Andrea. *Right-Wing Women.* New York: Putnam, 1983.

Dye, Thomas R. *Who's Running America? The Conservative Years.* 4th ed. Englewood Cliffs, N.J.: Prentice-Hall, 1986.

East, John. "The American Conservative Movement of the 1980's: Are Traditional and Libertarian Dimensions Compatible?" *Modern Age* 24 (1980): 34–38.

Edsall, Thomas Byrne. *The New Politics of Inequality.* New York: Norton, 1984.

————. "Republican America." *New York Review of Books,* April 24, 1986, pp. 3–6.

Edwards, Lee. "Paul Weyrich: Conscience of the New Right." *Conservative Digest,* July 1981, pp. 2–8.

Ehrenhalt, Alan. "Technology, Strategy Bring New Campaign Era." *Congressional Quarterly* 43 (1985): 2559–2565.

Eisenstein, Zillah R. "Antifeminism in the Politics and Presidential Election of 1980." In *Feminism and Sexual Equality: Crisis in Liberal America,* pp. 19–39. New York: Monthly Review Press, 1984.

Ellerin, Milton, and Alisa H. Kesten. "The New Right: What Is It?" *Social Policy* 11 (March-April 1982): 54–62.

English, Deirdre. "The War against Choice: Inside the Anti-Abortion Movement." *Mother Jones* 6 (1981): 16–32.

Epsing-Andersen, Gosta, Rodger Friedland, and Erik Olin Wright. "Modes of Class Struggle and the Capitalist State." *Kapitalistate* 4–5 (1976): 186–220.

Eudy, Ken. "N.C. Politics: Hunt, Mondale Are in Trouble." *Charlotte Observer*, September 16, 1984, p. 3B.

———. " 'Registered' Democrat May Mean 'But I'll Vote for Helms.' " *Charlotte Observer*, September 12, 1984, p. 1E.

———. "Sharply Drawn Images Define Senate Race." *Charlotte Observer*, November 4, 1984, p. 1A.

Evans, M. Stanton. "The Gospel According to Ayn Rand." *National Review* 19 (1967): 1059–1063.

———. "Raico on Liberalism and Religion." *New Individualist Review* 4 (Winter 1966): 19–25.

———. *Revolt on the Campus*. Chicago: Henry Regnery, 1961.

———. "Varieties of Conservative Experience." *Modern Age* 15 (1971): 130–137.

Evans, Rowland, and Robert Novak. "Is He the GOP's Future?" *Reader's Digest*, June 1982, pp. 108–112.

"The Faith of a Freeman." *The Freeman* 1 (1950): 5.

Falwell, Jerry. *Listen, America!* New York: Bantam, 1981.

Felsenthal, Carol. *The Sweetheart of the Silent Majority.* Garden City, N.Y.: Doubleday, 1981.

Ferguson, Thomas, and Joel Rogers. "The Knights of the Roundtable." *The Nation* 229 (1979): 620–628.

———. *Right Turn: The Decline of the Democrats and the Future of American Politics*. New York: Hill and Wang, 1986.

Fiorina, Morris P. *Retrospective Voting in American National Elections*. New Haven: Yale University Press, 1981.

Fitzgerald, Frances. "A Disciplined, Charging Army." *The New Yorker*, May 18, 1981, pp. 53–141.

Flake, Carol. *Redemptorama: Culture, Politics, and the New Evangelicalism*. New York: Penguin Books, 1984.

Forster, Arnold, and Benjamin R. Epstein. *Danger on the Right*. New York: Random House, 1964.

Frankl, Razelle. *Televangelism: The Marketing of Popular Religion*. Carbondale, Ill.: Southern Illinois University Press, 1987.

Gallup, George, Jr. *The Gallup Poll: Public Opinion 1986*. Wilmington, Del.: Scholarly Resources, 1987.

———. *The Gallup Poll: Public Opinion 1987*. Wilmington, Del.: Scholarly Resources, 1988.

Gamson, William A. *The Strategy of Social Protest*. Chicago: Dorsey, 1975.

"A Generation of the Intellectual Right." *Modern Age* 26 (1982): 226–460.

Georgine, Dan. "From Brass Knuckles to Briefcases: The Modern Art of Union Busting." In *The Big Business Reader,* edited by Mark Green and Robert Massie, Jr., pp. 91–110. New York: Pilgrim Press, 1980.

Germino, Dante. "Traditionalism and Libertarianism: Two Views." *Modern Age* 26 (1982): 49–56.

Gerson, Kathleen. "Emerging Social Divisions among Women: Implications for Welfare State Policies." *Politics and Society* 15 (1986–1987): 213–221.

———. *Hard Choices: How Women Decide about Work, Career and Motherhood.* Berkeley and Los Angeles: University of California Press, 1985.

Gilder, George. *Wealth and Poverty.* New York: Basic Books, 1980.

Ginsburg, Faye. *Contested Lives: The Abortion Debate in an American Community.* Berkeley and Los Angeles: University of California Press, 1988.

Gold, David, Clarence Y. H. Lo, and Erik Olin Wright. "Some Recent Developments in Marxist Theories of the Capitalist State." *Monthly Review* 27 (October 1975): 29–43, and 27 (November 1975): 36–51.

Goldman, Eric. *The Crucial Decade—and After: America, 1945–1960.* New York: Random House, 1960.

Goldstein, Richard. "The War for America's Mind." *Village Voice,* June 8, 1982, pp. 1, 11–20.

Goldwater, Barry. *The Conscience of a Conservative.* Shepherdsville, Ky.: Victor, 1960.

Goldwin, Robert, ed. *Left, Right, and Center: Essays on Liberalism and Conservatism in the United States.* Chicago: Rand McNally, 1965.

Goodman, Walter. "Irving Kristol: Patron Saint of the New Right." *New York Times Magazine,* December 6, 1981, p. 90.

Granberg, Donald. "The Abortion Activists." *Family Planning Perspectives* 13 (1981): 157–163.

Granberg, Donald, and Donald Denney. "The Coathanger and the Rose." *Society* 19 (1982): 39–51.

Granberg, Donald, and Beth Wellman Granberg. "Abortion Attitudes, 1965–1980: Trends and Determinants." *Family Planning Perspectives* 12 (1980): 250–261.

Gregory-Lewis, Sasha. "Stop-ERA: A Choice or an Echo?" *The Advocate,* November 2, 1977, pp. 12–15, and November 16, 1977, pp. 6–8.

Guth, James L. "The New Christian Right." In *The New Christian Right: Mobilization and Legitimation,* edited by Robert C. Liebman and Robert Wuthnow. Hawthorne, N.Y.: Aldine, 1983.

————. "Political Converts: Partisan Realignment Among Southern Baptist Ministers." *Election Politics* 3 (Winter, 1985–86): 2–6.

————. "Sex and The Single Issue Activist: Female Campaign Contributors in the 1982 Elections." Paper read at the meetings of the Southern Political Science Association, Savannah, Ga., November 1–3, 1984.

Guth, James L., and John C. Green. "The Christian Right in the Republican Party: The Case of Pat Robertson's Supporters." *Journal of Politics* 50 (1988): 150–165.

————. "Faith and Politics: Religion and Ideology Among Political Contributors." *American Politics Quarterly* 14 (1986): 186–200.

————. "God and the GOP: Varieties of Religiosity Among Political Contributors." Paper read at the meetings of the American Political Science Association, Chicago, September 3–6, 1987.

————. "The Moralizing Minority: Christian Right Support Among Political Contributors." *Social Science Quarterly* 68 (1987): 598–610.

————. "Party, PAC, and Denomination: Religiosity Among Political Contributors," Paper read at the meetings of the American Political Science Association, Chicago, September 1–3, 1983.

————. "Politics in a New Key: Religiosity and Activism Among Political Contributors." Paper read at the meetings of the Society for the Scientific Study of Religion, Knoxville, Tenn., November 4–6, 1983.

Hadden, Jeffrey K. "Religious Broadcasting and the Mobilization of the New Christian Right." *Journal for the Scientific Study of Religion* 26 (1987): 1–24.

Hadden, Jeffrey K., and Charles E. Swann. *Prime Time Preachers: The Rising Power of Televangelism*. Reading, Mass.: Addison-Wesley, 1981.

Hall, Bob. "Jesse Helms: The Meaning of His Money." *Southern Exposure*, January-February 1985, pp. 14–25.

Hamby, Alonzo L. *Liberalism and Its Challengers*. New York: Oxford, 1985.

Hamilton, Richard F. *Class and Politics in the United States*. New York: Wiley, 1972.

Hamowy, Ronald, and William F. Buckley, Jr. "'National Review': Criticism and Reply." *New Individualist Review* 1 (November 1961): 3–11.

Harding, Susan. "Family Reform Movements: Recent Feminism and Its Opposition." *Feminist Studies* 7 (1981): 57–75.

Harris, Louis. *The Anguish of Change*. New York: Norton, 1973.

Harrison, Bennett, and Barry Bluestone. *The Great U-Turn: Corporate Restructuring and the Polarizing of America.* New York: Basic Books, 1988.

Hart, Jeffrey. *The American Dissent: A Decade of American Conservatism.* Garden City, N.Y.: Doubleday, 1966.

Hayek, Friedrich A. *The Road to Serfdom.* Chicago: University of Chicago Press, 1944.

Heatherly, Charles, ed. *Mandate for Leadership: Policy Management in a Conservative Administration.* Washington, D.C.: Heritage Foundation, 1981.

Herbers, John. "Reagan Beginning to Get Top Billing in Christian Bookstores for Policies." *New York Times,* September 28, 1984, p. A23.

Herbert, Aubrey [Murray Rothbard]. "The Real Aggressor." *Faith and Freedom,* April 1954, pp. 22–27.

"Heritage Foundation Booms on the Right." *Group Research Reports* 26 (1986): 22.

Hershey, Marjorie Randon. "Single-Issue Groups and Political Campaigns: Six Senatorial Races and the Pro-Life Challenge in 1980." Paper presented at the 1981 meetings of the Midwest Political Science Association.

Himmelstein, Jerome L. "The Career of a Concept." Unpublished manuscript.

———. "Conservative Republicans in North Carolina." Unpublished manuscript.

———. "God, Gilder, and Capitalism." *Society* 18 (September-October 1981): 68–72.

———. "The New Right." In *The New Christian Right: Mobilization and Legitimation,* edited by Robert Liebman and Robert Wuthnow, pp. 13–30. Hawthorne, N.Y.: Aldine, 1983.

———. "The Social Basis of Antifeminism: Religious Networks and Culture." *Journal for the Scientific Study of Religion* 25 (1986): 1–15.

Himmelstein, Jerome L., and James A. McRae, Jr. "Social Conservatism, New Republicans, and the 1980 Elections." *Public Opinion Quarterly* 48 (1984): 592–605.

———. "Social Issues and Socioeconomic Status." *Public Opinion Quarterly* 52 (1988): 492–512.

Hodgson, Godfrey. *America in Our Time: From World War II to Nixon, What Happened and Why.* New York: Random House, 1976.

Hofstadter, Richard. *The Age of Reform.* New York: Random House, 1955.

Holt, James. "The New Deal and the American Anti-Statist Tradition." In *The New Deal: The National Level,* edited by John Braeman,

Robert H. Bremner, and David Brody, pp. 27–49. Columbus: Ohio State University Press, 1975.

Hook, Janet. "Georgetown's 'Intellectual Brokerage House.'" *Chronicle of Higher Education* 21 (December 8, 1980): 3–4.

Hoover, Herbert. *American Ideals versus the New Deal*. New York: Scribner, 1936.

Hout, Michael, and Andrew M. Greeley. "Church Attendance in the United States." *American Scoiological Review* 52 (1987): 325–345.

Hunter, James Davison. *American Evangelicalism: Conservative Religion and the Quandary of Modernity*. New Brunswick, N.J.: Rutgers University Press, 1983.

Inglehart, Ronald. *The Silent Revolution*. Princeton, N.J.: Princeton University Press, 1977.

Jacobson, Gary C. "The Effects of Campaign Spending in Congressional Elections." *American Political Science Review* 72 (1978): 469–471.

———. "The Republican Advantage in Campaign Finance." In *The New Direction in American Politics*, edited by John E. Chubb and Paul E. Peterson, pp. 143–174. Washington, D.C.: Brookings Institution, 1985.

Jenkins, J. Craig. "Resource Mobilization Theory and the Study of Social Movements." *Annual Review of Sociology* 9 (1983): 527–553.

Jessop, Bob. "Recent Theories of the Capitalist State." *Cambridge Journal of Economics* 1 (1977): 353–373.

Johnson, Loch, and Charles S. Bullock III. "The New Religious Right and the 1980 Congressional Elections." Paper presented at the annual meeting of the Southwestern Political Science Association, San Antonio, March 17–21, 1982.

Johnson, Stephen, and Joseph B. Tamney. "The Christian Right and the 1980 Presidential Election." *Journal for the Scientific Study of Religion* 21 (1982): 123–131.

Jonas, Manfred. *Isolationism in America*. Ithaca, N.Y.: Cornell University Press, 1966.

Jones, Charles O. "The Republican Challenge." *Society* 21 (July-August 1984): 21–24.

Jorstad, Erling. *The Politics of Doomsday*. Nashville: Abingdon, 1970.

Judis, John B. "Pop-Con Politics." *The New Republic* 191 (September 3, 1984): 18–20.

———. "The Right: Is There Life after Reagan?" *The Progressive*, October 1986, pp. 20–23.

Kater, John L. *Christians on the Right*. New York: Seabury Press, 1982.

Kellstedt, Lyman A. "Evangelicals and Political Realignment." Paper presented at the conference "Evangelical Political Involvement in the 1980s," Calvin College, Grand Rapids, Mich., October 17–18, 1986.

Kendall, Willmoore. *The Conservative Affirmation*. Chicago: Henry Regnery, 1963.

Kiewiet, D. Roderick. *Macro-Economics and Micro-Politics: The Electoral Effects of Economic Issues*. Chicago: University of Chicago Press, 1983.

Kinder, Donald R., and D. Roderick Kiewiet. "Economic Discontent and Political Behavior: The Role of Personal Grievances and Collective Economic Judgments in Congressional Voting." *American Journal of Political Science* 23 (1979): 495–517.

Kirk, Russell. *A Program for Conservatives*. Chicago: Henry Regnery, 1954.

Klatch, Rebecca. "Perceptions of Gender among Women of the New Right." Paper presented at the 1983 meetings of the American Anthropological Association.

———. *Women of the New Right*. Philadelphia: Temple University Press, 1987.

Kleppner, Paul, ed. *The Evolution of American Electoral Systems*. Westport, Conn.: Greenwood Press, 1981.

Knoke, David. "Stratification and the Dimensions of American Political Orientations." *American Journal of Political Science* 23 (1979): 772–791.

Kolko, Gabriel. *The Triumph of Conservatism*. Chicago: Quadrangle, 1967.

Kondracke, Morton. "The Heritage Model." *The New Republic* 183 (December 20, 1980): 10.

Kuttner, Robert. "Fat and Sassy." *The New Republic* 196 (February 23, 1987): 21–23.

———. *The Life of the Party: Democratic Prospects in 1988 and Beyond*. New York: Viking, 1987.

Ladd, Everett Carll, Jr. "Is Election '84 Really a Class Struggle?" *Public Opinion*, April-May 1984, pp. 41–47, 51.

———. "The New Lines Are Drawn: Class and Ideology in America." *Public Opinion* 1 (July 1978): 48–53, and 1 (September 1978): 14–20.

———. *Where Have All the Voters Gone? The Fracturing of America's Political Parties*. New York: Norton, 1982.

Ladd, Everett Carll, Jr., and Charles D. Hadley. *Transformations of the American Party System: Political Coalitions from the New Deal to the 1970s*. New York: Norton, 1975.

Ladd, Everett Carll, Jr., Marilyn Potter, Linda Basilick, Sally Daniels, and Dana Suszkiw. "The Polls: Taxing and Spending." *Public Opinion Quarterly* 43 (1979): 126–135.

Leland, Elizabeth. "Pocketbook Issues Decided the Campaign That Had Everything." *Raleigh News and Observer*, November 8, 1984, p. 15A.

Lemann, Nicholas. "The Evolution of the Conservative Mind." *Washington Monthly*, May 1981, pp. 34–41.

Leuchtenburg, William E. *Franklin D. Roosevelt and the New Deal*. New York: Harper and Row, 1963.

Liebman, Robert C. "Mobilizing the Moral Majority." In *The New Christian Right: Mobilization and Legitimation*, edited by Robert C. Liebman and Robert Wuthnow, pp. 50–74. Hawthorne, N.Y.: Aldine, 1983.

Liebman, Robert, and Robert Wuthnow, ed. *The New Christian Right: Mobilization and Legitimation*. Hawthorne, N.Y.: Aldine, 1983.

Lipset, Seymour Martin. "The Economy, Elections, and Public Opinion." *Tocqueville Review* 5 (1983): 431–470.

———. "The Elections, The Economy, and Public Opinion." *PS* (Winter 1985): 23–38.

———. "The Revolt against Modernity." In *Mobilization, Center-Periphery Structures, and Nation-Building*, edited by Per Torsvik. Bergen: Universitetsforlaget, 1981.

———, ed. *Student Politics*. New York: Basic Books, 1967.

Lipset, Seymour Martin, and Earl Raab. "The Elections and the Evangelicals." *Commentary* 71 (March 1981): 25–31.

———. *The Politics of Unreason: Right Wing Extremism in America, 1790–1977*. 2d ed. Chicago: University of Chicago Press, 1978.

———. "The Wallace Whitelash." *Trans-action* 7 (December 1969): 23–35.

Lipset, Seymour Martin, and William Schneider. *The Confidence Gap: Business, Labor, and Government in the Public Mind*. New York: Free Press, 1983.

Lo, Clarence Y. H. "Countermovements and Conservative Movements in the Contemporary U.S." *Annual Review of Sociology* 8 (1982): 107–134.

Lubell, Samuel. *The Future of American Politics*. 3d ed., rev. New York: Harper and Row, 1965.

Luebke, Paul. "Grass-Roots Organizing: The Hidden Side of the 1984 Helms Campaign." *Election Politics* 3 (Winter 1985–1986): 30–33.

———. "North Carolina—Still in the Progressive Mold?" *Raleigh News and Observer*, July 1985, special North Carolina quatercentenary edition.

Luebke, Paul, Stephen Peters, and John Wilson. "The Political Economy of Microelectronics." In *High Hopes for High Tech: The Microelectronics Industry in North Carolina*, edited by Dale Whittington. Chapel Hill: University of North Carolina Press, 1985.

Luker, Kristin. *Abortion and the Politics of Motherhood*. Berkeley and Los Angeles: University of California Press, 1984.

McBride, Stewart. "Leaning to the Right." *Christian Science Monitor*, April 2, 1980.

McCarthy, John D., and Mayer N. Zald. "Resource Mobilization and Social Movements: a Partial Theory." *American Journal of Sociology* 82 (1977): 1212–1239.

McConnell, Grant. *Private Power and American Democracy*. New York: Random House, 1966.

McCurdy, Jack. "A Reagan 'Brain Trust': Hoover Institution Finds It's in the Public Eye." *Chronicle of Higher Education* 21 (December 1, 1980): 3.

McLoughlin, William G. *Revivals, Awakenings, and Reform: An Essay on Religion and Social Change in America, 1607–1977*. Chicago: University of Chicago Press, 1978.

McQuaid, Kim. *Big Business and Presidential Power from FDR to Reagan*. New York: Morrow, 1982.

Magney, John. "Mountains, Molehills, and Media Hypes: The Curious Case of the New Conservatism." *Working Papers*, May-June 1979, pp. 28–34.

Malbin, Michael, ed. *Money and Politics in the United States: Financing Elections in the 1980s*. Washington, D.C.: American Enterprise Institute, 1984.

Mansbridge, Jane J. *Why We Lost the ERA*. Chicago: University of Chicago Press, 1986.

Markmann, Charles Lam. *The Buckleys: A Family Examined*. New York: Morrow, 1973.

Markus, Gregory B. "The Impact of Personal and National Economic Conditions on the Presidential Vote: A Pooled Cross-Sectional Analysis." Unpublished paper.

Marsden, George M. *Fundamentalism and American Culture: The Shaping of Twentieth-Century Evangelicalism, 1870–1925*. New York: Oxford University Press, 1980.

Mathews, Donald, and Jane DeHart Mathews. "The Threat of Equality: The Equal Rights Amendment and the Myth of Female Solidarity." Unpublished manuscript.

Mayer, George H. *The Republican Party, 1954–1964*. New York: Oxford University Press, 1964.

Menendez, Albert J. *Religion at the Polls.* Philadelphia: Westminster Press, 1977.

Merry, Robert W. "Growth Agent: Reagan Transformed." *Wall Street Journal,* September 13, 1985.

Meyer, Frank, "Conservatism." In *Left, Right, and Center: Essays on Liberalism and Conservatism in the United States,* edited by Robert Goldwin, pp. 1–17. Chicago: Rand McNally, 1965.

———. *The Conservative Mainstream.* New Rochelle, N.Y.: Arlington House, 1969.

———. "Richard M. Weaver: An Appreciation." *Modern Age* 14 (1970): 243–248.

———, ed. *What Is Conservatism?* New York: Holt, Rinehart and Winston, 1964.

Miles, Michael W. *The Odyssey of the American Right.* New York: Oxford, 1980.

Miller, Arthur H., and Martin P. Wattenberg. "Politics from the Pulpit: Religiosity and the 1980 Elections." *Public Opinion Quarterly* 48 (1984): 301–317.

Miller, Warren E. "A New Context for Presidential Politics: The Reagan Legacy." *Political Behavior* 9 (1987): 91–113.

Miller, Warren E., and J. Merrill Shanks. "Policy Directions and Presidential Leadership: Alternative Interpretations of the 1980 Presidential Election." *British Journal of Political Science* 12 (1982): 299–356.

Morgan, Dan. "Conservatives: A Well-Financed Network." *Washington Post,* January 4, 1981, pp. A1, A14.

Morley, Felix. "The Early Days of *Human Events.*" *Human Events* 34 (April 27, 1974): 26, 28, 31.

Mueller, Carol. "In Search of a Constituency for the 'New Religious Right.'" *Public Opinion Quarterly* 47 (1983): 213–229.

Mueller, Carol, and Thomas Dimieri. "The Structure of Belief Systems among Contending ERA Activists." *Social Forces* 60 (1982): 657–675.

Murphy, Charles J. V. "McCarthy and the Businessman." *Fortune,* April 1954, pp. 156–158, 180–194.

———. "Texas Business and McCarthy." *Fortune,* May 1954, pp. 100–101, 208–216.

Nash, George. *The Conservative Intellectual Movement in America since 1945.* New York: Basic Books, 1979.

Nelson, Michael, ed. *The Elections of 1984.* Washington, D.C.: Congressional Quarterly, 1985.

Neuhaus, Richard John, and Michael Cromartie, eds. *Piety and Poli-

tics: Evangelicals and Fundamentalists Confront the World. Washington, D.C.: Ethics and Public Policy Center, 1987.

Neustadtl, Alan, and Dan Clawson. "Corporate Political Groupings: PAC Contributions to the 1980 Congressional Elections." *American Sociological Review* 53 (1988): 172–190.

Newport, Frank M., and V. Lance Tarrance, Jr. "Evangelicals, Fundamentalists, and Political Issues in the 1984 Elections." *Election Politics* 1 (Winter 1983–1984): 2–6.

Niemi, Richard G., and Herbert F. Weisberg, eds. *Controversies in Voting Behavior.* 2d. ed. Washington, D.C.: Congressional Quarterly, 1984.

Nisbet, Robert. "Conservatives and Libertarians: Uneasy Cousins." *Modern Age* 24 (1980): 2–8.

———. *The Quest for Community.* New York: Oxford, 1953.

Nock, Albert J. "A Little Conserva-tive." *Atlantic Monthly* 158 (October 1936): 481–489.

Norman, Geoffrey. "Neo-Conservatism: An Idea Whose Time Is Now." *Esquire,* February 13, 1979, pp. 23–42.

"Northside Baptist Church and Dr. W. Jack Hudson Celebrating 30 Years of Service to the Carolinas." *Charlotte Observer,* September 6, 1984, special advertising supplement.

O'Connor, James. *The Fiscal Crisis of the State.* New York: St. Martin's Press, 1973.

Offe, Claus. *Contradictions of the Welfare State.* Cambridge: MIT Press, 1984.

"Organized Right Took a Beating in the Elections." *Group Research Reports* 25 (1986): 33.

Patterson, James T. *Congressional Conservatism and the New Deal.* Lexington: University Press of Kentucky, 1967.

Peele, Gillian. *Revival and Reaction: The Right in Contemporary America.* Oxford: Oxford University Press, 1984.

Peschek, Joseph G. *Policy-Planning Organizations: Elite Agendas and America's Rightward Turn.* Philadelphia: Temple University Press, 1987.

Petchesky, Rosalind Pollack. "The Antiabortion Movement and the Rise of the New Right." In *Abortion and Women's Choice: The State, Sexuality, and Reproductive Freedom,* pp. 241–285. Boston: Northeastern University Press, 1984.

Petrocik, John R. "Realignment: New Party Coalitions and the Nationalization of the South." *Journal of Politics* 49 (1987): 347–375.

Phillips, Howard, ed. *The New Right at Harvard*. Vienna, Va.: Conservative Caucus, 1983.

Phillips, Kevin P. *The Emerging Republican Majority*. New Rochelle, N.Y.: Arlington House, 1969.

———. *Mediacracy*. Garden City, N.Y.: Doubleday, 1975.

———. *Post-Conservative America: People, Politics, and Ideology in a Time of Crisis*. New York: Random House, 1982.

Pines, Burton Yale. *Back to Basics: The Traditionalist Movement That Is Sweeping Grass-Roots America*. New York: Morrow, 1982.

Piven, Frances Fox, and Richard A. Cloward. *The New Class War: Reagan's Attack on the Welfare State and Its Consequences*. New York: Pantheon, 1982.

Polsby, Nelson W. "Toward An Explanation of McCarthyism." *Political Studies* 8 (1960): 250–271.

Poulantzas, Nicos. "The Problem of the Capitalist State." In *Ideology in Social Science*, edited by Robin Blackburn, pp. 238–253. New York: Random House, 1973.

"Power, Glory, and Politics: Right-wing Preachers Dominate the Dial." *Time*, February 17, 1986, pp. 62–69.

Radosh, Ronald. *Prophets on the Right: Profiles of Conservative Critics of American Globalism*. New York: Simon and Schuster, 1975.

Ranney, Austin, ed. *The American Elections of 1980*. Washington, D.C.: American Enterprise Institute, 1981.

Reeves, Thomas C. "McCarthyism: Interpretations since Hofstadter." *Wisconsin Magazine of History* 60 (Autumn 1976): 42–54.

Reichley, A. James. "The Evangelical and Fundamentalist Revolt." In *Piety and Politics: Evangelicals and Fundamentalists Confront the World*, edited by Richard John Neuhaus and Michael Cromartie, pp. 69–95. Washington, D.C.: Ethics and Public Policy Center, 1987.

———. *Religion in American Public Life*. Washington, D.C.: Brookings Institution, 1985.

Reinhard, David W. *The Republican Right since 1945*. Lexington: University Press of Kentucky, 1983.

Ribuffo, Leo P. *The Old Christian Right*. Philadelphia: Temple University Press, 1983.

Rieder, Jonathan. *Carnarsie: The Jews and Italians of Brooklyn against Liberalism*. Cambridge: Harvard University Press, 1985.

"Right-Wing Drive to Control State Houses." *Southern Exposure*, January-February 1985, pp. 6–7.

Roberts, James C. *The Conservative Decade—Emerging Leaders of the 1980s*. Westport, Conn.: Arlington House, 1980.

Rogin, Michael. *The Intellectuals and McCarthy: The Radical Specter.* Cambridge: MIT Press, 1967.

———. "Politics, Emotion, and the Wallace Vote." *British Journal of Sociology* 20 (1969): 27–49.

———. "Wallace and the Middle Class: The White Backlash in Wisconsin." *Public Opinion Quarterly* 30 (1966): 98–108.

Roof, Wade Clark, and William McKinney. *American Mainline Religion: Its Changing Shape and Future.* New Brunswick, N.J.: Rutgers University Press, 1987.

Rose, Arnold M. *The Power Structure: Political Process in American Society.* New York: Oxford University Press, 1967.

Rothbard, Murray N. "The New Libertarian Creed." *New York Times,* February 9, 1971, p. 39.

———. "The Transformation of the American Right." *Continuum* 2 (1964): 220–231.

Rothenberg, Stuart, and Frank Newport. *The Evangelical Voter: Religion and Politics in America.* Washington, D.C.: Free Congress Research and Education Foundation, 1984.

Rothenberg, Stuart, and Richard R. Roldan. *Business PACs and Ideology: A Study of Contributions in the 1982 Elections.* Washington, D.C.: Free Congress Research and Education Foundation, 1983.

Rothmyer, Karen. "Citizen Scaife." *Columbia Journalism Review,* July–August 1981, pp. 41–50.

Rotunda, Ronald. "The 'Liberal' Label: Roosevelt's Capture of a Symbol." *Public Policy* 17 (1968): 377–408.

"Roundtable's President Ed McAteer Is Music Man of Religious Right." *Conservative Digest,* January 1981, pp. 2–7.

Rusher, William A. *The Rise of the Right.* New York: Morrow, 1984.

Sabato, Larry J. *The Rise of Political Consultants.* New York: Basic Books, 1981.

Sale, Kirkpatrick. *Power Shift: The Rise of the Southern Rim and Its Challenge to the Eastern Establishment.* New York: Random House, 1975.

Saloma, John T., III. *Ominous Politics: The New Conservative Labyrinth.* New York: Hill and Wang, 1984.

Scammon, Richard M., and Ben J. Wattenberg. *The Real Majority.* New York: Coward, McCann, and Geoghegan, 1970.

Schlamm, William S. "But It Is Not 1940." *The Freeman* 5 (1954): 169–170.

Schneider, William. "An Uncertain Consensus." *National Journal,* November 10, 1984, pp. 2130–2132.

Schoenberger, Robert A. "Conservatism, Personality, and Political Extremism." *American Political Science Review* 62 (1968): 868–877.

Scully, Malcolm. "More than GOP's 'Government in Exile.'" *Chronicle of Higher Education* 21 (December 15, 1980): 3.

"The 70's: Decade of Second Thoughts." *Public Opinion* 2 (January 1980): 19–42.

Shoup, Lawrence, and William Minter. *Imperial Brain Trust: The Council on Foreign Relations and United States Foreign Policy.* New York: Monthly Review Press, 1977.

Shupe, Anson, and William A. Stacey. *Born-Again Politics and the Moral Majority: What Social Surveys Really Show.* New York: Edwin Mellen Press, 1982.

Silk, Leonard, and David Vogel. *Ethics and Profits: The Crisis of Confidence in American Business.* New York: Simon and Schuster, 1976.

Simon, William E. *A Time for Truth.* New York: Berkley, 1978.

Skocpol, Theda, "The Legacies of New Deal Liberalism." In *Liberalism Reconsidered,* edited by Douglas MacLean and Claudia Mills, pp. 87–104. Totowa, N.J.: Rowman and Allenheld, 1983.

———. "Political Response to Capitalist Crisis: Neo-Marxist Theories of the State and the Case of the New Deal." *Politics and Society* 10 (1980): 155–201.

Slavin, Peter. "The Business Roundtable: New Lobbying Arm of Big Business." *Business and Society Review,* Winter 1975–1976, pp. 28–32.

Smidt, Corwin, "Evangelicals and the 1984 Election: Continuity or Change?" *American Politics Quarterly* 15 (1987): 419–444.

———. "Evangelicals in Presidential Elections: A Look at the 1980s." *Election Politics* 5 (Spring 1988): 2–11.

———. "The Partisanship of American Evangelicals: Changing Patterns Over the Past Decade." Paper presented at the 1986 meetings of the Society for the Scientific Study of Religion.

Smidt, Corwin, and Lyman Kellstedt. "Evangelicalism and Survey Research: Interpretive Problems and Substantive Findings." In *The Bible, Politics, and Democracy,* edited by Richard J. Neuhaus. Grand Rapids, Mich.: Eerdmans, 1987.

Smith, T. V., and Robert A. Taft. *Foundations of Democracy.* New York: Knopf, 1939.

"Special Issue: The State of Public Opinion in the States." *Election Politics* 5 (Winter 1977–1978).

Speer, James A. "The New Christian Right and Its Parent Company: A Study in Political Contrasts." In *New Christian Politics,* edited by David G. Bromley and Anson Shupe, pp. 19–40. Macon, Ga.: Mercer University Press, 1984.

Spinrad, William. "Power in Local Communities." In *Class, Status, and Power,* edited by Reinhard Bendix and Seymour Martin Lipset, 2d ed., rev., pp. 218–231. New York: Free Press, 1956.

Steeper, Frederick T., and John R. Petrocik. "Ratification of the Reagan Realignment: the 1986 Election." *Election Politics* 4 (Winter 1986–1987): 10–13.

Steinfels, Peter. *The Neoconservatives: The Men Who Are Changing America's Politics.* New York: Simon and Schuster, 1979.

Stockman, David A. *The Triumph of Politics: Why the Reagan Revolution Failed.* New York: Harper and Row, 1986.

Stone, Barbara S. "A Profile of the John Birch Society." *Journal of Politics* 36 (1974): 184–197.

Stone, Peter. "Conservative Brain Trust." *New York Times Magazine,* May 10, 1981, p. 18.

———. "The Counter-Intelligentsia." *Village Voice,* October 27, 1979, pp. 14–19.

———. "The I.E.A.—Teaching the Right Stuff." *The Nation* 233 (1981): 231–235.

Strauss, Leo. *Natural Right and History.* Chicago: University of Chicago Press, 1953.

Sundquist, James L. *Dynamics of the Party System: Alignment and Realignment of Political Parties in the United States.* Washington, D.C.: Brookings Institution, 1973.

Taft, Robert A. *A Foreign Policy for Americans.* Garden City, N.Y.: Doubleday, 1951.

"Tale of Two Right-Wing 'Think Tanks.'" *Group Research Reports* 25 (1986): 22.

"A Think Tank at the Brink." *Newsweek,* July 7, 1986, p. 87.

"Tide of Born-Again Politics." *Newsweek,* September 15, 1980, pp. 28–36.

Tilly, Charles. *From Mobilization to Revolution.* Reading, Mass.: Addison-Wesley, 1978.

Useem, Michael, "Business and Politics in the United States and the United Kingdom." *Theory and Society* 12 (1983): 281–308.

———. "Company vs. Classwide Rationality in Corporate Decision-Making." *Administrative Science Quarterly* 27 (1982): 199–226.

———. *The Inner Circle: Large Corporations and the Rise of Business Political Activity in the U.S. and the U.K.* New York: Oxford University Press, 1984.

Viguerie, Richard A. *The Establishment vs. the People: Is a New Populist Revolt on the Way?* Chicago: Regnery Gateway, 1983.

———. *The New Right: We're Ready to Lead.* Falls Church, Va.: The Viguerie Company, 1980.

Voegelin, Eric. *The New Science of Politics: An Introduction*. Chicago: University of Chicago Press, 1952.

Vogel, David. "Business's 'New Class' Struggle." *The Nation* 229 (1979): 625–628.

———. "The New Political Science of Corporate Power." *The Public Interest* 87 (Spring 1987): 63–79.

———. "Why Businessmen Distrust Their State." *British Journal of Political Science* 8 (1978): 45–78.

Warner, David. "Scaife: Financier of the Right." *Pittsburgh Post-Gazette*, April 20, 1981.

Weaver, Richard M. *Ideas Have Consequences*. Chicago: University of Chicago Press, 1948.

———. "Up from Liberalism." *Modern Age* 3 (1958): 21–32.

Weeks, Stephens. "Notes from the Underground." *National Review* 38 (September 26, 1986): 36–40.

Weidenbaum, Murray. "The High Cost of Government Regulation." *Challenge*, November-December 1981, pp. 32–39.

Weinraub, Bernard. "Foundations Support Conservatism by Financing Scholars and Groups." *New York Times*, January 20, 1981, p. 17.

Weinstein, James. *The Corporate Ideal in the Liberal State*. Boston: Beacon Press, 1968.

Weir, Margaret, Ann Shola Orloff, and Theda Skocpol, ed. *The Politics of Social Policy in the United States*. Princeton: Princeton University Press, 1988.

Welles, Chris. "The Supply-Side Cabal." *This World*, September 20, 1981, pp. 8–12.

Westby, David L., and Richard G. Braungart. "Class and Politics in the Family Backgrounds of Student Political Activists." *American Sociological Review* 31 (1966): 690–692.

Whitaker, Robert W., ed. *The New Right Papers*. New York: St. Martin's Press, 1982.

White, F. Clifton, and William J. Gill. *Why Reagan Won: The Conservative Movement, 1964–1981*. Chicago, Regnery Gateway, 1981.

Wills, Garry. *Confessions of a Conservative*. New York: Penguin Books, 1980.

Wolfe, Alan. *America's Impasse: The Rise and Fall of the Politics of Growth*. New York: Pantheon, 1981.

———. "Sociology, Liberalism, and the Radical Right." *New Left Review* 128 (July-August 1981): 3–27.

———. "Toward A Political Sociology of Reaganism." *Contemporary Sociology* 16 (1987): 31–33.

Wolfinger, Raymond E., Barbara Kaye Wolfinger, Kenneth Prewitt, and Sheilah Rosenhack. "America's Radical Right: Politics and Ideology." In *Ideology and Discontent*, edited by David E. Apter, pp. 262–293. New York: Free Press, 1964.

Wolfskill, George. *The Revolt of the Conservatives: A History of the American Liberty League, 1934–1940*. Boston: Houghton-Mifflin, 1962.

Wood, Michael, and Michael Hughes. "The Moral Basis of Moral Reform: Status Discontent vs. Culture and Socialization as Explanations of Anti-Pornography Social Movement Adherence." *American Sociological Review* 49 (1984): 86–99.

Wright, Erik Olin. *Class, Crisis, and the State*. New York: Schocken Books, 1979.

Wuthnow, Robert. "The Political Rebirth of American Evangelicals." In *The New Christian Right: Mobilization and Legitimation*, edited by Robert C. Liebman and Robert Wuthnow, pp. 168–187. Hawthorne, N.Y.: Aldine, 1983.

Wyman, Hastings J., Jr. "Yes, But Then Again, No: Social Issues and Southern Politics." *Election Politics* 4 (Summer 1987): 15–18.

Zoll, Donald Atwell. "Philosophical Foundations of the American Right." *Modern Age* 15 (1971): 114–129.

Index